CHILDREN OF THE VOLCANO

Finding Freedom and Making a Home for Three in Sicily

ROS BELFORD

september

1 3 5 7 9 10 8 6 4 2

First published in 2024 by September Publishing

Copyright © Ros Belford 2024

The right of Ros Belford to be identified as the author of this work has been asserted by her in accordance with the Copyright Designs and Patents Act 1988.

Typeset by RefineCatch Limited, www.refinecatch.com
Printed in Poland on paper from responsibly managed, sustainable sources by Hussar

ISBN 9781914613661
Ebook ISBN 9781914613678

September Publishing
www.septemberpublishing.org

To my mother, Patricia Belford, who showed me there were more interesting things in life than a tidy house. And to Izzy and Juno, who are continuing the tradition.

Author's note

This book is memoir. It reflects the author's present recollections of experiences over time. Some names and characteristics have been changed. Some events have been compressed and their order changed. As the author had her hands full with two little girls – and was not in the habit of walking around Salina with a voice recorder – some dialogue has been recreated.

CONTENTS

CONTENTS

Part II: Salina

STRETCHING COBWEBS

Salina, Spring 2023

I am going to break into our old house. Easy. I used to do it all the time, climb in whenever I forgot the key. There is this huge, long terrace looking down to the sea over the lagoon and its lopsided lighthouse, and I want to stand on it again. It feels like our souls are still in the house, and that even after all the years away, it still belongs to me and the girls, not the landlady, because we had loved it so much and created our messy, noisy, chaotic and colourful home there.

Try explaining that to the Carabinieri.

Hmm.

The Carabinieri would never understand. Not even Salvatore, who once backed the patrol jeep onto the box of shopping I had waiting at the port, squidging two kilos of tomatoes and inspiring a recipe I called *pesto al carabiniero*. By Italian law, Carabinieri cannot serve in their place of birth, and Salvatore came from Milan where the rules of ordinary capitalism hold good. But on the island, things are different. On the island, you can possess a house by living in it. Except that to do so you must demonstrate that there is no identifiable owner, and Juno and I met my former landlady, Maria Rosa, on the road to Santa Marina last week. She recognised me straight away, despite my long absence, stopping the car as she passed, as all the islanders do when they spot a friend. She opened the car door, apologising that her legs were no good now, so she couldn't stand up and embrace us. She looked into my eyes, then up at Juno, five feet ten in cut-off jeans, chestnut hair to her waist.

'Ismene? It can't be? Grown up already?'

Juno grinned, said, 'No, I'm Juno.'

Maria Rosa shook her head slowly. '*Come vola il tempo.*' How time flies. 'When I last saw you, Juno, you were a tiny little girl with wild blonde hair who never wore shoes.'

Juno laughed and pointed. Her feet are still bare.

'How old are you?'

'Twenty-one.'

'*Fidanzata?*'

Juno laughed. So far every islander we'd met had asked her if she's got a serious boyfriend. The day before, someone had even offered to find her a suitable island boy.

'*Per fortuna, non!*'

Maria Rosa looked surprised for a moment, then laughed. '*Hai ragione.*' You're right. 'Too many girls marry too young. You know one of your classmates has a baby already?'

Indeed we did. It was the talk of the island. Juno muttered something under her breath that might have been *nemesis*. She and the girl in question had never seen eye to eye.

'How long is it, Ros, how long since you left?'

Thirteen years. It feels like a lifetime and it feels like no time.

I walk up the lava-stone path that winds up to the house through olives and citrus trees. Sixty-seven steps and I know each one. There was a time when I bumped a double buggy up and down here four times a day. In the distance, I can see the lights of the night ferry carrying Juno away, back to Bristol, university and her fierce defences of Ancient Roman sex workers and Greek goddesses. At the tail end of the pandemic, she came to the island for a week, alone, returned and said: Mum, it's still home. The only place in the world that feels like home and where I can be exactly who I am. Please come back with me.

I'd been afraid to go back after so long away, worried that no one would remember me and that if they did remember, that they might feel let down, betrayed even, by my absence. Juno persuaded me to come. I never imagined I would stay on after she had gone.

I arrive at the blue metal door that leads to the terrace. The moon is shining through motionless clouds, the sky an eerie shade of steel. The ferry is still visible, its port light leaking like juice from an over-ripe pomegranate into the metallic sea.

I slip my sandals off. The lava is still warm from the day.

It's late. The village is in darkness. There's nobody about.

I crouch down and peep through the gap in the door. The one I used to use as a foothold whenever I forgot the key. In the moonlight, I can see the terrace is inches deep in bracts of bougainvillea brown as cornflakes and leaves from the lemon tree below where I used to hang balloons for the girls' birthdays.

No one has been living here.

It would be so easy.

I've done it so many times before. Left foot into the little gap. Swing up onto the wall, slither over, dangle down and jump.

I land on the ceramic-tiled bench built into the wall, the *bisuolo*, they call it, gritty on my soles with the sticky sand the sirocco blows from Africa. All island houses have a *bisuolo*. Somewhere to sit while you pod peas, watch the sea, eavesdrop on your neighbours. It was here I sat alone those dawns and midnights after the earth tremors, watching Stromboli erupt, looking at ultrasound scans of the seabed mapping its story of seismic violence, wondering what the hell I had done. My conscience had a field day weaving metaphorical life lessons out of the natural world. Being inside my head was like being back at school, found guilty by morality tales.

It had been like that since the day in Massachusetts, just after Christmas, when I told the children's father I was leaving him. By the time I left, a few weeks later, the adrenaline of conflict had subsided and I arrived in London with the girls in an amorphous, amoeba-like fuzz. It felt as if there was nothing much inside me any more, just the leftovers of a mistaken identity and an inner voice of ceaseless recrimination. To survive, I knew I had to make a decision.

Choose a direction. Jump. Sometimes all you can do is swim away from what you know you do not want. Then it's swim, swim, swim. Living in the present, looking forward, always forward, knowing you're striving for something, aiming at something, without really knowing what, without daring to think about what may be lurking beneath the surface, without daring to glance back, because look what happened to Orpheus and Eurydice.

All I knew back then was that I didn't want to bring the children up in London.

Perhaps it's not until you find safe harbour that you can let your mind dwell on the implications of your actions, and dare to confront the future as you really are and as it really might be, not simply make happy-lists. Once I got to Salina, I sat on this terrace night after night, teaching myself to tell the difference between the way the house responded to wind, thunder and jumping children, from the deep, earth-jelly swing of a tremor. I watch Juno's ferry slip behind the headland of Lipari. Was I more disturbed back then by living on a fault line or by the consequences of my decisions? Sometimes there seemed to be no difference.

Back then, I didn't know if I could create a life here for myself and the children. But life went on. Chaotically, as it is with kids, from hour to hour and day to day, fragile skeins of happiness and laughter accumulating like sand forming stone. The terrace became the heart of our lives. The girls learned to cycle and skate here, made tents of cushions and sarongs, houses of cardboard boxes, built wobbly towers of Kapla, citadels of Lego. I would sit here with Emma, then mother of two, now of six, drinking Yorkshire tea, exploring our lives – mine as a single mum, hers as the wife of an island fisherman – as the kids painted pebbles or made perfumes of stolen roses.

A beam of light, the sputter of an engine. I drop to the ground and peep over the wall. A solitary headlight on the road sixty-seven steps below. Someone on a Vespa. I wait for its tail light to disappear around a corner, then walk over to the kitchen.

The lock on the door is still broken.

I open it, stretching cobwebs.

4

The gap is just wide enough. You could step inside, avoiding the loose tile where the kids hid coins, and into the room where I worked on a laptop that fizzed with static from unearthed electrical wires. Next, the bathroom with its pink bathtub, where Izzy, inspired by a Horrible History of Cleopatra, once bathed in a month's supply of long-life milk. Those little heaps of white powder on the floor, the duct tape over the plug holes? Protection against the cockroaches that would creep in when the house was empty. Carry on and you'd move into the front bedroom, where you can lie on the bed and see nothing but the sea. A good place for daydreaming and crying.

But even without breaking cobwebs, entering is trespassing.

So back over the wall and slither down softly. Peep back. No footprints in the bougainvillea. A flash of orange by my knee. I wiggle a hand through the weeds and find the pebble the kids painted with an erupting volcano that we used as a doorstop. I put it in my pocket, slip my sandals back on and walk softly down the sixty-seven steps to the road.

Part I

FAVIGNANA

ORANGEADE

February 2004. A damp Saturday afternoon at Notting Hill Gate. Izzy is five, Juno two, and we are waiting for a bus in the rain, huddling inside the shelter. Someone has fired an air pellet, transforming the window into a giant web of shattered glass. It has been like this since we arrived in London five weeks ago, and every day there are more lozenges of glass on the pavement. There's a guy now, sunk inside a damp hoodie, fretting at a shard with a fingernail. Izzy watches him, entranced. His cuticles are picked raw. The lozenge falls, and she bobs down and picks it up. She's been collecting bus shelter safety glass, like she used to collect shells and sea glass on Good Harbor beach in Massachusetts. The glass isn't sharp, so I suppose the activity to be harmless. But as usual, there is an interfering old lady to disapprove.

'No, dear, it's dirty.'

Izzy glowers, holding the shard up to show Juno the tinge of sea green along its broken edge. 'Look, Juno, another diamond. We are rich!'

Nothing could be further from the truth. I have a royalty cheque from the *Rough Guide to Italy* due next week and that is it. Here in London, it will be gone in three months. Of course, I could ask the children's father but the break-up is so new, wounds still raw, that grey areas feel dangerous. Leeds? Where Mum and Dad are? The royalties would last longer up north but, much as I love my parents, much as they would love to have their grandchildren close by, I know that in Leeds I would disintegrate.

But I am in danger of dissolving here in London too. My mind feels like a bolus in a lava lamp, forming one shape then splitting, splitting again, morphing, disintegrating, reforming, then cutting loose and drifting out through ears and eyes and hair follicles, carrying us up as in a hot-air balloon, slowly, above the cars, above the traffic lights, up, past the floors of a tower block until our heads are dots, until London becomes like the map at the beginning of *Eastenders* and we are invisible. I've had bad times before, fragile times, but nothing quite like this. At least, not since I became a mother. But then, I say to myself, you've just made yourself a single mum.

'Mummy, look!' And we and the hooded man watch another lozenge of glass fall. Izzy picks it up. 'So beautiful!' The man is young but his eyes are bloodshot. He shakes his head and smiles.

The 52 to Kensal Rise pulls in, along its side a huge advert for Sunny Delight, a heavily advertised orangeade with which Izzy has become obsessed. With most of their toys still in storage, her TV watching has gone through the roof, especially as the only child-friendly aspect of the mirror- and laminate-lined apartment I've rented for a month is the Disney Channel.

She has been asking for Sunny Delight several times a day.

'So when?'

'When you're big.'

'How big?'

'Big.'

'But how big?'

'Nine.'

'Really, really? I can have Sunny Delight when I'm nine?'

'Uh-huh,' I say, lifting the pram onto the bus.

'How many years is that?'

I put the brake on the pram, swing her up too. Plant a kiss on her cold, wet nose. 'Four.'

'Four! That's not fair, that's forever, that's ...'

If things had worked out as I'd dared to dream, we'd have been off next week to the Mediterranean, eating and island-hopping from Greece to Italy. I was going to write a book called *Eating the Odyssey*, an adventure to pursue while I healed, something to focus on that would keep me busy, moving from place to place without too much time to think. Something that would reflect me back to myself as somebody I would like to meet, someone strong and brave, someone not prepared to settle for the path of least resistance. I was even excited. But over the past month, as publisher after publisher rejected the proposal, my glorious dream of spending a year in the wake of Odysseus has shrivelled.

I peer through the mucky bus window. It is raining in earnest now, water sheeting down the canopies of kebab shops and money exchanges. What the hell am I going to do? I can't believe that it was only just before Christmas that I pushed the pram across the iced sands of Good Harbor beach to the internet café to find an email from an agent, saying, '*Eating the Odyssey* is a wonderful idea, please don't show it to anyone else.' On the way home, we danced on sand that the ice had turned to fudge, Izzy twirling as I spun Juno, dancing turquoise seas, hot sun, olive trees, lemons, bougainvillea, the scent of jasmine, us in a garden gathering basil, picking pine nuts from cones, taking turns with a pestle as we made our own pesto. 'It's very important to remember,' I said to Izzy as we stood on the deck of the house, stamping snow and sand off our boots, 'that sometimes you can make dreams come true.'

Ha ha ha, says my whisper voice, shows how much you know.

The gutters of Ladbroke Grove are awash with dirty rainwater. Is London trying to tell me something?

I spent my childhood pursued by morality tales, narratives created not for the pleasure of storytelling but to teach you a lesson. School assembly was full of them. Robert the Bruce and his damn spider, and a weird one about William Colgate, the toothpaste inventor, making a financial arrangement with God. Most were variations on the theme of pride comes before a fall. Indeed, in 1970s Yorkshire, I was surrounded by relatives who seemed to think it was their job to teach kids not to get ideas above their station – cynical great uncles who wallowed in the anti-romance and misogyny of working men's clubs, and narrow-minded great aunts who thought that school-learning was a waste of time for girls, and tut-tutted over my low grades in needlework and the pricks of blood that spotted anything I sewed.

My parents were different. Mum made up adventure stories for us, an instalment every night, and dreamed of us having a sailing boat. She had sailed only vicariously, through the pages of *Swallows and Amazons*, and by the time she could afford a boat, we had all grown up, but she taught me that having dreams is OK. She wrote children's stories and *libretti* broadcast on Radio Leeds and YTV. She wrote reading books about children on a council estate, so that the inner-city kids she taught could see themselves in books. She showed me that ordinary people like us could achieve stuff.

Looking back, it seems strange that the morality tales from outside our family could have had such power. But then, I think, as the bus stops beneath a poster that reads 'BE SURE YOUR SIN WILL FIND YOU OUT', morality tales, like religions, find self-doubt as nourishing as bacteria do warm agar in a petri dish.

Dad left school at fourteen to be a watchmaker, but out of nowhere he developed a passion for opera and classical music. He and a friend hired a basement on an elegant Georgian square full of private doctors and barristers' chambers, furnished it with old cinema seats and built a seismic sound system with tombstones inside the speakers to play opera to any waif, stray, lost soul or cold policeman who happened to be passing. Dad showed me, just by the music that he surrounded us with, that there was a depth and complexity to life that went beyond the everyday, and that not everything could be put into words. He also taught me happiness was more important than ambition. Concerned, I think, that geeky kids got bullied, my parents bought me a radio for my eleventh birthday, tuned to Radio 1, and I discovered pop. One of my most joyous memories is dancing to 'I Feel Love' outside a souvenir shop on a school trip to London, but it was Monteverdi, Albinoni, Mahler, Rachmaninov, Britten who soaked up my teenage angst and made me feel that yearning was universal.

The bus jerks to a stop up outside Sainsbury's and I duck to dodge an elbow. As drenched people haul shopping aboard, I hear

Albinoni's *Adagio* playing in my head, so vivid I almost turn to check it's not some weirdo hugging a ghetto blaster. But I know it's not, just as well as I know it's not a telepathic message from Dad. It is simply music that I heard so often it is as much a part of me as my DNA. I look through the rain and wonder if it's not the conscious values and sensible rules of parenting that remain in your children for all their lives – helping them find resilience when things are tough – but your passions and dreams, the authentic ones that speak of who you really are, and that you transmit whether you are aware of it or not.

And what I love is Italy.

The first time I went to Italy, in the 1980s, I was shocked. I got off the train in Verona and it stank. It stank of drains and sewage and decaying cabbage and forgotten dishcloths, and I spent much of the first day trying to breathe through my mouth. Coming from a solid British city of brick and stone, stucco perplexed me, the way it flaked and crumbled, and soaked up the stains of rust and black mould. And so did the cracks between cobbles filled with cigarette butts and sunflower seeds.

But I loved the life on those cobbled streets. The colour, the sun, the light, the way Italians spoke with their hands, choreographing the air, and how kids played in piazzas while their parents had an *aperitivo* instead of being dispatched to bed by seven. I loved how people dressed like it mattered what they looked like – golden men in ochre trousers and women who walked like being gorgeous was nothing to be ashamed of, heels and bags selected to give just proportions to every outfit. No one had scuffed shoes or creased coat hems; even the punks had immaculately coiffed Mohicans. Far from not getting above your station, here they made an art of it. As I travelled from Verona to Venice then Padua and Mantua and Florence and Siena, bus drivers, shop assistants, market-stall holders and chambermaids not only knew but were proud of Giotto, Michelangelo, Raphael, Dante, Vivaldi, Puccini. Culture, it seemed, wasn't a class thing, it was an Italian thing.

I got over the flaking stucco. I even started to find something beautiful in the way the yellows, pinks and madders faded with the sun, and the plaster eroded to reveal the crumbled rubble and brickwork beneath. I loved the way that heavy rain would leave traces of ochre and rose stucco on the pavement below and I wondered if Italians had a more comfortable relationship with the idea of impermanence and accepted that the present is provisional. Perhaps that is what having a Roman amphitheatre or Renaissance duomo round the corner does to the psyche.

Time in Italy seemed less linear than it was at home, more of a space waiting to be filled with whatever delights the day might bring – exquisite miniature pastries behind the etched glass of an art nouveau window, a sliver of cantaloupe on a market-stall holder's knife, amber and pink spritzes on a waiter's tray, a flirty glance, a raised eyebrow, a tanned ankle in a tasselled loafer. Italians didn't mind waiting at the deli counter half an hour or more for a custom-made *panino*, and nor were they embarrassed to take up other Italians' time as they gave precise instructions to the *panino*-maker ... a touch of oregano, a *pizzico* of pepperoncino, *no*, the pecorino a little thinner, *yes*, so the light shines through, and just one artichoke, sliced thin, no thinner, and a sundried tomato left whole. Italians didn't appear to mind waiting at all. They chatted and laughed and joked, and time seemed fluid. Nor did they rush home after work for tea. They brushed their hair, reapplied make up, straightened their collars, sprayed on perfume and strolled, appraising shoes in shop windows, encountering friends by chance or design, stopping for an *aperitivo*. And then these glamorous people disappeared through heavy wooden portals in the flaking stucco walls, and, a few minutes later, between the slats of shutters, you could see lights go on.

I went back to England, learned Italian and practised by talking to imaginary Italian friends. I finished university and wanted to live in Italy, but I didn't quite have the nerve. It still felt like something for better connected, wealthier people than me. I started a PhD on T. S. Eliot and hated it, trained to be a teacher and hated it more, and then one day at a friend's house in the mid-1980s, I found a copy of *Cosmopolitan*. In among the fashion spreads and perfume ads was a half-page interview with a guy who had set up a series of guidebooks for travellers on a tight budget who were as interested in contemporary life and beaches as they were in high culture and history. The guy was Mark Ellingham; the series was the Rough Guides, and they had published four titles. Italy wasn't one of them.

'I could write one of these,' I said.

My friend spluttered over her cup of tea. 'They were advertising for writers for Italy last week, in the *Guardian*.'

Strokes of luck like that don't happen often, especially ones that could change your life, and I worked harder on that application than I had ever worked at anything before. I don't know how I would have coped if I'd failed. But thankfully, I didn't, and in September 1987 I was off, a backpacking travel writer living on a shoestring, unable to quite believe that this was my life, and that by the skin of my teeth I had escaped the ordinary.

It wasn't exactly glamorous. I spent a lot of time copying down bus timetables and museum opening hours and survived on bread, olives and oranges. I couldn't afford hotels, so slept in hostels, convents, campsites, even once a commune, where I helped two members of a Bulgarian heavy metal band sell contraband cigarettes. But it wasn't humdrum. Even the simplest things in Italy seemed resonant with history, culture, tradition. Making coffee in a little hob-top Moka instead of with a spoonful of Gold Blend; joining the elderly ladies scrubbing clothes on a stone washboard by the village fountain; buying food from market stalls where not only was everything seasonal, but the provenance of the vegetables was scrawled on labels, suggesting that everyone knew that the broccoli from village A was better than that from village B.

Over the next decade, I carried on making trips to Italy, no matter whatever and whoever else was in my life. While pregnant I sang Spice Girls songs with a radio producer as we walked through a disused train tunnel on the way to Spoleto. The first time I went as a mother, Izzy was not quite one, and so fussy with her food that she was becoming seriously underweight, and I was beginning to panic.

'Let's see how she is when you get back from Italy, and in

the meantime try not to worry,' said my lovely paediatrician, patting my hand. Doctor O'Connor turned out to be right. The first lunchtime, with Izzy sitting on my knee, the waiter placed a steaming dish of tagliatelle with truffles on the table. Izzy breathed in, grabbed a handful and stuffed it into her mouth.

MYTHOLOGICAL
RESONANCES

That evening, in Kensal Green, when the girls are asleep, I sit in the kitchen eating pasta and pesto and begin to think. Just because *Eating the Odyssey* hadn't worked out doesn't mean that nothing could. I have my royalties coming and the pound is strong against the euro. We could just go and live in Italy. If I am careful, we could almost manage on the royalties alone. But whereabouts? I know and love Rome, Florence, Venice and the art towns of Tuscany and Umbria, but they are expensive, and the past year, living on the coast of Massachusetts while the children's father set up a business importing Indonesian furniture, had been a revelation. On the beaches of Cape Ann I discovered that if you have sea and sun, you don't need much else when children are young. Sandcastles, sea glass, beachcombing, sea creatures, fishing nets. They play and you get odd moments to lie in the sun, swim, even to read.

But I know it is more than that. I had discovered that out-of-season beaches are good places to be alone without feeling lonely, good places to think without staring into nothingness. On Cape Ann, I learned that there were fears, dreams, memories that I would have been afraid to contemplate in a room, even in the countryside, that I could face up to without flinching by the sea. Living in an old wooden house on Good Harbor beach, I found that the sea made things bearable that otherwise might not have been. The wild seas were exhilarating, waves crashing with therapeutic abandon

17

against the rocks, and calm seas were a salve, the shifts in light, mood, colour compelling me to stand still for a moment, swallow the lump in my throat and look at what was before me. It wasn't some hackneyed notion that the sea put life into perspective; it was more visceral than that. During those awful months when the relationship was crumbling, my reflex responses to the sea reminded me that feeling wonder at the beauty of the world can be enough.

However, although I need to know that solitude is available, I am not a recluse. I am not self-sufficient enough to have no one with whom I can share emotions, opinions, ideas, anxieties. I need to go somewhere I will meet people. I love the buzz of small-town evening life in the Mediterranean. And the chance to dress up sometimes. I am an outdoor person, and even in my prettiest clothes I am happier in a pavement café watching life pass by than in the finest of bars or restaurants.

I would like a fishing harbour. It's not just that I like fresh fish; it's the culture, with its ancient roots and rhythms, the boats, the nets and the fact that all is dictated by the vagaries of the weather. It could be a fantastic education, I think as I wash the dishes, to live in a community where the girls would learn that they were not in complete control of their surroundings. It might foster respect for the planet, and perhaps help them to grow up questioning the metropolitan world most people we know inhabit, with its mania for instant gratification and aspirational consumption. And wouldn't it be great for them too to be able to eat only local, seasonal fruit and veg, as an antidote to supermarkets where anything is available all the time? *OK, reality check.* I make myself a camomile tea and go to sit in the window. Currently, the only vegetables they will eat are potatoes and cucumbers, but surely that would change surrounded by the fantastic colours and smells of an Italian market? We could grow our own vegetables. I have never successfully grown anything but surely it can't be hard in Italy.

Finally, I think, I might have to forget about following Odysseus, but I am fascinated by the way classical mythology gives the sense of tapping into a common humanity that stretches back over the millennia – the fear of illness and death, the dread of betrayal, the dream of love, the fear of harm coming to loved ones, the struggle to understand life and what it means, and how to live well.

So, the sea, the sun and Italy. But I can't think of anywhere along the coast that I want to live. I've seen the chic, over-populated seaside towns of Tuscany, Liguria and Amalfi; the dreary Adriatic coastline, with kilometres of featureless sand punctuated with grids of sun loungers and umbrellas. I remember some nice little coves in Puglia, but the interior depressed me, motorways slicing through agri-industrial fields of wheat, and dead flat hectares of olives and vines.

But that is all about me, not the girls, and though it is probably true that the kids have a nicer time when their parent is happy, is that really a valid argument for taking them away on what could essentially be a very long holiday? On the other hand, who can argue that a childhood by the sea, absorbing another language and culture, would not be a fantastic basis for the rest of life?

I open my notebook and write a list:

Sea and sun

Quiet beaches

An old town or village – evening *passeggiata*, some life

Fishing harbour

Primary school

House with a sea view

Garden? Grow fruit and veg?

Ancient, preferably mythological resonances

Accessible and cheap

Over the next week I read. I google. Beaches. Fishing villages. Coastal reserves. Houses to rent by the sea. I pore through guidebooks, cut out photographs from magazines and research places on the web. I look at maps, at low-cost flight routes, call friends. That we should head somewhere in Italy, obvious. But apart from that, I wasn't getting anywhere. It is all too random.

I rang Mum.

'Do you really think this is a good idea?' she said. 'After all, it's nearly time for Izzy to start school.'

Exactly. I am surrounded by friends buying houses in the catchment areas of the state primary schools with the highest Ofsted scores or going to church every Sunday to try to get their kids into the local C of E school. Children as young as five are sent to private maths and English tutors, music lessons, drama lessons, language schools, in the hope that at eleven, they will secure scholarships at public school. And in case they don't, parents are feverishly saving money to add to the school fee accounts grandparents have been persuaded to open. Anything rather than see their children end up in the community school, where, if the stories passed between parents pushing their kids on swings in the park are anything to go by, our offspring will spend their days writing misspelled essays, getting stoned in the toilets or being laughed at for over-achieving and threatened with broken bottles.

'You're a mother now,' says Mum. 'You can't just carry on living like a nomad. And you don't even seem to know where you want to go.'

So even Mum thinks I am being irresponsible and selfish. Perhaps she is right. She'd dreamed of having a boat but had put us first, worked hard to pay for music lessons, roller skates, seaside holidays in a fisherman's cottage.

Living by the sea in Italy is what *I* want, how *I* want to be a mother, but how can I know if it will be good for the girls or not? Is it egoistic to think what I could offer them, alone, in some Italian paradise, would be more than the museums of London and one of Ofsted's top-rated primary schools?

After Mum rings off, I look back at my notes and despair. Perhaps, I think, we should just go to Italy for a few months and have a look. So I start to plan a journey right around the Italian coast. I am frantic. Manic. Gripped by the fear that if I pause for a moment, or think too much, I will end up spending the rest of my life in Kensal Green.

I write to a magazine editor. Could I write a series of monthly columns following my travels around Italy with two young kids as I look for the perfect place to live? She emails straight back. 'No.'

I pull out my list again. If we can't go everywhere, I will have to choose somewhere.

'There are plenty of beautiful places in England,' my mum had said.

I look back at my list. The Northumberland coast, Cornwall, even the Scilly Isles would not cut it. I want an outdoor life that does not involve technical fabrics, battling the elements and swimming in freezing water, and I want an abundance of fish, fruit and vegetables that does not involve ice freight, Israeli poly tunnels or overpriced farmers' markets. And, pretentious or not, I want to inspire the girls with my love of classical history and mythology, and give them a sense at first hand of the roots of Western culture.

Then, a few days later, the magazine editor emails. 'I need a piece on the tuna massacre, the *mattanza*, on the Sicilian island of Favignana. £320. Are you interested?'

Sicily. I have never been to Sicily. Of course I am interested. Not in the tuna massacre, nor even in the fee, which will barely cover our flights, but because it feels like destiny has stepped in. The cost of living in Sicily is low, isn't it? And the sun shines all year. *What about the Mafia?* said Mum. I look to see what my colleagues Jules Brown and Rob Andrews had written in the *Rough Guide to Sicily*. 'The Mafia is usually an in-house affair, hardly likely to affect travellers.' I google Favignana and find images of turquoise seas, white beaches, golden cliffs that looked as if they'd been sculpted by a Cubist. I also read about the *mattanza*. Every spring, bluefin tuna leave the Atlantic for the warmer waters of the Mediterranean, swimming through the Straits of Gibraltar and along the Tunisian coast to Sicily, where the fishermen of Favignana trap them. We had to be in Sicily in May, when the tuna arrived. The rest would follow.

CINNAMON

The forecourt of Palermo airport is crazy-paved with taxis. They are parked at all angles and at each a driver stands shouting and gesticulating with a cigarette at an open door. Every single car has its engine running. It is humid, the air a steamy soup of petrol fumes and cigarettes, and the girls huddle together in their double buggy.

'But I thought you said we were going to the beach,' Izzy says, tapping the pink plastic Barbie bucket she has carried all the way from London.

'We are. This is just the airport.'

'Look at all those people smoking. Don't they know they will die?'

A swarthy man squeezed into tight white jeans and a yellow jacket saunters up, smoking a pungent cigarillo.

'Die,' says Juno, staring.

Izzy looks at the man, splutters pointedly, then buries her face in her bucket. The man looks a little uncomfortable.

'Palermo?'

'Cover your face, Juno, or you will die,' Izzy's voice booms from inside the bucket. Juno is staring at the cabbie, fascinated by the smoke coming out of his mouth. Izzy nudges her. 'Your bucket, Juno, put it over your face, quick, there's a stinky man!'

Juno snorts.

'Palermo?' he repeats, a little weakly.

'No,' I say, 'Cinisi.'

'Cinisi?' He raises an eyebrow. Cinisi is a two-bit seaside town, best known as the birthplace of Mafia boss Gaetano Badalamenti, who used his influence back in the early 1960s to ensure that the airport was built right on his doorstep. 'Ah.' He looks puzzled, then suddenly smiles, nodding at the buckets. 'Cinisi beach?'

'No, Cinisi *stazione*.' An obscure station on the main line from Palermo to the west of Sicily, which I'd discovered after poring over maps and train timetables. Ten minutes from the airport, so no need to waste forty euros on a taxi into Palermo. I look at my phone. The last train of the night is due in twenty-five minutes. We better get a move on.

'Cinisi *stazione*. Forty.'

Outrageous. I turn and gesture to another taxi driver.

'Twenty then.'

I offer ten and we agree on fifteen.

There are no seatbelts. The girls kneel at the open window, arms outstretched, faces to the wind, cheeks glowing, the hot air whipping at their hair as the car hurtles along the motorway. Accustomed to being buckled into car seats, this is the first time in their lives that they have travelled unrestrained in a car, let alone one travelling at high speed.

'No car seat, no car seat!' chants Izzy, stretching her arms out wide. Their father, my mum, everyone I know in England, would be horrified.

Juno opens her arms wide too, then flops back onto my knee, giggling uncontrollably. Well, I think, I came here because I wanted to give them freedom. I guess this is it. Freedom has risks.

Without slowing down, the taxi takes a sharp turn off the motorway, sending the girls tumbling onto my lap in a tangle of arms and legs. They scramble back to the window as we tear down a long, straight, dazzlingly lit and totally empty street of pale, flat-roofed buildings garlanded with sagging strings of grimy bunting, dust billowing behind us. I've been travelling in Italy for twenty-five years but have never seen anything like this. We turn off at a piazza where improbably tall, skinny palms sway in the breeze, then zigzag along narrow, dark, unlit streets lined with crumbling ochre cubes. Where are the pavement cafés, I think, where are the beautiful people strolling the streets eating ice cream?

The station is unmanned, the ticket machine vandalised. The taxi driver, placing the suitcase at the edge of the platform, tells me not to worry – I can get a ticket on the train. Then he points at a digital display above the platform. The last train to Trapani is half an hour late.

'That way,' he says in English, pointing behind the station. 'Pizza.'

The pizzeria is in a flat-roofed building of polished pine, brightly lit, with Louis Armstrong soaring from the speakers. It is Sunday night and it is jam-packed with loud tables of teenagers, louder tables of families and a sole courting couple cowering at a table for two in a dark corner below a Swiss cheese plant thick with dust. The clock on the wall says 9.30. That must be why the streets are empty. Everyone is at dinner. Give it another hour and they'll all be out again, strolling aimlessly, looking beautiful and eating ice creams till gone midnight.

Two immaculately dressed children with Etruscan eyes slide over and stare shyly at Izzy and Juno, who respond by hiding behind my back. I order Fanta, beer and two margheritas, which I take out to the platform. The girls, sitting in the pram, fall silent with the first mouthful, which has a surprising note of cinnamon. The Arab influence on Sicilian cuisine, dating back to, what, the ninth century? They also brought mosaics, science, almonds, ice cream. I sit down on the bench beside the pram and wonder why I hadn't thought of persuading my editor to commission an article on the traces of Arab cuisine in Sicilian cookery. I would far rather write about this cinnamon-scented tomato sauce than a tuna massacre.

A bell shrills, violating the silence, and the train hurtles out of the darkness, kettle-drumming through body and soul like the climax of Elgar's *Nimrod*. A door yawns open head-height, spilling white light onto the platform. There is no way I can lift the buggy so high and I stand there frozen, but then a man springs down from the train, and swings the case, the buggy and the two girls aboard, as I watch in a daze. He then graciously offers me his hand and I step up onto the train.

'*Grazie*,' I say. '*Grazie mille*.'

The man has sun-wrinkled, burnished skin, roasted deep like a chestnut, and green eyes. He is wearing a green and black striped Bertie Wooster blazer and a baseball hat.

'Sebastiano,' he says. You can see straight away that he is used to smiling, his leathery face as supple and creased as a pair of thirty-year-old brogues, and he smiles now, doffing his cap to the girls. I feel my heart rate calm. He is totally bald and his pate, several shades lighter than his face, is a riot of freckles. The girls gaze shyly at him, hand in hand, as he bows low, rather gravely, then replaces the cap.

He slides open the door into a compartment and turns to me.

'Are you going all the way to Trapani?'

'Yes,' I say, 'we want to go to Favignana.'

We walk inside the compartment, leaving suitcase and pram in the corridor. The only other passengers are a crewcut youth with deep-set eyes who glowers as we enter and a middle-aged woman in rhinestone-studded jeans, who smiles gap-toothed at the girls. The compartment is decorated with silver wallpaper embossed with circles that remind me of a bad migraine and the floor is scattered with greasy screws of brown paper. As the train lurches, a can rattles down the aisle, leaving a snail-trail of Coca-Cola behind it.

'Favignana,' says Sebastiano. 'That's where I'm from.'

Tired now, the girls lie on their tummies and gaze sleepily out of the window at the passing lights.

'Do you live there?'

'Sometimes. Sometimes not.' He seems on the verge of a confidence but appears to decide against it. 'So, what about you? Why Favignana?'

'I'm a journalist,' I say. 'I'm here to cover the *mattanza*.' A great word, 'cover', with its implication of objectivity and impartiality. Puzzled, Sebastiano looks at the children, who have now drifted into sleep. I guess he is wondering what the hell I am doing bringing two tiny kids to watch a bloodbath.

I tell him I am combining work with looking for somewhere to live, quiet and unspoilt, by the sea, where I can bring the girls up far away from city life.

'Favignana is quiet,' he says, 'and some of it is beautiful, but I don't know if it would be a comfortable place for a stranger. The people, you see ...'

'The people?'

'You'll see.' He sits down across the aisle from me and looks out of the window. I can see his reflection and wonder if he is looking at it or through to the night. I close my eyes and breathe deep, hurtling through the night between one life and another. As well as the turquoise seas and golden cliffs, my research has left me haunted with images of savage men, choppy seas, frothy water pink with blood, and a net known as the chamber of death. When there are enough fish inside to make a kill worthwhile, the net is raised and the bluefin are stabbed to death. Worse, a book I read about the *mattanza*, by a journalist who had an affair with a tuna-fisherman, describes her lover diving into the chamber of death after the kill.

I know I am going to hate the *mattanza*. Bluefin are under serious threat, their numbers decreasing year by year, and the World Wildlife Foundation has called for a moratorium banning bluefin tuna fishing in the Mediterranean. As I was packing for Sicily, £2.5 million was paid for a single bluefin at the Tokyo fish market. 'Imagine a market selling tiger meat,' I heard a marine conservationist say on Radio 4.

Until the beginning of the twentieth century, there were working *tonnara* or tuna fisheries all around the coast of Sicily, each one running its own *mattanza*. The narrow strait between Favignana and the adjacent island of Lèvanzo is one of the easiest places in the Mediterranean to trap the fish and the only place in Sicily where the *mattanza* has survived. I open my eyes and stare at my reflection in the train window. If the *mattanza* hadn't provided an excuse to get away from London, I would never have agreed to write about it.

JOYRIDE

Although it is after midnight, Trapani station is bathed in dazzling light, the air heavy and warm. The girls are fast asleep. I lean on the pram for a moment and breathe in deeply. This is Sicily. We made it.

It's one of those surreal Fascist-era stations – all repeating arches and nifty vanishing points – built by Mussolini all over Italy. I've been arriving at stations like this since I was eighteen years old and every time, they take the wind out of my sails. I imagine I'll step off the train as beautiful and inscrutable as Botticelli's *Primavera*, yet instead I end up feeling like a dispossessed mannequin from a De Chirico canvas. By now, I should know better, but frilly dreams are part of my secret armour and sandbag resignation never did anyone any good.

Scant voices and footsteps echo, brittle, as the last few passengers scurry home. I guess I had imagined Sicily would be different, more exotic and sensual. But so far, the only sign of its Arabic past has been that taste of cinnamon in the pizza sauce at Cinisi. I pull up the handle of my suitcase. Did it never occur to Il Duce, I wonder, as I push the pram with one hand and drag the suitcase with the other, how demoralising it might be to travel the length of the peninsula, only to arrive somewhere that looked exactly like the place you had left? Perhaps he hoped that by building the same station over and over again, he could convince Italy that it was a single, homogeneous nation.

Except that it wasn't.

And isn't.

For example.

I emerge onto an even more startlingly lit travertine piazza, deserted except for a couple of seedy looking guys with gelled spikes smoking outside a snack booth. So far, so normal. Then I look around for a taxi. And there isn't one.

Name me any other city in Italy where you arrive on the last train of the night to discover there is not a single taxi waiting.

Determined not to panic, I drag pram and suitcase the length of the forecourt, then walk back to see if, by a miracle, there is a taxi there that I hadn't noticed the first time. Or one that has returned from taking people wherever they might go on a Sunday night in Trapani. Nope. *Niente.*

So. I'm here, at midnight, in a town I don't know, alone with two young children and no way of getting to the hotel I booked. Great start. Then, I notice a sticker with a taxi number stuck to a small cupboard bolted to a lamppost. My English SIM doesn't work in Italy, so I try to keep calm as I write the taxi number on the back of my hand, swing the pram round, drag the suitcase behind me and trudge back to the concourse to look for a public phone. There's a row of them in a corner, six of them. I pick up each receiver, one by one, and naturally every one of them is dead.

Heading back to the taxi rank I talk to myself, slowly, softly, deeply, like a suicide counsellor. There's no need to despair. Step down from the window, there is hope. You have a hotel booked; you have a map. It will be hard walking to the hotel, with the pram and the suitcase, but the children are sleeping and you are strong. Step away from the window now, step down, carefully now, step down and take a deep breath ...

'Excuse me, are you all right?'

I leap about a mile into the air. Just as well I am not standing at a window on the twentieth floor.

It's Sebastiano from the Cinisi train, bowing like a Shakespearian courtier, doffing his baseball cap as if removing the cosy from an egg.

He replaces the cap. '*Allora*, what's wrong?'

'There are no taxis,' I say, 'and none of the payphones are working, so I can't call one.'

He pulls out a mobile phone the size of a brick and I read out the taxi number from the back of my hand.

'It's ringing!'

My spirits rise. Then almost immediately fall. I tap Sebastiano on the shoulder and point at the little metal cupboard on the lamppost. Inside it, a phone is shrilling.

I take Sebastiano's phone and call the hotel. A woman answers and, in a voice cloying as *dulce de leche*, says she can't help. Why can't she help? I ask. Isn't it a normal thing for a hotel to call a taxi for their guests?

A *dulce de leche* hum, then silence.

I feel panic start to rise.

Concern flashes over Sebastiano's face, which he swiftly masks with a smile, revealing his gold incisor. 'So, what are you going to do? I mean ...' He hesitates. He's probably terrified I'm going to come back with some tragic story of existential angst or, worse, the truth of partner-leaving. He breathes in slowly, cups his hand over his mouth and stares into the distance. Poor guy, he probably wishes he'd never spoken to me.

One of the guys from outside the snack booth walks over to Sebastiano and mutters something. White lamplight falls on a hefty forearm.

'What did he say?'

'He offered to be our taxi.'

I am not sure. It seems a bit bloody risky. Sebastiano seems unsure as well, but as far as I can see I have no choice, unless I really do want to walk two miles to the hotel.

Sebastiano lays a hand on my shoulder. 'I think I better come with you.'

The snack booth guy walks away and returns a few minutes later in a battered Fiat 500 with a mangled radiator grill. There is no way two adults, two children, the pram and the suitcase are all going to fit in. I look at Sebastiano. The harsh light reveals the skull beneath his skin. He is older and looks frailer than I realised.

'We'll have to do two trips,' he says. 'First you and the girls, and then me, the pram and the luggage.'

As we carry the girls into the car, they wake up.

'Where are we?' Izzy sits up straight, alert, anxious. 'What's happening? What are those wires?' She points at a spaghetti of multicoloured wires spilling out of the dashboard.

Oh great. A joyriding taxi.

The man sees me looking, grins gappily and, raising a bushy comma of an eyebrow, pulls a key out of his pocket and off we go, lurching through deserted side streets full of muttering retreats that T S Eliot would doubtless have appreciated had he been a Trapanese. At last, we pull up in a narrow street outside a revolving door at the top of a flight of steps neatly covered with red baize. I pay the driver and flee inside. The lobby is all shiny toffee marble and gilt-frame mirrors. Juno trots off towards an ornamental kumquat tree and has just started to pick the fruit when a plump lady with a blonde coiffeur walks in wafting clouds of perfume so recently applied that the alcohol catches my throat. She frowns, hand on hip, and peers at the children over half-moon diamante reading glasses on a heavy gold chain.

'Hold your brother's hand.' The *dulce de leche* voice. Hold Juno's hand, I translate. Izzy obeys and Dulce de Leche beams approval. Juno pops a kumquat in her mouth, bites it, then spits it out onto the gleaming marble.

'YEEUK.'

'Sorry,' I say, bending down to scrape up the pulp with a used tissue.

'They are very beautiful.' Dulce squeezes out a smile. 'Very blonde,' she says in caramel English. '*Come si dice.* How do you say – "cute"?'

Izzy, clearly taken with the idea of cuteness, looks at their reflection in the mirror, wipes a smear of kumquat from Juno's face and takes hold of her hand. Then she spots a bowl of sweets on the reception desk.

'Who are those sweets for, Mummy?'

'For people,' I say, digging out the passports.

'Not for children?'

'For children too, but you have to wait to be asked.'

Izzy stares at the sweets and then smiles again at the lady, exuding cuteness with every fibre of her five-year-old being.

'*Ah, gioia, vuoi una caramella?*' She passes the bowl to the children.

'*Caramella*,' says Izzy, taking a pink one.

'*Caramella*,' repeats Juno, taking a fistful.

Great. Their first Italian word is 'sweet'.

A phone shrills and Dulce de Leche answers, then passes me an ornate Bakelite and ormolu receiver. It is Sebastiano. The taxi has still not returned and he is worried. I reassure him we have arrived safely, and he rings off.

The lift clanks slowly up to the room. It's on the fourth floor. Huge, with cold ceramic tiles on the floor, lit by long-life bulbs protruding from faded lampshades. Above the double bed is a little plaster statue of the Virgin Mary. As I open the creaky shutters a car drives past. The thin glass rattles.

The children are asleep by the time there is a quiet knock on the door. It is Dulce de Leche with our suitcase. She has left the pram downstairs. Is that OK?

'Yes,' I say, 'but Sebastiano, our friend?'

'He says goodnight, and good luck,' says Dulce. 'He thought you might be sleeping and didn't want to disturb you. A kind man, I think. Un *vero angelo custode*.'

Angelo custode. Guardian angel. Indeed.

'But I needed to pay for his taxi.'

'Don't worry, *Signora*. There are still some people here who like to help.' I'm tempted to ask why she wasn't one of them, but instead I say a polite goodnight.

I lie on the bed in the dark, listening to the children breathing. If my phone worked, I'd be texting now. Telling the full story to my friends. And to the children's father: Arrived safely in hotel.

Which I suppose is true.

If abridged.

CANTALOUPE

There is a hydrofoil to Favignana at midday, which leaves time to explore Trapani first and find a café for breakfast. We step out of the hotel. The city swims, translucent as a mirage. A collage of white, sand, rose, ochre shifts without perspective against the cobalt-blue sky. There is a smell of salt and in the distance, I can hear a pneumatic drill. Izzy and Juno, faces shiny with suncream, screw up their eyes against the dazzle.

I strap them into the pram and we set off. There is no pavement so we have to walk in the middle of the narrow street, past parked cars with paintwork scarred and peeling like sun-blasted skin. A couple of Vespas whizz past a hair's breadth away, then a battered white Panda approaches and slides to a halt. It can't get past. I look through the windscreen at a youth with a very short fringe gelled flat to his forehead. He points to a tiny gap between two cars. Multiple ear-piercings, shiny football shirt, tattoo. Better do what he says. I swing the nose of the pram into the niche, but it still sticks out too far. The guy gets out, looks at the pram, frowns. A musky scent of ripe melon fills the street. Probably his hair gel.

Suddenly he grins. If he were a cartoon character, a lightbulb would be hovering over his head. He squats down beside the pram, takes a deep breath, braces himself and with a hulloo of *Pronte, bambine?* swings it high over his head, shouting *Evvia!* As the girls squeal with excitement, he carries them and the pram over the car. His muscles are not trembling one iota.

32

He sinks down into a squat and sets the pram down gently on the cobbles.

'*Grazie*,' I say.

'Can he do that again?' says Izzy.

'Again, again!' shouts Juno.

He raises a finger.

'*Aspetta*.' Wait.

The guy opens the hatchback and lifts a bright blue tarpaulin. The boot is full of cantaloupe melons. He selects one, sniffs it and puts it back. Picks up another, sniffs deeply and smiles.

'This one good.'

'Thank you.'

'*Arrivederci*.' He smiles, slamming the boot as I wedge the melon into the pram hood. He has no front teeth.

We turn a corner into a broad pedestrianised *corso* drenched in sun and paved with mellow limestone. It feels like stepping onstage. At its head is a huge, Spanish-looking church, its façade so intricately carved it could have been the work of a silversmith. Rising above us is a cathedral built of grainy golden sandstone. I can't resist touching the stone, rough-textured and glinting. After months of living with London brick, I get that lovely feeling of continuity, of life going on, whatever happens, that being somewhere ancient can give you. As I stand there, several women – some plump, some slight, none of them reaching higher than my chest – emerge from the church's gloomy innards, all of them clutching carrier bags of fish. They look at us suspiciously, then quite obviously begin to discuss us. They may be doing it *sotto voce* but their gestures are a giveaway. They are like a Greek chorus.

All eyes on me.

Little shake of the head and disapproval first at bare legs, then at bare arms, followed by gathering their shawls tighter over their shoulders.

All eyes on the girls.

Sentimental smiles: 'So blonde. So beautiful. But so underdressed.'

Eyes back to me and more head-shaking:

'What does she think she's doing, letting children out in May, when there's wind (heads swivel to a nearby palm tree, leaves trembling in the breeze), dressed only in cotton dresses?'

Back to the girls again: 'So blonde, so beautiful. But what a strange pram. Two seats. Are they twins, do you think?'

'No, they're different sizes.'

'That happens, you know, with twins. One of them eats all the food, takes up all the space and is born huge. The other a little runt.'

'And in the worst cases, one twin eats so much and takes up so much space that the other twin dies. Imagine that. Killing someone before you're even born.'

'Well, I'm not sure it's killing. It's nature. Destiny.'

'God's will.'

They all cross themselves, carrier bags of fish swinging wildly.

Eyes back to the pram again for more head-shaking and the odd tut-tut: 'Ugly. Khaki, what kind of colour is that for two little blonde girls? And built like a tractor.'

'She should have an engine fitted.'

General hilarity, cackles and nudges.

They should be used to strangers in Trapani. The Spanish ruled for centuries, laying down the law and sowing terror. Way before that, there were the Arabs and the Normans, and before them Romans and the Phoenicians. Back in Phoenician times, there was a temple above the city where men proved their devotion to the goddess Astarte by sleeping with holy prostitutes. And down the coast, on the island of Mozia, is a graveyard where the Phoenicians sacrificed their first-born children to the goddess Tanit. So, on reflection, it's not surprising that the Trapanese are a bit suspicious of strangers. Port people are often like that. Places of arrivals and departures, with an ever-shifting population of strangers. The locals feel threatened and treat the newcomers with suspicion, cheering themselves up by making them the butt of secret jokes. Underlying it, the fear that the strangers will seduce their women, steal their children. In fact, it's not only ports that are like that. I think of Lincolnshire villages, of the Eastern European agricultural workers, the tut-tuts of locals finding *kiełbasa piaszczańska* in the fridge at Tesco Express.

We walk on down the *corso*, past exuberant Baroque palaces with scrolly balconies from which you can imagine mantilla-ed Spanish ladies peeping out at the world, pale, from behind ivory fans. There are no pavement cafés and the shop fronts look as if they have not changed since the 1930s. Mannequins in dusty windows wearing sensible tweed suits, a gorgeous art nouveau bookshop and what can only be described as an emporium of candy, walls lined with trays of banana chews, strawberry marshmallows, gummy cherries, liquorice spirals, candy fried eggs and sour peaches. Quick as a flash I swing the pram around and cross to the other side of the street, past several narrow doorways with beaded fly curtains, each with a faded red stencilled sign in the stark capitals of Fascist-era Italy saying *macelleria, paneficio, vino olio* – butcher, baker, wine/oil. None has a window. We stop at the *macelleria* and peep through beads. A blood-smeared marble counter, half a cow hanging from a hook and, in the zinc display fridge, chickens with their heads and feet, coils of fat sausages, slabs of liver and, oh dear, a skinned rabbit.

'What's that?' asks Izzy.

'Rabbit.'

'A real rabbit?'

'Yes.'

'He's still got his eyes. How can people eat that?'

'You've eaten rabbit.' A huge plate of her grandfather's venison and rabbit stew less than a week ago.

'But … that wasn't the same. It didn't look like a real rabbit.'

I can see there is a grave risk of my daughter becoming a vegetarian. Which wouldn't be a problem, except that she refuses to eat any pulses, and still only eats potato and cucumber. She's not particularly keen on cheese either, unless it is Philadelphia, and she's pale and skinny enough as it is. But if I've brought her here in part to see what real food is about, I'm going to have to bite the bullet.

'Izzy, did you realise that all meat comes from animals?'

She looks at me aghast. 'What? Do you think I am stupid or something? Of course I know meat comes from animals, it's just, you know, at Sainsbury's the meat doesn't look so... animalish. That rabbit looks just like a pet rabbit that has had its fur taken off.'

She has a point.

We are getting hungry now and there is still no sign of a café. I turn around and head back the way we came, deftly avoiding the sweet shop. The old bids are still outside the church, admiring a toddler dressed in a pink padded ski suit, sitting in a nice normal pram with a frilly white parasol, pushed by a weary-looking mother in a pilled electric blue tracksuit smoking a cigarette. The bids look pointedly from suitably dressed Sicilian child to dangerously undressed English kids, and one of them takes a deep breath. Fearing a lecture on how to dress your child, I quickly ask where the market is and they point up a broad street that is being repaved. I thank them and make a swift retreat.

The street is billowing with dust, echoing with the sound of pneumatic drills, and to get along it I have to squeeze through passageways of plastic orange netting that keep getting snagged in the pram's side. Eventually we arrive at a semicircular colonnade packed with tarpaulined fish stalls, its cobbled pavement slippery with ice and water. There are tuna and swordfish twice the size of Izzy, heads sliced off to reveal the deep red and rose-pink flesh, silver anchovies layered like butterflies on sheets of paper. Surprisingly, the girls are fascinated. Perhaps it's only fluffy, furry things that they object to eating.

Admiring the rose-fleshed tuna, I ask the stallholder if there is news of the *mattanza*.

'News?' he asks.

'Are we still in time?' The timing changes from year to year depending on when the tuna arrive, and the numerous phone calls I made before I left had established nothing except the need to wait and see.

'Still in time?' He laughs, revealing a keyboard of huge, perfect teeth. 'Eh,' he calls over to the neighbouring stallholder, a tall, skinny man with a long, lugubrious face and bulging eyes who is butterflying anchovies. 'This lady wants to know if she's still in time for the *mattanza*!'

General hilarity.

'You'll be lucky if there *is* a *mattanza* this year,' says the toothy man.

Uh-oh.

'Why?' I start scrabbling for my notebook, then realise I left it in my suitcase at the hotel.

'Why? You want to know why? Hey, Giuseppe, she wants to know why.'

The lugubrious man looks over. 'You want to know why, *Signora*?' he says slowly. His voice is very deep and extremely despondent. Imagine Will Self reincarnated as a Sicilian fishmonger.

'Mmm,' I say.

'Well, it's not really for us to say. But there have been, some – shall we call them problems?'

'Problems?'

'Yes. Problems. *Interessi*.'

'*Interessi*?' Is that a euphemism for Mafia? I dare not ask.

'Problems,' he says and turns back to filleting anchovies. That, quite obviously, is all they are willing to say.

Meanwhile, the girls have wandered over to another stall and are happily munching through the free samples. We try smoked tuna, swordfish bresaola, even a salty tuna salami. There are sheep cheeses too – a creamy ricotta which Izzy declares is better than Philadelphia – and open trays of currants, sultanas, almonds, pine nuts and salted capers. I buy ricotta, currants, sultanas and almonds, a tiny jar of orange blossom honey and a loaf of crusty bread, and, giving up hope of finding a café, we set off back to the hotel to collect our bags.

MAGNESIUM GLARE

Through the scratched Perspex window of the hydrofoil, I can see Favignana slumped against the sky like a sleeping dinosaur. The sky is as heavy as a hot, damp sheet, and the sun glares like burning magnesium, leeching the sea of colour.

The boat slows its engine, lowers its wings into the water and chugs slowly into the port. Juno is asleep, face smudged with drying ricotta, t-shirt scattered with melon seeds, a hunk of bread clenched in her fist. Izzy is regarding with admiration the purple plastic mirror shades worn by an amply proportioned lady standing in front of us carrying a lilac cardboard box of cake, elaborately tied with gold ribbon.

'Nice sunglasses,' says Izzy. 'I'd like some like that. And, oh, Mummy, have you seen that her bag matches her shoes? And her jacket matches her skirt. Why do you never look smart like that?' I look at Izzy's paragon of chic. Coral polyester suit. That's a tad too tight, I think bitchily. Black patent handbag with gold chains. Pudgy feet in black patent high-heeled pumps, also with gold chains.

'And she smells lovely,' she whispers, then moves closer to the lady, breathing in deeply. The lady looks at me, frowns and raises a plucked, irritated eyebrow. 'Mum, why do you never wear perfume?'

The hydrofoil bounces against a row of old tyres strung along the quay, as a docker catches a rope and secures it around a rusty capstan. With a clatter, a metal ramp is pulled up from the dockside.

The coral polyester lady, pointing through the window, leans down to whisper something to her husband. A miniature man with a *tanguero*'s moustache, wearing a mustard shirt that is too big at the collar, he is twiddling an unlit cigarette in one hand, which he lights as soon as a crew member in a yellow t-shirt swings the door open. The only other passengers to disembark are a nun with a vinyl briefcase held together with fishing twine, a young man with semicircular eyebrows in a royal blue beret and sky-blue shirt with epaulettes and a frail old man with a tartan shopping trolley full of Tupperware containers and aluminium foil parcels.

I peer through the door. A small harbour full of brightly painted fishing boats. I pause, blinking. It is humid as well as hot; the sky glares still with that grubby white light. My hair is sticky on the back of my neck and beads of sweat sprout behind my knees. I bump the pram onto the metal ramp and reach a hand back to Izzy, who falters at the door, looking down at the slice of sea churning between the boat and the slimy wall of the quay.

'*Non preoccuparti bambolina, ti aiuto io.*' The man in uniform swings her up into his arms, holding her tight, pulling the suitcase behind him, and sets her down on the quayside.

'*Ciao, bambolina.*'

Izzy looks at me. 'What does *bambolina* mean?'

'Doll.'

Her eyes darken, and she turns back to the man and glares. 'I am not a doll.'

He raises his marvellous eyebrows quizzically.

'*Io non sono una bambola,*' I explain.

He laughs. 'Like Cinzia Oscar,' and he begins to sing. '*Nun so'* '*na bambola,*' adding, 'Famous song,' when he sees me looking puzzled. He swivels his hips, '*Napoletana,* like me,' then shimmies over to a small blue and white electric golf cart, and, clasping hands to heart and gazing in fake anguish at the heavens, sings, '*E me lasse sóla sóla.*' And you leave me all alone. Then he jumps into the car. As it wheezes off across the piazza, I see the words 'Polizia Penitenziaria' written on its side. I had forgotten that the island is home to a high-security prison.

The other passengers walk up past the fishing boats to an empty street overlooked by a row of stark houses with scuffed walls and tiny windows. It is noon and even in the angles where the walls meet the paving stones, there is not a sliver of shadow. A brief squall of wind whips along the quayside, whisking up dust, dead leaves, losing lottery tickets. A black car rounds the corner and the couple climb inside. I watch it swing off up a narrow side street. The old man pulls his trolley slowly across to a small blue bus and climbs on board. We follow him. The bus door is open but there appears to be no driver. I peer inside. The old man is leaning against the window, one hand on his trolley, eyes closed. The driver is fast asleep in the back seat.

There is a timetable on the bus stop but it is so faded that I can't read it. I don't know where I want to go, anyway. The guidebook lists one smart hotel in town, way beyond my budget, and a couple of campsites with bungalows. Hmm. Sleeping on a campsite with two kids is not my idea of a good time. Serves me right for being so pig-headed back in London. I could have scribbled down the numbers of a couple of B&Bs. Or even, God forbid, made a booking, rather than heading off with the notion that after years of having to plan every itinerary as if it were a military campaign, it was more romantic and authentic to allow happenstance – or even destiny – to shape my travels.

There are some rusty signs bolted to the harbour wall. The two campsites from the guidebook, the hotel from the guidebook, another campsite and a *villaggio*. Damn. A *villaggio* is to Italy what Pontins was to England. I worked in one outside Blackpool the summer I was seventeen, replenishing tureens of packet soup, instant mash and stewed gloop in the self-service canteen. Wages were low, accommodation and food free, the application procedure lackadaisical. Which made it the ideal hideaway for the denizens of the northern English underworld who needed to lie low. You soon learned to spot the folk with aliases – they blanked for a split second when you called them by name. It was bad enough in Blackpool. What the hell would it be like in the Mafia heartland?

Then, as I turn back to the girls, something catches my eye. I look back. There's a visiting card sellotaped to the corner of the *villaggio* sign. Eureka! A room-to-rent place called Villa Antonella. I write the phone number down and go to look for a telephone.

The first has no ringing tone, despite repeated bashing of the keyboard, but swallows fifty-cent coins with alacrity. The next takes only prepaid phone cards. The third has no handset. Grumbling, I push the pram up one of the side streets, dragging the suitcase behind me. Shutters are closed. The only signs of life are the sound of cutlery on plates, and the voice of a TV newsreader, reading the news as fast and feverishly as a horse race commentator.

The street ends and we are in a vast piazza dominated by a huge sandstone church, domes and cupolas soaring above blank Baroque façade. An antique-looking blue and white enamelled sign says Piazza Matrice, which means Matrice must be the name of the church. I've never come across this before. It must be a Sicilian thing. But what does it mean? Matrix? The church as an intricate web from which no one and nothing can escape? Or does the word derive from *madre*, and mean mother church? A Christianised version of the Mother Goddess, giver and protector of life? Could it be that ancient fertility cults of Phoenician Tanit and Greek Aphrodite live on?

All over the Mediterranean, as Christianity took hold, churches were built over pagan temples, and the attributes of pagan goddesses were taken over by Christian saints and the Madonna. Still today, there are festivals in which a Madonna is 'born' from the sea, like Aphrodite, or shown holding ears of corn, like the fertility goddess, Ceres. Agnostic as I am, right now I can think of nothing nicer than stepping inside a cool, dark church, heavy with incense and having a lovely long nap on a pew. But the church is closed of course, presumably while the priest has his lunch and siesta.

I look around the piazza. No sign of a shop or café, just lots of closed shutters. There's an inch of shade now, under a broken red canopy on the far side, so we walk over and squeeze ourselves underneath it. The wall is cool and smooth. I press my wrists against it and close my eyes.

'This wall is made of glass, Mum,' says Izzy.

I open my eyes.

'What?'

'Look.' She spits on her hand, gives the glass a vigorous rub with the hem of her dress and peers through.

'There are people inside.'

I bend down and look. Half a dozen or so men, sitting at tables, leaning against a bar, smoking.

The door is round the corner. I shove it open and go inside, pulling the pram behind me, leaving the case outside. The air-con is whining ineffectually and the TV buzzes like a trapped wasp, as a discreetly tanned newsreader continues to rattle out the day's events. Several of the men peel their eyes from the screen to look at us and the barman gives us a kind of chin jerk by way of acknowledgement. I chin jerk back, order Cokes and we sit down at a sticky Formica table.

As we drink, a blonde woman in a silver thong bikini comes on screen, spinning a glittery wheel. Izzy giggles.

'Look, you can see her bottom. Look, Juno, quick, you can see that lady's bottom.'

She jumps up and wiggles her behind. The screen cuts abruptly to a dishevelled reporter with come-to-bed eyes wearing a leather jacket. He's standing on a small piazza bordered by the sea, on which fishermen are laying out nets. Something the reporter says causes cynical laughter to ripple through the bar, followed by some heated discussion, but the only word I can make out is *mattanza*, before the screen flicks back to Mr Rent-a-Newscaster.

'Was that Favignana?' I ask the barman. Everyone turns to look at me.

He jerks his chin upwards a tad, his face so utterly impassive that it's impossible to tell whether it means yes or no.

'Yes? Favignana?' I say in Italian, looking at the other guys. 'Is there news of the *mattanza*?'

They laugh. There's a pause. Eyes turn to a guy with the bridge of his glasses mended with an Elastoplast. He sighs and takes a deep breath. 'That guy on the TV? Who said 16 or 17 May?' He pauses, drawing deep on his cigarette. 'That guy knows nothing.' More knowing laughs, accompanied by long, slow chin jerks, so I decide to drop the subject of the *mattanza*, and ask if anyone knows if there is a phone nearby that works. More laughter, then the man with the Elastoplasted glasses asks where I have to phone.

'Here, Favignana.'

He passes me a clunky mobile phone. 'Please,' he says in English, looking round at his mates for approval. I dial the number. Another phone rings and I step outside so that I can hear.

'*Pronto.*' A man's voice.

I ask if he has a room, how much it will be. It's cheap. Cheaper than I hoped. So I accept and ask how to get there.

'It's a bit of a way. Where are you?'

'Piazza Matrice, in un bar.'

'Piazza Matrice, in un bar?'

The bar door opens. A man with white hair pokes his head around.

'*Piazza Matrice in un bar*? With two children?' He says in heavily accented English. '*Salve, sono Salvo*. Villa Antonella.'

CÉZANNE BEACH

Villa Antonella is not actually a villa but a pine cabin in the garden of a modern white house on a dusty road about three kilometres outside town. Salvo lives in the house with his wife Antonella, their grown-up children and a two-year-old afterthought (well, actually accident, says Antonella laughing huskily and adjusting her cleavage) called Pascuale, who follows Juno around a goldfish pond, shouting *bimba! bimba!*

The cabin is as hot as an oven and as skinny as a barge, with two sets of bunkbeds built into the walls. At one end is a kitchen with a two-ring gas hob, a mini-fridge and a sink. At the other, a door leads into a cubicle with a loo and shower. It smells of varnish and I can see several mosquitoes asleep on the walls, but we collapse inside gratefully and fall asleep.

I wake up a couple of hours later to the girls bashing their buckets with spades to an insistent chant of *Beach! Beach! Beach!* It's five o'clock. What I should really be doing is food shopping and, more to the point, finding out how the hell we get into town and back. I open the door and look out. The sky is still dirty white, and the air is close and humid. A swim would be so nice and shops in Sicily stay open to eight. I tie the buckets to the pram and pack a bag with swimming gear.

Salvo points us along a *strada bianca*, a white dust road that winds between golden drystone walls of eroded tufa sandstone across flat, arid fields run wild. The girls trot ahead, darting from side to side, poking their fingers into the holes that pit and pock the stone walls. It is more natural cement than stone, so soft you can carve it with a fingertip, and they discover trapped within entire semi-fossilised shells. In places, it has eroded from the inside out – like a semi-frozen ice cube, with a sharp crust but no centre – creating perfect hideaways for bright green lizards. Dust lies in the folds of leaves along the roadside.

We reach a little bay. It's a Cubist beach designed by Cézanne, a crescent of soft sand fringed by a series of shallow rectangular pools, the tufa cliffs above covered with a series of square niches. It is all far too neat to be natural and I wonder when the tufa was quarried. Were the workings Roman? Or did they date back to the early twentieth century, when tufa from Favignana – soft, light and easy to cut and work with – was used to rebuild Messina after it was flattened in an earthquake. The water is shallow over the tufa, tiny fish dart here and there, and the girls play naked, intensifying the Cézanne-effect, as they lie and loll in the warm pools pretending to be mermaids. I go for a swim. The water is cool, translucent, and I dive, swimming hard until I am tired, then sink onto the beach.

I'm about to strip off my wet bikini when I spot a cloud of dust back along the coast path. I sit on a rock, watching. It's getting closer. A silver car. Something big and hefty, a 4x4. It draws to a halt directly above the bay and a man gets out. Too distant to see his face, but he has a wild shock of long, white-blond hair. He reaches into the car and brings out a pair of binoculars. Just as well I didn't strip off. I look again. The binoculars are trained on the water. I peer out to see what he could be looking at but can see nothing but the sea. I stand up and, though I have my back to him, am convinced that he has trained the binoculars on me. I shiver, pick up a sarong and wrap it tight.

'Mum, Mum' – Izzy is tugging at my sarong – 'I've been calling and calling. Look what Juno has found.' It's a scarlet starfish, still alive, its stiff tentacles misshapen as if they had been bitten off and regrown.

I glance back at the coast path as the silver car drives away. We get dry, ready to carry on exploring, and I convince the girls that not only would it be cruel to keep the starfish in a bucket but that it would make a very boring pet, so they return it to its rock pool and climb into the pram. The track cuts inland and I push them on, now looking out to sea, now looking down over the wall, at the wind stirring the tips of pine trees far below. I'm not really concentrating, so it's some time before it dawns on me that the pine trees are growing in the bottom of a deep ravine. I stop the pram and lean over the wall. There, way below, is a garden, hidden within a gorge of golden tufa rock formations. Columns and arches rise in the dappled shade of the pine trees, sprouting geometric agave, flopping aloe, and prickly pears with flowers like gaudy pink pan scrubs. There are flights of steps carved into the rock, and two of the columns have been linked by a stepped bridge, giving the place the air of the Willow pattern. Another disused quarry. I lift the girls up so they can see too and try to work out if it's possible to get down into the garden.

Suddenly Izzy starts. 'Listen, Mum, what's that?' She jumps down from the wall and looks around.

'What, what, what?' shouts Juno.

'Shh,' hisses Izzy, putting a finger over her lips. 'Listen.'

Juno nods seriously and puts her hand over her mouth.

We listen.

Mewing. High pitched and fragile.

Juno jumps up and down, tugging at my skirt, 'Look ...' she mouths, eyes huge.

A pale ginger kitten the size of a hamster and as skinny as a famine victim is walking shakily along the top of the wall. It has a bony little face and its eyes are glued shut. Sensing our presence, it trembles.

'What are we going to do, Mum?'

I don't know. I hate cats. If we leave it, it will either die of starvation, fall into the gorge or walk onto the road and be run over by a car. I don't hate cats that much. If we could open its eyes, that would help, at least it could see, but I am way too squeamish to pick up a feral kitten with oozy eyes. What the hell do I say to the girls?

'Mum, answer!' says Izzy. 'What are we going to do?'

'I don't know.'

Pathetic.

As we watch, the kitten totters and falls onto the verge. Sooner or later, it is going to wander into the road. I can hear a car approaching now.

'Stand in front of the kitten, so it can't get onto the road. There's a car coming.'

A white Fiat Punto is approaching slowly. Izzy takes a decisive step into the road and flags it down. The car stops and a young man wearing a straw trilby leans out of the window, white linen shirt billowing in the wind.

I'm sorry, I explain in Italian.

'It's OK,' he says in perfect English. 'Now, what's wrong, and how can I help?'

We tell him about the kitten and he gets out of the car to take a look. Carefully he picks the kitten up, holds it firm in his palm and, taking a bottle of water and a tissue, gently wipes its eyes.

'Can we have the kitten as our pet, Mummy? Please?'

'Not really,' I say. 'We don't have a house yet, don't even know if we are staying here.'

'Please, Mummy...'

'No, we really can't.'

'Now,' the man squats down and talks to the girls, 'would it be OK if I adopted the kitten and you came to visit it sometimes?' He looks at me. 'Hi, my name's Michel. I've just opened a new bar; it'll be good luck to have a kitten. The bar's called Zazzamita, that's dialect for gecko. It's miles away from town and no one can find it, so I'm driving around the island putting up signs.' He points to the car boot, where there is a pile of wooden arrows spray-painted with ZZZ.' He turns to the girls. 'I have two little girls who speak English and baby twin boys. You must come and play. I'm going into town now if you want a lift.'

With the kitten in the boot and the pram tied to the roof, we drive back into town, stopping at every junction while Michel and the girls tie ZZZ signs to trees and lampposts. Michel's family, he explains, is from Favignana but they now live in Siracusa, where

Michel works at a university for American students. He, his wife and his children are spending the summer break on the island.

'I don't like not doing anything, so we decided to open the bar.'

As we reach the outskirts of town, we drive past a row of bleak, two-storey terraced houses overlooking a street where two kids are playing football with an empty Coke can. Parked outside one of them is a silver Range Rover. As we drive past, I notice it has Swiss plates.

'So,' I say, feigning nonchalance, 'Favignana is quite an international place?'

'What? The Swiss plates? Nah. That's just tax avoidance.'

ULYSSES'S RICOTTA

'Well, this is a bit of a mess, isn't it?' Izzy, accustomed to the shiny aisles of Sainsbury's, stands in the entrance of Favignana's *supermercato*, surveying two cauliflowers yellowing at the bottom of a fridge.

She's right. It looks more like a discount warehouse than a supermarket. I squeeze the trolley into a narrow aisle lined with towers of toilet rolls in torn shrink-wrap. The next aisle tunnels between cardboard boxes with holes ripped in their sides to reveal the cans, jars and packets within. Only half the items have been priced. I pull a packet of pasta out of its box and hold it up to see what shape it is. Curls like the helix of an ear. *Spaccatelle*. As I turn it over to find the price, I am sure I can see something move inside. I look again. At the bottom of the packet, an extended family of ants are at dinner, industriously grinding the pasta to dust.

'Look at this,' I hiss to Michel, hoping Izzy won't notice. If she does, she'll never eat pasta again.

'Eh! Eh, Alberto,' Michel calls out to the back of the shop. An earnest-looking young man with a sharp frown line and round glasses, wearing chinos and an immaculate turquoise polo shirt, walks up. 'What you doing, running an antique shop or a supermarket? Look at this pasta.'

Alberto looks at the pasta and grimaces. 'Expired last century. I'm sorry. We've just taken over and things are in chaos. It's already half past seven and the ferry bringing the fruit and veg is late. But come and see the deli counter. At least we've got that sorted.'

And indeed they have. Row upon row of salamis and hams, cheeses speckled with black pepper, chilli, oregano, rocket. Trays of sundried tomatoes, olives, capers. Jars of mushrooms, aubergines and anchovies in golden oil.

Alberto goes round the back and washes his hands.

'Give her some ricotta,' says Michel.

Alberto leans over to a mound of quivering white ricotta.

Michel looks over his shoulder, as if to check no one is listening. 'No, no, Alberto,' he says quietly, '*la ricotta vietata*.'

Alberto looks at me, then back at Michel. 'Are you sure we can trust her?'

'I'm sure. And Alberto, she speaks Italian, so she understands everything you are saying.'

Alberto makes a kind of embarrassed Prince-Charles-like hiss-grin and disappears through a swing door. I don't have a clue what's going on. *Vietata* means forbidden. What the hell is forbidden ricotta? Michel looks over his shoulder, steps closer.

'It's ricotta that doesn't adhere to EC standards,' he says under his breath. 'It's made on a local farm. The recipe goes back to Ulysses.' Never having associated Homer with cheese recipes, I am now even more confused.

Alberto reappears with a white plastic bag sealed with a knot, and hands it to Michel. Michel nods and slips it into the cotton bag he wears over his shoulder.

'You finish shopping. I'll see you down the street in ten minutes.'

While we've been at the deli counter, the fruit and veg has arrived. I get red-green cherry tomatoes, a huge bunch of basil, rocket, melon, nectarines and small flat peaches. I find a nice packet of twenty-first century pasta, a jar of local honey, orange juice, olive oil, wine.

Outside, Michel is across the road, talking to a butcher in a blood-smeared apron and shorts sitting outside his shop on a wooden chair that has no seat. Michel introduces him as his uncle. Izzy peers at him curiously, then turns at Michel.

'Why has his chair got no seat?'

CHILDREN OF THE VOLCANO

Michel translates. The butcher rubs an unshaven chin and grins at Izzy.

'Because if I take the chair to the carpenter, what would I sit on while I waited for it to be repaired?'

We buy sausages and then, across the road, I spot a bakery. We buy a long crusty loaf of bread studded with seeds and half a kilo of chocolate chip cookies, or *cokkies*, as the bakery calls them. I won't let the girls start on the biscuits but tear off strips of bread for them. At home, the girls refuse to eat the crust, but they eat this thick, crunchy crust as if it were a biscuit. Then we move on to the crumb, creamy yellow, dense, toothsome and— I squeal. Running through it is a vein of tiny green grubs. I look closely. No sign of movement. Well, I don't suppose there would be after being inside a hot oven. I look again and gingerly pick one out with a fingernail. It's a seed. I taste it. Fennel. Amazingly, the kids declare fennel seeds to be yummy, and have eaten half the loaf by the time Michel drops us back outside Villa Antonella. As we get out, a silver Range Rover emerges from a side road. Before it drives away, I spot the CH sticker on the back and a cloud of white-blond hair through the window.

ANGEL HAIR

There was a storm in the night. We heard it approach, the rolls of thunder getting louder and louder, and felt it too, sharp currents of cold wind shaking the windows, slipping through gaps between the cabin's wooden planks like an impish poltergeist, upturning the tumbler of wild flowers, sending paper napkins flying, turning the pages of an open book. As we were eating Michel's uncle's sausages, the rain arrived in a violent deluge that cascaded off the cabin roof. Then, just as we were starting on the chocolate chip *cokkies*, there was a flash of white-blue light, and a deafening crash of thunder that catapulted the girls straight into my lap. Then the lightbulb flickered and went out. We all screamed. The darkness was complete. I managed to carry them to a bunk and we all lay there, snuggled together, eating *cokkies* and counting the seconds between lightning flashes and thunder claps until the storm passed and the light flickered back on.

But the morning is magnificent. Clear, blue sky, fluffy white clouds, a gentle breeze. As I attempt to wash up yesterday's dinner plates in lukewarm water, the kids devour ricotta, fresh fruit and honey for breakfast, then run around filling a basket with bougainvillea blossoms that had fallen in the storm, scarlet, magenta, purple, white. A page from my Sicilian dream. Although it's tempting to head to the beach in this magnificence, I know I have to do something about trying to find a house to rent. If I continue paying holiday accommodation rates, the royalties will be gone in a month and it'll be back to Kensal Green.

Salvo tells me the best way into town is to walk to the Cézanne beach and turn left instead of right.

The *strada bianca* is dazzlingly white today, flowers Crayola bright. There are lemon yellow dandelions, egg-yolk yellow thistles, tangles of mauve, purple, lilac, pink and – best of all – clusters of a spongey cactus-like plant with blowsy magenta and pineapple yellow flowers like strippers' tassels. The sea today is turquoise, transparent, with indigo shadows. The girls skip ahead.

The track reaches Cézanne beach and we turn left to follow the coast towards town. There are wild roses, petals covered with fine, white, sticky powder. *Salt is on the briar rose.* I lick a petal. It is just ever so slightly salty. Cool. I can send a postcard to my old Eliot supervisor saying that far from having abandoned academia for the superficial world of magazine journalism, I am in Sicily tracking down real, live objective correlatives. Who said literary research had to be confined to libraries? Poor guy, stuck in Manchester watching his garden rust.

The shops are just opening as we arrive back in town, shuttered doors on the piazza rattling up to reveal a fishmonger, a baker, an ironmonger and a shop called simply *Casalinghi*. *Casalinga* is housewife, a rather bizarre word with – to my ears at least – pornographic overtones of Italian *lingua* (tongue) and Sanskrit *lingam*, and whenever I hear it, I imagine voluptuous Italian mammas with sexy underwear beneath their gaudy housecoats stripping off while their kids are at school to indulge in languid sex with the postman on the sofa. I peep through the bead curtains. Pots, pans and lots and lots of plastic bowls and buckets. Not a frilly thong in sight. *Casalinghi* must be goods for the housewife. Wonder what the Italian feminists have to say about that?

I look around the piazza. Elderly ladies in black leaving the church, young mums in tracksuits pushing prams, a lady in a pineapple-print housecoat and sunglasses gesticulating melodramatically as she laments to a friend. Another woman walks up to her and rests a hand on her shoulder, and the lady in the pineapples raises her sunglasses to show a bruise on her eye. The friends sigh as we walk past. *Such is life*, I hear them say. I touch my eye and flinch.

We cross over to the fishmonger. There is an entire tuna fish, twice my height, suspended from a hook in the ceiling, gleaming steel blue, with a neat triangular wedge cut from its side revealing glistening crimson flesh. The fishmonger enters through a red and white plastic curtain at the back, patting the tuna gently on its flank as he greets us, as one might a favoured horse. The girls stare in silence.

'From the *mattanza*?' I ask. Its eyes are still bright.

'*Mattanza*? What *mattanza*?' he says, 'That's the only *mattanza* you're likely to see this year.' He points at the walls, whose ceramic tiles are painted with an idyllic scene of merry fishermen standing in a long, low boat stabbing shoals of leaping tuna. Izzy and I move closer to take a better look. There's no hint of carnage, just a few subtle splashes of blood, such as you might find on a Renaissance crucifixion.

I look at the ceramic fishermen. Centre stage, javelin raised, is a man with a shock of blond curls that would not look out of place on a Renaissance angel.

'But what's going on?'

'Not very much. That's the problem. The trapping nets are down, the ones that the tuna swim into, but the nets for the chamber of death are still spread out by the port. And without those, they can't pull the tuna in.'

It is May. The tuna will have passed through Gibraltar's Pillars of Hercules and be charging across the Mediterranean, bellies full of eggs, ready to spawn in warm, shallow waters off Favignana.

'Is that not too late?'

'Far too late.'

'And why?'

'You mean, why are they late when they've been doing this for over a thousand years?' He grins, revealing teeth dark and eroded like weather-gnawed dolly pegs. 'Well, last year it didn't happen at all.'

'But why?'

'*Problemi.*' And with that, he turns into the back of his shop.

As we turn the corner into a broad, cobbled street, I spot a fluorescent orange sign saying *affitasi*, to rent, pinned to a hefty wooden door. A rusty wrought-iron arch in a wall of tufa, pale honey in the sun. Two storeys, with a little tower. But there's no phone number on the sign, no agency name, nothing. I knock on the door and hear it echoing through the house, knock again. Nothing. There's no one around on the street to ask either. We'll come back later.

I decide instead to do a little dutiful journalism and check out the chamber of death, so we head down to the port where a large piazza beside an abandoned warehouse is covered with nets, kilometres of them, doubling, tripling, quadrupling back on themselves. A couple of fishermen with long, greasy locks, copious facial hair and large bellies lean against the back of a three-wheel Piaggio pickup, breakfasting on beer like heavy metal roadies. We peep into the warehouse. Shafts of light through broken windows slash the darkness revealing a pile of broken polystyrene trays, a tangle of rope, deep metal vats, piles of rusty cans. It must be the old tuna cannery.

In the nineteenth century, Vincenzo Florio, one of Italy's most powerful industrialists, revolutionised the tuna industry in Sicily, buying up *tonnara*s and redesigning the traps. Catches broke all previous records and Florio perfected the art of canning tuna in oil (he invented the key-opening can), found ways to use every last scrap of tuna (fancy playing football with a tuna eye?) and exported worldwide. In the 1870s, his son, Ignazio, bought Favignana and the island flourished as never before. Ignazio built a magnificent belle époque villa, installed electricity and would watch the *mattanza* from a canopied red velvet throne on a boat of tropical wood, fitted with a Persian carpet, powered by ten oarsmen. An image of Cleopatra swims into mind. *The barge she sat in like a burnish'd throne.* I wonder what the *tonnaroti*, the tuna fishermen, made of this super-rich gentleman.

Tuna was shipped in from all over the world to be canned on Favignana and, at its height, a thousand people worked in the cannery. Like the Rowntrees and Cadburys in England, Florio was a benevolent employer, providing a free nursery, breastfeeding breaks for mums and a playground for children. But as over-fishing led to dwindling fishing stocks, it no longer made sense to can tuna in Sicily, and in 1981, the cannery closed. The impact on Favignana was devastating. Before the arrival of Florio, tuna fishing had simply been a seasonal occupation that co-existed with farming and quarrying tufa. But for over a century, the entire economy of the island had been built around tuna. Twenty-five years on, I think, Favignana has still not found its way. They are trying tourism, opening campsites, but the island is too scruffy to attract the smart set. Almost every field I have seen is abandoned and the island is riddled with derelict farmhouses. There are even rumours that the prison is going to close. It's a sad story, I think, a salutary lesson in the dangers of globalisation. I hear a rat scuttle and leave.

Back in the sunshine, I squat down to look at the nets. They are heavy, woven tight, each hole barely more than a finger's width. As I stand up, the silver Range Rover rounds the corner and draws up by a small wooden hut. The door opens and out of it steps the man with the angel curls. He stands there, staring straight at me, to my eye oozing lazy insolence and the desire to humiliate, like a medieval feudal lord accustomed to exercising his *droit de seigneur*. I stare back. I narrow my eyes. I can do insolence too. His hair is undeniably beautiful, blond, spiralling and tangling into a cloud, the kind of hair that should indeed belong to a Renaissance angel. But his face? Rough, red, leathery skin, broad clumsy nose, and a ludicrous thin mouth with a slight downturn. He reminds me of someone. I try to remember who. A Renaissance prince? A Nicaraguan freedom fighter? A heavy metal star?

No. I've got it. I look at him, hoping to God he can read my mind.

Les Dawson in drag.

And if you don't know who Les Dawson is, matey, I'll send you a photo.

And then it hits me. This must be the guy the journalist had an affair with – an *avventura* he called it when he left her and went back to the mother of his youngest child. The hair is unmistakable, but she described him as charismatic, rugged and chiselled. The idea of anyone ever finding this guy attractive seems so absurd that I am overcome by the desire to giggle, and just about manage to swing the pram around, so that when the laughter erupts – in an extremely undignified and spitty splutter – I have my back to him.

Unfortunately, at that point, I remember I am supposed to be writing about the *mattanza* and that, as a responsible member of the British press, I should be getting out my notebook and interviewing the man. Building up a close and trusting relationship with this inheritor of tradition so that I can get the inside story, go out on the boat, report on what it is like to be bathed in tuna blood. Hell, there is no way on Earth I am going to talk to that oaf.

I take a deep breath, get hold of myself, turn around and am just about to leave the piazza when a dark, bearded man sputters round the corner on a rusty child's bike. He pulls up next to the Swiss Range Rover and walks over to the blond guy. Broad and spare, with grim, deep-set eyes, he is built on such a scale the world seems to shrink around him. He distorts all sense of proportion – the bike is, I realise, full-sized – and he dwarfs the blond oaf as they stand together looking at the nets, the blond guy speaking occasionally, pointing something out, the dark giant nodding in sombre silence.

This is not a world I want to or can enter.

And I don't feel like laughing any more.

MANNEQUIN

I turn the pram and walk back to see if there is anyone at home in the *affitasi* house. The door is ajar. Eureka! I knock, and then it creaks open, revealing a flight of undulating stone stairs paved with delicately painted tiles. They are old, cracked, pale blue and dark yellow on white, minute swirls and curlicues ending in tiny grotesque masques and cherubs with puffed-up cheeks. I knock again. Wait. No answer.

I step inside and call up, '*C'è nessuno?*'

This is the Italian equivalent to 'is there anybody home?' but it literally means 'is there nobody?', a contradiction in terms that makes me think of austere De Chirico piazzas, peopled by desolate figures hovering on the cusp between mannequin and human. I shudder, thinking of the piazza when we arrived, shadowless at noon, with its blank buildings, imperious church, harsh sirocco light, my stranger's sense of menace. I look back at it now. It's another world. There's a pickup laden with fruit, a couple of old guys selling huge bunches of leafy greens from the boots of their cars, and people zigzagging here and there, bustling in and out of shops, stopping to queue and chat.

I call again, '*C'è nessuno?*'

Still nothing, so, parking the pram in the entrance, and taking Juno in my arms and Izzy by the hand, I walk slowly upstairs, pausing again to call, louder this time.

'*C'è nessuno?*'

We round a corner. There's a narrow door, open. I peer inside

58

and, in the gloom, can make out what appears to be an old bread oven, tiled with the same tiles as the stairs. The floor of the room is covered with rubble. Cobwebs hang in the corners, heavy with dust. I jump at the sound of a throat being cleared. Izzy grips my hand tight. There is a man walking downstairs towards us. Thin, with a moustache, and a few greased strings of copper red hair combed across his bald head. He is wearing a brown striped acrylic sweater.

'*Salve.*' He has a reedy voice, expressionless, like a badly played oboe. He flicks his eyelids like a reptile.

'*Salve,*' I say with a broad smile. 'I've been calling. I saw the *affitasi* sign and am interested in renting. I'm sorry we just walked in ...'

He pats the air. I am not sure if it is to reassure me or because he can't stand the sound of me talking. Another eyelid flick. '*Venite.*' Come. He has scant, colourless eyelashes.

We follow him upstairs into a large whitewashed room with a domed ceiling flooded with light. Other rooms lead off, all of them with the same gently domed ceilings. The floors are covered with encaustic tiles; the furniture is dusty but beautiful, the bedsteads iron and painted with flowers. There's a little kitchen and steps up to a dusty cement roof terrace, with a glimpse of the sea. At the other end of the street is a dour octagonal building with a green Perspex corridor running around the top. As I watch, a man paces along the corridor. It is hard to see him clearly through the pea-soupy window, but I begin to think he is carrying a submachine gun.

'What's that place?' I ask.

'That place?' he says reedily. 'That place is the prison.'

Hmm. A medieval castle would have been prettier but, hey, this is real life. And most medieval castles began life as prisons, anyway. With conditions far worse than that one. We can live with a prison.

'High security. Many Mafia. And *terroristi.*'

'Oh.'

'You go in there, you never leave. It's underground in concrete cells with neon lights for the rest of your life.'

Izzy's eyes narrow.

The tour of the house continues. We cross the terrace to the tower, with another bedroom leading to a sparkling new white bathroom with a huge bathtub. I ask the landlord about the room with the bread oven and he says it needs restoring, but yes, if we like, we could restore it. He shows us the cellar, cool and dank, drips echoing from the water cistern sunk below it. I think about the prisoners.

It's perfect. Well, except for the view of the prison. But it's bound to be too expensive.

'How much is it?'

'Five hundred.'

Shit. Over €2,000 a month. Almost as much as we were paying in London.

'OK.' I nod sadly. 'Too much.' Izzy and Juno are sitting under the table, whispering. 'Thank you. It's a very nice house,' I smile, 'but too expensive. Come on, girls.'

'But we want to live here,' says Izzy.

'We can't,' I say, 'too expensive.' I pick up Juno and nod to the man. '*Arrivederci.*'

'Four-fifty?'

'I'm sorry, it's still too much. *Arrivederci e grazie.*'

I turn and we walk down the stairs.

'Four hundred. Four hundred euro. That's only a hundred a week. I'll include electricity.'

Oh my God, he's talking monthly, not weekly. Four hundred euros a month. It's nothing. Better not show my amazed delight, though. I turn back to him. 'OK,' I say slowly. 'Four hundred is possible. But for how long?'

'How long do you want? One month, one year, two years, eight years?'

'A year at least. Maybe even two.'

'Two years?' His eyes glint beadily.

'Yes, two years.' If we decide not to stay, I think, we can always rent it out to friends. Won't be difficult at that price.

'And I ask for one month's deposit, one month in advance.' His eyes flick to closed, the lids tremble.

'Of course.'

His eyes flick open. 'And when do you want to move in?'

I explain we are in holiday accommodation at the moment, so as soon as possible.

He looks at his watch. 'This afternoon? Seven o'clock? And you bring me eight hundred euros?'

A bit quicker than I imagined. I'd thought a few days at the least. But, hey, that's great.

'Fine. Agreed. Eight hundred euros at five o'clock this afternoon.'

As I walk away from the house, it strikes me this may all be a bit dodgy. Perhaps he isn't even the owner of the house? What if he just broke in? Or was there reading the electricity meter when we showed up and decided to take advantage of the situation?

'Mum,' says Izzy, 'I don't like that man.'

'Oh, well, don't worry. We don't have to be his friend. He's just the owner of the house.'

'Hmm,' she says, 'but tell me this, how did he know that the prison has concrete cells and neon thingy lights?'

I search for a plausible explanation.

'Well, let me tell you, Mummy. It's obvious. He must have been in prison.'

FISHING WITH
HELICOPTERS

It's still early, not even mid-morning, and the piazza is full of women darting here and there with bags of shopping. As we pass, the guys selling wild greens from their car boots are joined by a man with a polystyrene crate of fish tied to the back of his bike, silver, pink and gold, none of them bigger than my palm, eyes beady. Perfect fish for soup but if we are moving house tonight, then making a *cacciucco* is probably not the wisest option. Nevertheless, finding a home deserves celebration, so I take the girls across to a café in the piazza and order ice creams and a cappuccino. The ice creams are so huge that, for a while, even Izzy is lost for words.

I take a tiny sip of cappuccino, letting the bubbles burst on my tongue. I am happy. Utterly content. As a teenager, I used to think that the moment you realised you were happy was also sad, because it contained within it the recognition that happiness is fleeting. But now I think differently. I think that realising you are happy is just a way of fully and absolutely celebrating it. Back in London, I was bored and restless, possibly depressed, haunted by the fear of discovering that I was a failure and drudgery is inescapable. Now, from a distance, I wonder if I had internalised my ex's daily barrage of fault-finding until it became indistinguishable from my own conscience. 'You were nothing until you met me,' he had said once, and my biggest fear was that he was right. But now, I think, licking a sugar lump dipped in foam, I know he was wrong. The boredom, the restlessness, even the depression were simply signs of my refusal

– a visceral refusal fired by every fibre of my being – to accept a life lived without beauty, fulfilment and intensity.

Here, alone on the island with my girls, with no friends, no internet, no radio or TV, I have been completely absorbed. I am enthralled by this weird sunny place where I have seen rock eroding from within, pasta shivering to dust and walked above the tops of pine trees. I feel alert and alive meeting people who might reveal themselves within minutes as angel or adversary. Despite the Neanderthal fishermen, despite not really having a clue what is going on, I feel fully myself, stimulated, engaged. I take a last sip of cappuccino. Of course I am alert. I am fully and solely responsible for my children. But there's more to it than that. Wonder has come back into my life. I needed this, to be in a place where every day takes the senses on a rollercoaster of turquoise sea, scarlet starfish, searing sun, knee-grazing rock and the taste of fennel seeds.

I think about the *mattanza*. My sensible voice is telling me to get a grip and do the interview. But I don't want to enter that masculine world. It repels me. I am here with my kids and feel as if I am shedding layers of ... what? Protection? Armour? Layers that have accumulated over the years of fending off criticisms from a man who thought he knew best, slow as sand becoming stone. I imagine a half-formed fossil with the creature inside still breathing.

I guess I should get organised to move house but the weather is so beautiful, with a whisk of a breeze and the blue sky dancing with fluffy white clouds, that I decide to head to the beach. This time, we follow the signs along the white road to Cala Azzurra and end up in a gorgeous, golden horseshoe bay, the cliffs soft and sea-scooped, the water violet-blue. The rock crumbles like shortbread to the touch and it is covered with the names of lovers. They obviously don't do graffiti here, instead they carve their names on this cliff.

'The names of the dead,' pronounces Izzy, and won't hear any different.

Above the cove is a beach bar. Having already given the girls ice cream for elevenses, I had managed to distract Izzy on the way down. But, scampering ahead of me as I trudge back up the track with Juno on my back, she naturally spots it. She comes rushing back.

'Guess what, Mum, there's—'

'A café. Yes,' I say. It's hot and although I need to be careful with money, the idea of an iced drink in the shade is completely irresistible.

We sit on the terrace looking out to sea, drinking Coke and eating crisps. Behind us is a huge black-and-white photograph of the *mattanza*. This time, the fishermen stand in a broad, flat-bottomed boat, javelins drawn as they stab tuna leaping and squirming in the chamber of death. The blond guy is centre-shot, all B-movie action hero. Muscles tensed as he stabs the stake with gusto down deep into his victim's flesh. Beside him is the dark giant. He seems to be sliding the stake into the tuna, as if he were killing gently, making a necessary but regrettable sacrifice. If the *mattanza* is not happening, I think, then there's no story. I could just ring my editor now and tell her. I suppress the little whisper voice telling me that if the *mattanza* is not happening, then that is a story, too.

We head back home, along a different white road this time, following the coast and looking out across the narrow strait to the island of Lèvanzo. The wind has dropped and the water is like glass. Orange floats trace the layout of the nets below, a floating rectangular floorplan of a corridor of rooms clear as a dot-to-dot. If the nets for the *camera della morte* are still in the port, these must be the nets that act as holding rooms for the tuna before they are released into the death chamber. I think of one of Keats's letters where he describes the mind as a 'large Mansion of Many Apartments', in which we slowly feel our way through darkened rooms.

In the distance, I notice a column of smoke. As we approach, I see that the fire is burning in the garden of a small bungalow, tended by a bald figure with a bare torso. I lift the girls up to watch and, hearing their voices, the man turns.

'Eh!' he says, smiling and walking towards us. His torso and upper arms are pale, the rest of him hazelnut brown. Tattooed at the top of his right arm are a Chinese junk and a dolphin. He has clearly recognised us. I am a second or so behind. Then I get it. The polished leather skin, the gold incisor.

'Sebastiano!'

I tell him we've found a house, been to some lovely beaches and that we will stay here.

'Even if the *mattanza* doesn't happen?'

Especially if the *mattanza* doesn't happen, I think. I pause and take a deep breath. I know that when I ring my editor she is going to want to know why it isn't happening, and I can hardly tell them I have no idea. 'Do you know why, Sebastiano?'

'Well, last year a container ship drove through the *camera della morte*, so they lost all the fish. Now they have no money, and they can't afford to pay anyone to help, so they had to mend the net themselves and it's taking a long time.'

'And that's why they are late?'

'Exactly. But if you want to know more, I can take you to meet my cousin, Alessandro Sammartano.'

Pram roped to the roof of Sebastiano's ramshackle Fiat 500, we set off. Sebastiano drives in the middle of the road, his speed depending on the pace of the conversation, slowing down as he thinks, speeding up as he talks, slamming on the brakes as we pass a pair of elaborate wrought-iron gates, then reversing back up the road and through them to park under an enormous carob tree.

'Who's there?' A tall, elegant old man with a walking stick, whose grey suit cannot hide legs as heartbreakingly fragile as a flamingo's, takes a tentative step out of the shadows. We get out of the car. Juno clambers onto my hip, Izzy hides behind me.

'Alessandro?'

'Is that you, Sebastiano?' He squints against the harsh light, and I see that one eye is milky from blindness. Sebastiano explains who I am and why we are there.

'Container ship? Nonsense.' We are walking below a flaking villa with a balustrade terrace, where, once upon a time, I imagine Sammartano ladies in long silk dresses sipped vermouth. Alessandro Sammartano looks over at Sebastiano, who is helping the children make a fairy house under the carob tree. 'My cousin would believe in anything,' he says, leading me across a garden of geraniums grown wild. 'There was no container ship. The problem is worse than that. The problem is fishing with helicopters.'

I follow Alessandro into a long barn with a vast stone sink running along one wall. 'There is no fish because the Japanese have been fishing with helicopters. They go out in trawlers, with cages behind them, and above them fly helicopters scouting for tuna. We don't stand a chance. The *mattanza*, you know, was a battle between man and fish. We used our intelligence to trap the tuna but then we had to kill them, one by one. Man against fish. Being against being. Flesh against flesh.' I think of the photo of the bearded giant, the sense of necessary sacrifice as he slides his stake into the tuna. 'They are in direct contact, physical contact, with the fish and as they kill them, they are washed in their blood.' Alessandro continues, 'After the *mattanza* is over the *tonnaroti* swim in the *camera della morte*, as if it were a ritual bath – a recognition perhaps that man and nature are one. Fishing with helicopters is like modern warfare. The target is a dot on a screen and there is no connection.'

Alessandro walks over to the sink. 'Come over here if you want to understand the respect we have for tuna. Here we preserve the eggs of the tuna, in the same way that people have been doing for thousands of years. We salt them, leave them to cure for a week, then we wash them three, four times until the water runs sweet and clear. After that, we press them under blocks of tufa until the very, very, *very* last drop of liquid has gone, and then we wash them again, press them again, and put them in the sun to dry for two weeks, maybe three.' We step out into the sun, where Sebastiano and the girls are making shadow animals on the wall. 'Nowadays,' Alessandro continues, 'this is a delicacy, precious, because there is so much work, so much time involved, but the eggs used to be simply protein, survival, all that was left for the islanders to eat after the flesh of the tuna had been sold to the wealthy. Times have changed.'

He gazes out across the arid landscape to the sea. A bee buzzes past, birds sing and I can hear the whine of a Vespa in the distance. The sky has the intense blue of late afternoon; the sun is low, our shadows long. It is so quiet. I am moved by this quiet, dignified man, stirred by his stories of the *mattanza*, beginning to glimpse that there may be more to understand than I had thought. But it still doesn't change me not wanting to write about it.

PLAYTHING OF THE GODS

'But how can I write a receipt?' The landlord shrugs his shoulders and proffers me his empty palms. 'There is no paper in the house.'

We turned up as arranged, to find him waiting for us on the stairs. I gave him the money; he handed me the keys and then he made as if to leave. All very easy but I'd just given him €800.

He remains, as if frozen in 'mere plaything of the gods' mode, adding a downturned mouth for effect. Izzy nudges Juno and copies him, and they collapse on the floor in giggles.

I grimace. 'Oh ho, matey,' I mutter to myself, scrabbling in my bag, 'you weren't counting on your new tenant hulking around as much in her bag as Mary Poppins.' Since we started travelling, I have become a walking child's activity centre, with a constant supply of paper, pens, balls, finger puppets, books, snap cards, magnets and Blu Tack. It's all a bit of a mess and when I bring out Juno's scribbling book, it is spotted with stains from a half-eaten ham panino. I find a page that is not too greasy, and hand it over to him with a pen. He sits down at the dining table and writes rapidly, pausing to ask how to spell my name, which he writes in block capitals. He stops again.

'*Codice fiscale?*'

Weird. He's gone from not wanting to give me a receipt at all to wanting my tax code.

'I don't have one yet,' I lie. 'I'm waiting for it.'

He shrugs, signs the piece of paper and slides it over to me. Apart from my name, it is completely illegible.

After he has gone, we explore the house. The kitchen has several battered aluminium pots and a cupboard full of chipped plates, cups and glasses. Fine, we can manage. Then we go into the bedrooms to decide who is going to sleep where. At that point, it dawns on me there is no bedding. In a wardrobe, I discover four hard, lumpy pillows. And that is it. I look at my watch. It's half past seven and the shops close at eight.

There's a woman across the street dressed in a housecoat printed with watermelons, sweeping the pavement outside her house. I ask her where I can buy sheets.

'The market, tomorrow.'

I explain I need sheets now for tonight.

'Well,' she says doubtfully, 'there *is* a shop in the piazza ...' This is clearly one of those sentences that is going to finish either with her reservations about the shop in the piazza or about its owner. Or both. But I don't have time for that.

'Where in the piazza?' As few of the shops have names or window displays, tracking down the right one is time-consuming.

'Oh, you know, by the church. After Tano and Argentino but before La Palermitana.'

'Um. I'm sorry. I don't know Tano, Argentino or La Palermitana.' I step into the road, so that I can see into the piazza. 'Can you show me?' She follows me into the road and points vaguely to a row of fly-curtained doors across from the church.

We trundle over. The first fly curtain belongs to a bar, where a barwoman is painting her nails. The second is some kind of ironmonger. Stepping through the curtain of the third, we enter a tiny shop where a small, middle-aged blonde lady is doing a crossword puzzle. Apart from a rack of housecoats and plastic mules, all I can see are boxes. I ask if she sells sheets. She looks disapprovingly over her reading glasses at Izzy, who is slipping one of Juno's rather grubby feet into a man's plastic beach mule.

'*Non toccare,*' she snaps. Don't touch. Then she turns to me and points at the boxes. 'Sheets. There.'

There are shelves and shelves of dusty flat white boxes, each bearing a price in lire. I ask for two double sheets and four singles, and she reluctantly leaves her puzzle book and starts pulling out boxes. Most of them are empty. By the time she has discovered that her entire sheet stock consists of four plain, white linen sheets, and that the only towels she has are rough things thin as tea towels or fluffy red hand-towels embroidered with candles and sprigs of holly, the children have slithered unseen into a back room crammed with racks of bikinis, beach bags, sarongs and, oh lordy, a box of pink Disney princess sunglasses, which they are now trying on. If I tell them off, the woman will look, so I stay quiet, and turn my attention to helping her convert lire prices to euros. After all, it's only four years since Italy switched currency. I glance back at the girls, who are now sashaying before a mirror, Juno with a shocking pink D-cup bikini bra on her head, Izzy with a shimmering sarong around her shoulders. I gesture to Izzy to not let the lady see what they are doing, to take the clothes off, put the sunglasses back. Izzy points at the sunglasses, then looks at me pleadingly.

I mouth an OK, and she springs into action. She stuffs the clothes under the rack, grabs Juno's hand, and they sidle back towards the counter, each wearing a pair of heart-shaped sunglasses.

'Very cute,' says the lady, '*due bambole bellissime*.'

I pay up and we walk out of the shop.

'We are not dolls.' Izzy stamps her foot.

It is only then that I notice they are each wearing a pair of brand-new Barbie flip-flops. Stolen Barbie flip-flops. And that their battered old Clark's sandals are still inside the shop. I hesitate. We are going to be living less than 100 metres away. It's a tiny island. There is no alternative. I have to go back in there, retrieve their old shoes and buy the bloody flip-flops.

'Take those flip-flops off and wait here,' I growl at the girls. Each flip-flop is now stamped with a grubby footprint. I walk into the shop, delving for my purse, and hold up the flip-flops, trying to look apologetic.

The lady laughs, possibly because she has just got another twenty euros out of me.

'*Che monelle ...*'
Monelle ... must look that one up in the dictionary. *

---

* *Monella* means naughty – it is quite affectionate, but not as
affectionate as the English scamp or scalliwag, for which there
seems to be no Italian equivalent.

MADONNA OF THE TUNA

Within a few days, the house looks like every home we have ever lived in. Toys, books and clothes strewn across the floors, Izzy's paintings and Juno's muddy daubs pinned to the doors and walls, and – thanks to the fact that we have to cross the bare concrete roof terrace to get to the shiny white-tiled bathroom and back – an awful lot of grubby footprints. One rare rainy day, Izzy runs out of paper, so we paint a life-sized princess on her whitewashed bedroom wall. And another and another, until there are eighteen princesses and one Pippi Longstocking. Whitewash is cheap and I figure we can easily paint over them when we leave.

We start every day with *ricotta vietata* and honey on toast, together with whatever fruit is ripe. In May, there were the last of the oranges, so full of juice that I just squeezed them into glasses for the kids with the palm of my hand. Now there are cantaloupes sweeter than sugar, cherries, nectarines, peaches, watermelon, figs. When Izzy asks one morning how ricotta is made, I realise I have neglected my quest to bring her up understanding the link between farm and plate. I ask Alberto at the supermarket if he thinks the farmer would mind if we went to see ricotta being made.

'Of course not,' he says, 'go by any evening about six. Just ask for Peppe.'

The farm, says Alberto, is by the Madonnina on the road to Cala Azzurra.

*

Three days in a row, as the sun drops and the shadows lengthen, we take the road to Cala Azzurra – and end up in Cala Azzurra. Not a bad place to be at sunset, watching the blue of the bay get more intense by the minute, as Izzy keeps a look out for graffiti-artist ghosts, but not what I had planned. The problem is there is no sign of a church along the road, so I call by the supermarket to ask whether, by chance, there are two roads from town to Cala Azzurra.

'No,' he says, 'just one, or at least, just one that's not a dirt track.'

'But I couldn't find the Madonnina.'

'Well, it's there. Or at least it was this morning.' He grins. 'But it is quite small. Well, very small. It's on the right and it has flowers outside.'

We set off yet again, walking on the right side of the road this time. About ten minutes out of town, we come to a small junction. There, decorated with neat plastic greenery and bunches of artificial flowers, is a tiny monument with three domes topped by three tufa crucifixes framing a painting of the Madonna with child. She's a Mediterranean Madonna, with black hair and dark eyes, and, as Izzy notices straight away, she has a real gold ring in her ear and a real gold ring on her finger. Juno clambers up into my arms to take a look, tries to steal a plastic rose, knocks a vase over and then looks at the painting and stops.

'Fish.'

'Silly Juno,' says Izzy. 'Ladies have babies. Not fish.'

I take a look and can't quite believe what I am seeing. 'Izzy, jump up and have a look.'

I stand there with a girl on either hip. The Madonna is cradling a tuna. Izzy leans over and touches the Madonna's ring.

'Just seeing if it would be easy to steal it. I mean, if we took it and put a toy ring there, I bet no one would notice.'

Opposite the Madonna and her fish-baby is a rusty gate. Behind it is a farm, an Escheresque assembly of pale tufa cubes linked by external stone staircases, its surreal geometry ruined a bit by the motley collection of crumbling outhouses and tumbling lean-tos clustered around it. The yard is scattered with turds, mosquitoes buzz above a tufa tank full of scummy water and a newborn kitten trembles in the shadows. Steam is emerging from one of the lean-tos and we peer inside. There's a simmering cauldron full of blue, white liquid, a stone sink, several ancient-looking sieves and a witch-like broomstick. I can see why the EU health and safety inspectors might not approve.

An old lady sitting at the top of the flight of stone steps that leads to the living quarters waves at us.

'Is Peppe here?'

'On his way back. Won't be long. Would you like some water?' She turns to the girls. '*Succo di frutta?*'

'*Succo di frutta*,' says Izzy. 'Suck the fruit. Must be fruit juice. *Sì.*'

The lady fetches two cartons of peach juice and inserts the straws.

'See,' says Izzy, looking at me, 'Italian is quite easy, really.'

There's a tinkling of bells, and a flock of mustard-coloured sheep with rasta locks and striped noses are herded into the yard by a man with a thatch of white hair sitting astride a mud-caked Vespa.

'Now,' says the lady, looking at the girls. 'You can watch, but you have to be quiet or you'll frighten the sheep.' She puts a finger on her mouth. '*Zitta.*' Be quiet.

'*Zitta.*' Izzy nods gravely.

'*Zitta*,' says Juno.

I smile. Finally, a useful addition to their vocabulary.

We stroll down the steps back into the yard. Izzy keeps behind me, clutching my skirt, peeping out tentatively. Juno, squawking with excitement, wriggles free of my hold and walks slowly towards the flock. She's about the same height as the sheep and gazes curiously into their eyes. Peppe watches her quietly, smiling, then catches her eye, puts a finger to his lips and points at a blue plastic bucket. Slowly, carefully, she tiptoes over to the bucket and brings it to Peppe, who squats down and milks the first sheep. His jeans, boots and arms are covered with a thin wash of translucent white whey. Juno kneels down next to him, head on one side, watching everything he does, and he keeps glancing across at her. They both have eyes of the kind of blue that change with the colour of sky or sea. They are acting as if they have known each other a lifetime.

When the last sheep has been milked, Peppe places the bucket next to Juno and indicates that she is to look after it while he takes the sheep back to the field. She stands on guard, serious, rigid, as if the island is full of sheep-milk thieves. When Peppe returns, he picks up the bucket and leads the way to the smoke-blackened lean-to, where we discover a smaller, squatter, fatter version of Peppe wearing a too-tight checked shirt and cowboy boots. Peppe pours the new milk into the steaming cauldron, then leans back against the wall. 'My brother,' he says, without enthusiasm. 'He used to live in Germany.'

'*Guten abend,*' says the brother.

'*Guten abend,*' I return.

'*Ich Deutschland.*'

'*Ich England.*'

'Peppe.' He points, then pulls his mouth into a moue of disapproval, and shakes his head. '*Alles Favignana.*'

Which, as far as I can work out, makes no sense at all, but probably means that he thinks Peppe is an oaf who has lived on Favignana all his life and knows nothing of the world.

'*Käse ist gut.*'

'*Käse ist gut,*' I repeat.

'*Käse ist sehr gut.*'

I can see this going on for ever. 'Peppe,' I plead, 'I don't really understand German. Can't we just speak Italian?'

'See,' says Peppe to his brother, 'your German sucks. She doesn't understand a word you're saying.'

Peppe reaches out for one of the witch's broomsticks, turns back to the cauldron and stirs the liquid. Izzy is watching on tiptoe and I lift Juno up so she can see.

'Willow,' says Peppe, pointing to the brush, as he draws it delicately through the liquid, gathering the specks of curd together. He turns to Izzy and nods at a sieve on the sink.

'*Mi porti questo?*'

'*Sì,*' says Izzy and hands him the sieve, then watches as he scoops up the curds and carries them, still steaming, over to the sink, taps them into a white plastic basket sitting on the stone drainer, and presses them down with the heel of his hand squeezing out the excess whey.

'*Tuma,*' he says.

The first, creamiest curds, which can be eaten as a fresh cheese or aged to make pecorino. The excess whey dribbles down a runnel into a bucket, which Peppe pours back into the cauldron. Then he makes a tiny pot of *tuma* for us to try and we eat it, hot, with our fingers. It's creamier and heavier than ricotta, with a peculiar, though not unpleasant, squeaky rubbery texture a bit like halloumi. Chewing gum cheese, Izzy calls it.

As the sky darkens, Peppe continues stirring, his face shadowed in the late evening light, slow, patient, lost in what he is doing, a look of infinite tenderness on his face. If I'd had a camera, it would have made a chiaroscuro worthy of Caravaggio. If I was any good at photography, that is. Peppe sees me shifting my weight from one leg to the other and, with the grace of a host offering me a Louis Quinze chair, fetches me an empty orange crate to sit on. But the girls, bored now, requisition the crate and run out into the yard shouting poo! poo! as they search, giggling, for a turd-free patch where they can place it.

Peppe reaches for a bottle and pours a generous dash of colourless liquid into the cauldron.

'What's that?' I ask.

'Seawater.'

'Seawater?'

'I use it to set the ricotta, instead of rennet. It's what Polifemo did.'

Now I remember. Polyphemus, the one-eyed monster in the Odyssey, kept sheep and made cheese. So that's what Michel was talking about that first evening in the supermarket. It seems like a lifetime ago.

Meanwhile, I can hear gleeful cries from the farmyard of 'sheep poo!', 'cow poo!', 'horse poo!', 'caterpillar poo!'. Caterpillar poo? I look out to the yard. The girls dart around the farmyard, seemingly trying to identify turds.

A car draws into the gateway, closely followed by another. A man and boy get out of the first, carrying a stainless-steel pressure cooker; a frail-looking woman in early pregnancy follows, carrying a Tupperware bowl and a spoon.

'Again, Mariuccia?' Peppe nods at the pregnant woman.

'The only thing I want to eat, Peppe, is hot ricotta.'

Peppe nods now at the father and son and they pass him the pressure cooker, which he fills with steaming ricotta. He does the same for the lady, who leans against the stone sink and eats slowly, straight out of her Tupperware, blowing each spoonful to cool it. Another car arrives, and then another, so that soon there is a small queue of islanders snaking across the yard, clutching containers to hold the *ricotta vietata*. As the last car pulls away, the earnest little supermarket manager arrives with his arm around the girl from the checkout.

Peppe looks up from the cauldron and gives the manager a little chin jerk.

'*Ciao, Papà.*' The girl comes over and gives Peppe a peck on the cheek.

'Peppe's your dad?' I ask, unnecessarily.

ANKLE SOCKS

Every morning and lunchtime, Izzy leans over the roof terrace wall watching children carrying immense, brightly coloured rucksacks walking along our road on the way to and back from school. I decide it's time to enrol her. She needs to start to make friends, learn Italian. And she rather fancies a rucksack. I ring the school and they tell me to come along. So, adding her passport and birth certificate to the junk in my bag, we leave the house. I've been reading Pippi Longstocking to them every night and Izzy has insisted on wearing odd socks, one green, one orange, in tribute.

It is visiting hour at the prison and we pass a desolate queue of visitors, most of them women, several of them North African, all clutching carrier bags of food. They watch us as we approach; the kids singing some nonsense as they sit side by side in the pram. I can see the school on the other side of the road but I don't want to cross, in case the women think we are avoiding them. They lower their eyes as we pass – all but one, a young woman with a toddler clutching at her skirts. Our eyes meet and I can see her swallowing hard, tears in her eyes. I am sure that for her we must represent a normality that seems unattainable.

I whisper *ciao* to her and we cross over to the school. It's a style of architecture that, after a couple of weeks here, I already recognise as Sicilian municipal. There are cracks in the wall, peeling paintwork, windows you know will rattle in the wind and a roof that is bound to leak. There's no playground, just a wobbly pavement with huge clumps of pink and yellow stripper's tassel succulents sprawling through the cracks.

We are shown inside by a smiling man with a mop and bucket, and wait in a corridor inexplicably decorated with a series of photographs of forest fires, each puckering away from its frame and beaded with condensation. The secretary, a sympathetic-looking woman with freckles and frizzy ginger hair, looks dewy-eyed at Juno, fast asleep and peony-cheeked in the pram, and shows us into her office, where a gaudy print of a doe-eyed Madonna with a red-glitter heart sits on top of a pile of ergonomic computer keyboards. While she goes to fetch some papers, we sit down and Izzy's eyes alight immediately upon the wooden crucifix on the wall behind the secretary's desk.

'Mummy, there's something I've never really understood.'

'Yes?' I say warily, wondering what's coming.

'Why was Jesus killed on a cross?'

'I'll tell you later.'

But once Izzy has a question between her teeth, there is no stopping her. 'I mean, Mummy, why didn't they find another way to kill him, if that's what they wanted to do?'

'Izzy ...'

'Hanging, or electrifying, like they do in America, or shooting or ... stabbing, again and again and again, like those men in the chamber of death. In fact, Mummy, I've been wondering, do you think Saddam will be killed, because I was thinking maybe his parents were horrid to him? So perhaps it wasn't his fault that he was horrid too.'

The Iraq war was at its height when we were in America, Izzy already a sponge for adult conversation, and my determination to answer all her questions as honestly as I could resulted in Saddam becoming her bogeyman. She hadn't mentioned him for months but something – the violence of the tuna massacre, maybe – must have triggered a memory.

I am rescued from having to psychoanalyse Saddam Hussein by the secretary returning with a pile of papers. She informs me school is every morning from 8.30am to 1pm, and then adds proudly that in line with recent government recommendations, there is also afternoon school twice a week for the five-year-olds.

'But what do mothers do if they work?'

'Oh?' She looks baffled. 'Well, *boh*, most of them don't, and if they do, *boh*, there are grandparents.'

She hands me a pile of forms. I plod my way through them, trying to make sense of the bureaucratic Italian, and all goes smoothly until she hands me the final form. It is to say whether I want Izzy to study religion.

'It's an option not to study it?'

'Of course, for *Mussulmani* and *Ebraici*.' Muslims and Jews.

'So the children study only Catholicism?'

'No. In the fifth year, they study other religions.'

'But is the teaching dogmatic?'

Once again, a look of pure bafflement.

I'm struggling with the Italian now and manage something like, 'Are they taught about the Catholic religion objectively, or is it like church?'

'Well ... let me see ... well, *allora*, let me put it like this. The teacher is a nun.'

I hesitate for a moment, then tick the YES box. If Izzy is going to be brought up in Italy, she'll need to understand what Catholicism is about. And that you can't steal jewellery from the Madonna.

The secretary looks at her watch and tells us there are some children of Izzy's age doing afternoon school, so we head back past the forest fires to the classroom. The walls are decorated with Disney characters, each two metres high, and flowers made of coloured card. I look closely. Not a glob of glue or wobbly line in sight. Three little girls wearing pink overalls and abundant hair decorations are colouring in a photocopied hot-air balloon. The kind of activity known in the primary school my mum used to teach at as a wet-playtime activity – undemanding, no educational content, no preparation necessary, but it keeps the kids quiet. Also to be used on occasions when the teacher is tired/stressed/hungover.

I look at the teacher, who is thin, dark and beautiful, and

reminds me of a portrait on an Etruscan tomb. She's sitting sharpening pink pencils, and seems perfectly wide-awake/relaxed/clear headed. She introduces herself as Maestra Anna. I watch the kids work. I am half amazed, half appalled. These are five-year-olds, colouring in so neatly that when they have finished, the page looks to have been Photoshopped.

They look up and scrutinise Izzy, eyes ending on her odd socks. They nudge each other and whisper.

'Maestra Anna, why is she wearing odd socks?' asks a frail-looking girl with a large, pink hairband.

Maestra Anna looks at me, uncomfortable.

'She likes Pippi,' I say.

'Pippi Calzelunghe?'

'Yes.'

'And you let her wear odd socks?'

'Yes.'

'Hm. My mum wouldn't.'

'Neither would mine.'

'She wouldn't think it was right.'

'It's not right.'

'No, it's not. It's not normal.'

They stretch out their legs from under the table. Six skinny brown ankles clad in identical frilly white ankle socks.

'They're very neat,' I say, pointing to their colouring in.

'Oh, yes.' Maestra Anna smiles. 'But they should be. They've been here for three years.'

'Did they do those?' I point at Cinderella and Snow White.

'Goodness me, no,' says Maestra Anna. 'On the walls, it needs to be perfect, as an example. So we teachers do that.'

Liberal arty extremist that I am, Izzy has never been allowed a colouring book, resulting in many a tantrum at WH Smith. She is beaming, unable to believe that she is going to a school where she actually *has* to colour in a picture. She sits down and begins to work on her balloon, so absorbed she just gives a nod when I say goodbye.

As I push Juno and the pram home across the piazza, I bump

into Sebastiano. He seems tense, keeps glancing anxiously over his shoulder.

'The agent wants to see you. He's been looking for you.'

'The agent? What agent?'

'The estate agent. For the house.'

'But I didn't deal with any agent. I don't understand.'

'That house is for sale and he is the agent.'

FLAK JACKET

Confused and worried, I follow Sebastiano's directions to the estate agent's office, while he pushes Juno around the piazza. A large bald man with a complexion the colour and texture of orange peel, dressed in an over-ironed polyester flak jacket, is talking into a Bakelite phone at an immense desk littered with scraps of paper. Each is covered in microscopic writing and makes me think of the miniature books the Bronte sisters made as children. I hover at the door. He summons me in imperiously, waves me to a squishy leather swivel chair and puts his hand over the mouthpiece.

'You need to get out of that house. Sit.' He then turns his back and continues with his call. He has a mild lisp and his voice echoes in his mouth, the effect somewhere between nasal foghorn and subwoofer.

What the hell is going on? I knew I shouldn't have just handed over the money. What if, as I feared, the so-called landlord was just some random passer-by?

The agent finishes the call and puts on a pair of red-framed glasses that make his eyes look as if he has a serious thyroid problem. He leans across the desk.

'I repeat,' he says in English. 'You need to get out of that house.'

His breath stinks. I am hot, sweaty and trembling, but I have to calm down and find a way through this. There is a powerful-looking desk fan right next to me. I fantasise about switching it on, sending his miniature meticulous papers flying across the piazza.

I take a deep breath. 'I've paid two months' rent and I also have a receipt for eight hundred euros.'

'A fiscal receipt?' he gloats.

'We also had a verbal contract.'

'In Italy, a verbal contract is worth nothing. If you rent a furnished house, you can be ejected like that!' He clicks his fingers.

'Sicily is part of Europe and covered by European human rights legislation. People can't just do whatever they like.' I feel about as effective as Mary Poppins trying to reason with Hannibal Lecter.

The agent smirks. I want to hit him but I know about bullies. The important thing is not to lose control.

'And perhaps you could explain,' I say, letting my fingers hover over the fan switch, 'where you come in. I don't understand.'

'You don't need to understand anything.' He leans across the table. 'You just need to do what you are told.'

'I'm hot,' I say, finger positioned on the max button, 'do you mind—'

He grips my wrist like iron.

'This is summer. This is Sicily. If you don't like heat, go home.'

I shake my wrist free. As I walk out the door, I pass a Stetson hanging on a hat stand and remember that in medieval Sicily, a law was passed granting the *tonnaroti* immunity from all legal processes, including murder.

Sebastiano is in the piazza, nervously waiting for me, as Juno, wide-eyed, licks a melting chocolate ice cream.

'Did you clarify things?'

'No, I'm completely confused. Who is this scumbag, anyway?'

'Be careful. You don't understand. You don't understand what he can do.'

I trudge home, peel off Juno's chocolate ice cream-soaked clothes and put her in the bath. As I soap her down, I realise my hands are trembling. Sebastiano looked rattled, frightened even, and he is from the island and knows the score. So much for standing up for myself. It would have been far wiser to be deferential to the agent and at least to try to get to the bottom of what the hell is going on. I get Juno out of the bath, pull the plug and dry her, taking comfort in her wriggly warmth. I am completely out of my depth, I think, as I get her dressed again, knocked for six because I have just met someone who has told me to do as I am told or else, because the law is irrelevant. The bath is ringed with a murky brown tide mark, which I wipe away with a thick cloth, slowly, deliberately. Of course, I'd read up about Mafia culture before coming to live here, but I had innocently assumed that if *mafioso* ways didn't affect tourists, they would not affect ordinary people living out their ordinary lives. I stand up. The bath is white again. Maybe we should just give up, go back to London. I shove Juno's chocolatey clothes in the washing machine then call Michel.

'Who is this guy, your landlord?' he says. 'What's his name?'

'Russo.'

'Russo, eh? OK, leave it with me. I'll see what I can do.'

When I collect Izzy from school a couple of hours later, Maestra Anna, looking a little bemused, shows me her work. She has covered her balloon with flowers and butterflies, and put Pippi Longstocking in the basket.

DEAD PEOPLE PLAYING STATUES

That evening, as we walk across the piazza, Juno, who has missed her afternoon nap, falls asleep, and Izzy is sandwiched between two little girls with large blue eyes and wavy dark hair, who take hold of her hands and go skipping off across the cobbles towards the Matrice.

'Well, that didn't take long.' It's Michel, in pyjama trousers, linen shirt and straw trilby, sitting in a café with a Campari spritz and a bowl of pistachios beside a double buggy in which two cherub-faced twins lie sleeping. We watch the three older girls whispering to each other on the steps of the church. 'Those two are Charlotte and Hayley, in case you needed to ask.'

Charlotte points towards the open door, and the girls collapse into giggles.

'You look like you need a drink.'

I sit down, nodding. 'Trying to make decisions.'

'Decisions?'

'Not sure if it's a good idea to stay.' The waiter brings my spritz and I take a huge, icy gulp.

'You can't let him get away with this. If good people are frightened to stand up to the bastards, nothing will ever change. In Siracusa now, as soon as anyone opens a new shop, there is a visit.'

'A visit?'

'A visit. From a certain kind of visitor. The skill is to work out if it's just a punk chancing it or someone with backing. If it's a punk,

86

the most effective action is to take him into a back room and mash him.'

'And if it's Mafia?'

'Most people pay up. But some don't. They don't pay but they don't open their shop either. They put a sign in the window to say they can't open because of demands. People like that douche-bag agent, they're not Mafia, they're not even really punks. They're just bullies. But bullying is what Mafia culture is all about and it has filtered through the whole of society. They have to learn that bullying doesn't work.'

'That tuna guy, Michel, with the blond curly hair and the Swiss Range Rover. What's he's up to?'

'Clemente? Ros, you have to understand that Clemente is an icon.'

'He's the one in charge of the *mattanza*? The *rais*?'

'No, he's not. The *rais* is that giant guy, Gioacchino, but it's Clemente who's famous. He's like a rock star, and not just on Favignana. There's a story he was up in Turin once, parked in a no-parking zone, came back to find a warden writing out a ticket. When the warden looked up to see Clemente, he went *Oh my God you're the Favignana tonnaroto*, and tore the ticket up.'

'You mean I shouldn't ask questions like that?'

'No, I mean you *should* ask questions like that. Just not out loud to anyone except me.' He cracks open a pistachio and hands it to me. 'Remember my uncle, the butcher with the chair? Know what he always told me when I was a kid? Never tell anyone anything because you never know who you are talking to.'

And I brought the kids here looking for freedom. 'OK.'

'Take the *mattanza*. What have you been told?'

'Problems, *interessi*, whatever that means. Japanese hoovering up all the tuna. Then they clam up.'

'Well, it's like this. The fishing rights are owned by a wealthy family and every year, they rent out the right to fish to a cooperative of *tonnaroti*. It's worked like that, just about OK, for a few years, but with over-fishing the catch has got less and less, and the co-op has been losing money hand over fist. This year, tempers got frayed, there was a huge row and two rival co-ops set up – one run by the *rais*, one by Clemente. Neither of them could afford to work alone, neither of them could agree what to do, and by the time the argument was sorted, it was too late and the tuna had already passed.'

'So why put the nets down?'

'Well … the rumour is that they have this plan to apply for UNESCO intangible cultural heritage status, and they won't get it if they don't put all the nets down.'

These fishermen and their traditions, basking in their mythical status like ageing rock stars, repel me. I can't stand the way Clemente looks at me with that *drôit de seigneur* insolence in his eyes, as if assessing me on a scale of potential sexual pleasure. Encountering Clemente takes me back to being a teenager cringing during Sunday tea in front of the telly at Carry On films; to being a student, when a young woman waiting alone in a northern pub was read by the beer-bellies at the bar as 'here comes a lass looking for a good time'. I take a last sip of Campari. Hopefully, one of the most significant achievements of feminism will prove to be the obsolescence of the male predator. If the predatory male is no longer attractive or necessary, he will eventually die out.

'They've even been talking about selling tickets to tourists.'

That is when I make a decision. Tomorrow I am phoning my editor. I *will* write about the *mattanza*, but not as a travel piece. I'll offer her an op-ed on the links between traditional culture and male oppression on a Mediterranean island. I have heard raised male voices behind closed doors, women's voices pleading in response, and I have seen too many women hurrying home too quickly, fearing the consequences of lunch being late. There was the woman with the bruised eye and her friend thinking it was normal. I worry that on this small island, cut off from the world, locked in the ancient practices of *mattanza* and Mafia, domestic violence may not simply be rife, but accepted.

I look over at the church. The girls are now nowhere to be seen.

'Oh god, the girls, Michel, where are they?'

'Don't worry, this isn't London. They're fine.'

As he speaks, Izzy and Hayley come running out of the church, screaming, and belt over to us.

'That church is full of dead people,' they say breathlessly.

'Charlotte says.'

'All these dead people, playing statues.'

'In fancy dresses.'

'With blood on them.'

'One lady has a knife in her throat.'

'She was murdered.'

'By a vampire.'

'And they come to GET you at night.'

'And carry you to the chamber of death.'

'Izzy and Hayley, calm down. She's just trying to scare you,' says Michel. 'Charlotte, act like you're six for once.' He passes her a bag. 'There's paper and crayons. Now, if you all sit down quietly and draw while we finish our drinks, I'll get you ice creams.'

PYJAMA PARTY

It is almost dark by the time we get home. The town is quiet and in the distance, I can hear the last hydrofoil of the day approaching, the clatters and clanks as it docks. I turn the corner into our street and stop, sharp. The landlord is standing outside the door.

'*Buonasera*,' I say dully.

'Now you, you English, you listen here,' he shouts, his voice high pitched and agitated, 'you just get out.' He jabs at the air. 'Get out of my house, now.' He jabs again, stepping towards me. 'Get out, you hear?' He jabs me now. '*Capisci?* Get out, get out, get ow … ?' He jumps back and lets out a squeak, as a large hand appears from nowhere and clamps itself over his acrylic-jumpered wrist.

'Michel!' Izzy and Juno squeal.

'Just a minute, girls,' says Michel, who now has a fistful of acrylic sweater bunched up under the landlord's chin. 'Now listen to me, here, you scummy little rat, do not ever even think of threatening a friend of mine again, OK?' He gives him a shake. 'Understood?' A sharp shove and the landlord scuttles away like a frightened crab.

'I only came because Izzy left this behind on the table,' and he hands me a drawing of a man with the landlord's unmistakeable string of hair and orange moustache, behind bars, arms, legs and neck shackled.

The next morning, we are awoken by a knock at the door. I peer down over the terrace. It's Michel. 'You got a moment?' he says

90

fiercely, barely controlling his anger. 'We're going to the Carabinieri to report that bastard Russo. I've been talking, asking questions. He's got other properties and is always making problems for his tenants, that guy. He's got to learn a lesson.'

I bundle the girls into the pram and we walk up to the Carabinieri barracks, a small, ochre building with heavy grates at the window and a sign saying 'no access, military zone' on its wall. We ring the bell and a kindly, Greek-looking officer opens the door. Michel explains the problem.

'Ah, yes.' He smiles. 'Russo. He's been here already. To report that he has tenants who won't move out of his house. He claims the lady's friend was aggressive.'

'Only because I found Russo threatening her.'

'Listen,' says the guy, 'don't worry, the *Maresciallo* will be able to sort it all out. Can you come back at 2.30?'

On our way back home, across the piazza, I spot Sebastiano and wave. He pretends he hasn't seen me and hurries away.

'We look like we're going to a party,' says Izzy.

We are sitting side by side on a bench in the waiting room at the Carabinieri. Michel in his usual pyjama trousers and straw hat, me in green lizard-pattern kitten heels and a pink silk dress, Izzy and Juno with hair shining for the first time since we arrived, wearing new white dresses sent by their granny. A *bella figura* offensive, the result of three agonising, scream-punctuated hours of bathing, shampooing, hair-brushing and drying. The landlord sits slumped in a corner in his pilled acrylic with a large vinyl briefcase on his knee. I deliberately do not look at him but out of the corner of my eye, I can see that Izzy is staring at him.

'Mummy, Michel,' Izzy whispers. 'Do you know what the horrid landlord just did?'

'What?'

'He combed his hair!'

'Great,' says Michel, raising his eyebrows. 'That means we've intimidated him.'

The smiling Greek pokes his head round a door to tell us we

can go in to see the *Maresciallo*. Dressed in jeans and t-shirt, with a shaved head, the *Maresciallo* greets us with iced politeness. He has cold, grey eyes, SAS material if ever I saw it, an inscrutable type who I am sure would be capable of killing. He says good afternoon in English then acts as if I am not there – whether because I am a foreigner or a woman I do not know. He listens as Michel and the landlord give their versions of what has happened, then fixes his gaze on the landlord.

'You cannot, Mr Russo, agree to rent a house, take money from a tenant and then change your mind because an estate agent has told you that you were an idiot to rent the house for so little. It is a fair rent and you need to make a contract. Whether you have a contract for six months, one year or two years, is immaterial. Either party has to give the other two months' notice.'

'I'm sorry,' stutters the landlord. 'Two months, I don't understand.'

It takes the *Maresciallo* five attempts to explain to the landlord what two months' notice means, by which time his air of cool is showing signs of evaporating.

'And you cannot claim that someone has been aggressive to you, if you, at that very time, are manifesting a great deal of aggression towards their friend.' The landlord looks daggers at Michel.

Hands are shaken, leaves taken, and the landlord walks out of the room.

'Is he going back to prison now?' asks Izzy.

The *Maresciallo* smiles for the first time.

EMPTY NETS

It is sunset. Three weeks after the summit at the Carabinieri. I am sitting on the beach while the girls make a sandcastle. There are two boats out in the straits, weaving back and forth above the nets. Have they trapped a few tuna after all?

While the girls play I think about the things on Favignana that disturb me. Unnerving me more than the landlord is the hold that the agent seems to have. It was he who made the landlord act as he did, he who intimidated Sebastiano so much that he turns his back now every time our paths cross – afraid, I assume, of the consequences of being seen talking to me. I worry about bringing my girls up in a place where they might learn that it is wise to do what bullies tell you.

I look at the girls, covered with sand, collecting shells in their Barbie buckets, intent. I love the weather, the beaches, the food, the feeling of being somewhere that holds itself apart from the rest of the world. I love the simplicity of living on a small island, with only so many places to go and so many things to do. I love waking up, stepping out and just seeing what the day brings, free of negotiations and arguments and compromises, free of the need to justify what I want to do or not do. I love watching the girls applying their creativity and curiosity as they interpret this new world, where everything is unfiltered, almost as strange for me as it is for them, and they have to make sense of things for themselves. Aged five, two and forty-three, I feel as if we all three see the world more clearly for not having inherited it, but for having landed up here and having to suss it out. I think it is this that makes every day so exhilarating.

The school dismays me, though. Its prissiness echoes what I've noticed around town, a paranoid attitude to child-raising powered by the need to dodge the ever-present scary monsters of catching cold, grazing a knee, dying of starvation, bursting into tears or looking unrespectable. I'm fed up of seeing mothers hollering at kids for running in case they sweat, for climbing in case they fall, for taking off a jumper if there's the slightest breeze in case they die of pneumonia. I'm fed up with seeing grannies shovelling food into the mouths of overweight kids, of giving them sweets and Coke whenever they whine, of kids being told they can't play in case they get their clothes dirty, can't take their shoes off in case people think they are *marocchini*, Moroccans. There's a weird attitude towards girls as well. I heard a grandmother congratulate her granddaughter on looking 'sexy' the other day – the little girl was dressed in a pink cropped top and mini skirt and was about four years old.

Maybe I'm acting like a petulant kid, dragging the girls to the other side of Europe, then moaning because life still isn't perfect. Maybe it is ridiculous, dangerous even, to always be seeking more. Maybe I am just someone who will never be satisfied. But then, I think, I've never been a mother before. It's the most important thing I've ever done and I have to carry on following my instincts because there is nothing else to follow. If I am happier than I can ever remember being, then that must mean something. If I accept that Favignana hasn't worked out, it doesn't have to mean I have failed nor that the adventure has to end. Maybe I could see Favignana as just a step on a journey. Maybe once the summer is over, we should go and look and see what the rest of Sicily is like.

I hear a car draw up, the slam of a door, the crackle of static. The blond-haired fisherman is leaning against the silver Range Rover, binoculars trained on the boats, talking into a walkie talkie. I turn back to the boats and realise they are not checking nets, but drawing them in, empty.

INTERMEZZO

CHILDREN OF
SHADOWTIME

The summer rolls on, too hot for thought, too hot to do anything but spend mornings and evenings on the beach, the afternoons at home with shutters closed. Juno has her birthday, a frugal one, with a ten-euro present of a sand kit comprising plastic wheelbarrow, buckets, moulds and spades, which I hang from the pram twice a day as we walk to the beach. The willpower involved in living life under a roasting sun cancels out awareness of anything but the present.

But just as I am beginning to face the fact that the royalties will not last for ever, Rough Guides ask if I can update their Sicily book. It's on a six-month deadline, and the first part is easy – travelling around Sicily to see what has changed since the last edition. I've done this kind of work scores of times and figure I can do it with the children in tow. Not only that, but the timing is perfect. I can combine updating the guidebook with looking for a new place to live. The second part will involve hours at the computer, checking that every phone number, address, price and opening time is correct, and there is no way I can do that with Izzy and Juno at home. If I am going to make the deadline, then by January Izzy needs to be in school and Juno needs to have a babysitter (can I afford it?) or be in nursery school. First though we need to start exploring Sicily.

As summer tips into autumn and the days get cooler, I feel my energy revive along with the resolve to leave this island of machismo and intimidation. In five months our only new purchases are bedsheets, flip-flops and the beach toys, so it takes less than a morning to pack, but three days to paint over Pippi and the princesses. As I close the door to leave, I can still see them dancing ghostlike through three coats of whitewash.

We take the ferry to the mainland, I hire a car and we head along the Sicilian coast. We find crescents of golden sand, wind-sculpted dunes, tiny white-pebbled coves, strands of glinting quartz, dramatic cliffs, splintered pinnacles and arches of natural rock. But, inevitably, just outside the frame are oil refineries big as small cities, cement and breeze-block resorts of jerry-built villas and apartments, fields of sun-yellowed poly tunnels, motorway viaducts and everywhere – on the sands, on clifftop paths, caught in the roots of pine trees shading the ruins of an ancient Greek temple – shoals of plastic bottles, cigarette butts, beer bottles, crisp packets, condoms and baby wipes. I am getting anxious and the cynical whisper voice has returned, mocking the blind romanticism that has me ending up, time after time, on another trashed beach.

Taking notes for the guidebook with two children for company is harder than I thought. I am tired, stressed, edgy, and on top of that endlessly asking myself if I am doing the right thing in being so determined to stay in Sicily. I accept that some degree of anxiety when taking a big decision is generally quite a good thing, prompting a healthy dose of reflection and self-questioning. But the voice in my head is relentless, refiguring every blight on the landscape as if it were an allegorical step on a journey in a medieval morality tale designed to demonstrate what happens to people who want too much. I can hear them all: sour teachers, Yorkshire uncles, my ex – their criticisms and put-downs accumulated somewhere at the back of my head, quieter recently than has often been the case, but always ready to spring to the surface whenever self-doubt erodes my armour. *Ideas above her station, that one. She strayed off the path of toil and duty and ended up wandering into the maw of hell.* What will come next? Monsters and dragons?

I get a grip. What the hell am I doing, seeing the damaged world as if it were a comment on the decisions I am making, like a medieval peasant believing that natural disasters were divine punishments? Surely, turning the outside world into a metaphor is a kind of warped arrogance? But it is not as simple as that. If we were not stirred by the beauty of the real world, how could we ever have imagined paradise? Our sense of spirit and soul, religion, meaning, all have their roots in the Earth. If the beauty of nature stirs within us a sense of the sublime, of transcendence even, then perhaps we accept that beautiful places that have been trashed do not only symbolically reflect our imperfections but are evidence of our guilt. And that is real, not a metaphor – or real as well as being a metaphor. I look at plastic detritus on the sand and think of John Donne. *True paradise I have the serpent brought.*

On a beach near Siracusa, I sit watching the girls make a house out of a sea-scoured plastic crate for the Guatemalan worry dolls we bought at a hippy stall. They have stuck stalks of sea parsley in the sand for trees and made a swimming pool out of an aerosol cap. Juno is helping one of the worry dolls slither down a slide of wave-buffed plastic. Inside the house, the tiniest doll lies on a bed made of a shard of bathroom tile. Izzy is at work on the kitchen, positioning bottle tops on a chunk of polystyrene. This stuff will never disappear, just be ground up by the sea to become micro-plastic particles so small they will be ingested by fish and, I suppose, eventually by us.

This morning we left the coast and climbed up to the remains of a Bronze Age settlement in a magnificent silver-gold limestone gorge honeycombed with caves, the only signs of human habitation niches carved into the bare rock to hold oil lamps, candles or keep food out of the way of rodents. They lived lightly on the planet back then. History teaches us to be awed and thrilled when elements of ancient civilisations are discovered. But, I think, perhaps we should be even more in awe when ancient civilisations leave no traces on the Earth; if their homes, art, temples, weapons, lives were biodegradable; if the only traces they have left are in our DNA.

As the girls and I look for our home, it strikes me that 'home' is where it all began, the need for a permanent settlement marking the beginning of humans making an impact on the planet, an impact that eventually became so enormous that we have created our own epoch and become a monstrous force on a geological scale.

The sun is high, the sky biting blue as we drive away from the gorge and up the coast, across a fertile plain dense with citrus groves. Oranges and lemons hang heavy on the trees, sky and sea seem freshly washed and hung out to dry by a wind from the north. Far below the road, breakers crash on grey quartz beaches. In the distance is Etna, already snow-capped, charcoal puffs of volcanic gas dragged like paint across the sky by the wind. There is no way we are going to live on an active volcano, but there is also no way we are going to drive past an active volcano without taking a closer look.

Three thousand metres high, Etna is impossible to ignore, and every one of the many peoples who have lived in Sicily has had to absorb it into their worldview. The Greeks thought it the forge of Hephaestus, god of fire; that Zeus had buried a monster below it and that the eruptions and earthquakes were a result of him struggling to escape; that Homer's one-eyed Cyclops lived here, keeping sheep, making cheese and hurling thunderbolts. To the Romans, Etna was a goddess who gave birth to twin gods of thermal geysers, while in medieval Sicily, some believed it to be the entrance to hell, others to Avalon. An Islamic poet saw Etna as a woman and wrote a love poem: 'I am the lava, you are the fire that melts me.' These days, Sicilians call Etna *iddu*, him, or *u muntagna*, the mountain, as if to give it a name would be to invest it with too much power.

In 1693, a violent eruption triggered earthquakes which destroyed a string of towns stretching for over 100 kilometres across southeast Sicily. Although nothing on a similar scale has happened since, volcanic activity is frequently severe enough to close the airport in nearby Catania.

We stand in a car park 2,000 metres up Etna, surrounded by souvenir stores, and look up at its peak hidden in cloud. Alone, I would walk, but even I will not push a pram up a volcano, so we take the easy way – a cable car. Halfway up the mountain, the cable car swims into a white void. The temperature plummets, and the cabin stops dead and hangs shuddering over a slope of lava in a wind that howls as I have only heard it do on the Yorkshire moors, shooting shafts of icy air through ill-fitting windows. Our hooded fleeces and cagoules do nothing to keep out the cold.

I am just beginning to worry when the cable car cranks into action again and lurches on. Out on top, I peer through the station windows at impenetrable white fog. The bucolic Sicilian autumn of the foothills seems like an improbable dream. I open the door and the girls jump into my arms, screaming, burying their faces in my waterproofed chest. The wind is iced, relentless, lashes my eyes with volcanic grit. Across a road thick with ash, I can see a jeep waiting to take us to the active crater. Instead, I step back inside the station and close the door. It feels like we are somewhere humans are not meant to be. We jump into the next cable car and leave.

For most of humankind's existence, the assumption has been that we are at the centre of the universe. The theory of the Anthropocene involves a seismic ontological shift. Humankind is no longer the passive inheritor and observer of the Earth but is determining its future. Volcanic eruptions may halt aircraft, destroy villages, rain lava, but it is our actions that will dictate how fast the planet speeds towards a point where life is no longer sustainable. One of the most interesting Anthropocene projects is the Bureau of Linguistical Reality, a search for new words that help us to understand, to conceptualise – and to come to terms with – the emotional and intellectual impact of manmade climate change. One is 'nonnapaura', 'the desire for your children to have children of their own, at the same time as fearing that the world your grandchildren will inhabit will be full of dangers rooted in climate change'. Another is 'shadowtime', defined as 'a feeling of living in two distinctly different temporal scales simultaneously… Shadowtime may occur when one is preparing a meal for their child and suddenly realises that an endemic flower that had evolved over 42.7 million years has gone extinct within their child's lifetime'.

Shadowtime is also, I think, the attempt to understand geology as a human being rather than as a scientist. When your point of reference is a human lifespan.

We get into the car and drive back down the volcano, getting out to look at the charred skeletons of orchards and vineyards smothered in savage frills of solidified lava, a farmhouse sunk to its bedroom windows in lava, metres thick, with the texture of elephant skin. We are driving through a landscape people have seen change before their eyes.

I drive on. There is no way we are going to live anywhere near an active volcano. The girls have fallen asleep and I am tired too. I join the motorway. The coast here is built up, hugged by railway as well as autostrada, clogged with ramshackle seaside resorts. I am afraid that time is running out. Am I looking for a perfection that doesn't exist? Should I try Tuscany? Go back to England? Give up? Maybe Favignana wasn't too bad after all. Perhaps I have to accept that you don't get pristine beauty and remoteness without a few Neanderthal attitudes.

Yesterday, Michel sent me a message to say a fisherman had caught a poisonous Japanese puffer fish off Favignana. Even if I could find a paradise, it would only be apparent, the sea harbouring plastiglomerates and synthetic dress fibres, native fish floundering, alien species brought in on the hulls and in the ballast waters of big ships from China, colonising new seas. As I look out to sea, a rust-red container ship slides along the horizon.

FAULT LINE

On a bridge above Messina, the traffic grinds to a halt. Ahead of me, a ghastly pink apartment block is rammed across the head of a gorge and below it, the city spills down, haphazard, to the narrow strait that separates Sicily from mainland Italy. The wind whisks the water into staccato waves, like egg white on the way to becoming meringue, and ferries slide back and forth like shuttles. I wonder how many laments that monstrous pink apartment building has provoked from tourists caught in traffic jams. *How could they? Have they never heard of planning regulations?*

Messina is a dust-mote in the eye of those, like me, seeking the quaint, the picturesque, the *authentic*. Which is surely to misuse the word authentic. Because, after all, what are those oil refineries, shopping malls, breeze-block resorts and shoals of litter but the signs of authentic everyday life, symptoms of the universal desire for progress, improvement, security? It is only too easy for me to look down my eco-conscious nose at Messina, but there is a good reason why it is one of the ugliest towns in Italy.

At 5.21 on the morning of the 28 December 1908, Messina was struck by an earthquake, 7.5 on the Richter scale. Seconds later, a huge tidal wave crashed into the coast. The city was devastated and between 80,000 and 100,000 people died, but as the records office was destroyed, the precise death toll will never be known. After the earthquake, the survivors were housed in hastily erected prefabricated shacks, known as *baracche*. Many of these are not only still standing, but still inhabited. To the *messinesi*, however, the apartment blocks that so affront my aesthetic taste would have signified something else. What apartments like this pink behemoth offered was dignity.

I am depressed, despondent, in danger of becoming paralysed by a feeling of helplessness. Our ideas of what constitutes a dignified life – an income, enough to eat, a safe, clean home that offers protection from the elements – might be incompatible with the survival of the planet. I look over my shoulder at the girls, tangled together, fast asleep. If I really cared about the planet, I shouldn't even have had kids.

As a child, I assumed the Earth was unchanging, that it could be taken for granted, was simply the stage on which life was lived. Then in the 1970s, Leeds council sand-blasted the charcoal black Victorian buildings that defined the city. My school, the library, the neo-Baroque town hall were revealed to be made of golden sandstone. Looking back, I think the intended message from the council must have been that Leeds was a thriving modern city, not a relic of the industrial revolution. Stinking polluted rivers and canals were cleaned up, abandoned factories, former wool mills and warehouses converted into prime real estate, sink estates demolished, and the kinds of restaurants that journalists in London wrote about opened on streets that had been no-go areas for as long as anyone could remember. And so it seemed, back in the 1970s and 80s, that if things got dirty, we could clean them up, turn back time. But now we know we can't.

An ecologically irresponsible choice, but nothing in my life has made me so human – or care as much about anything, including the future of the planet – as having children. What would the beauties of the planet signify were there no humans to observe them, feel their souls lifted and filled with wonder? Raw still from my stand against the machismo of Favignana, I can't help but see some link between bullying and exploiting the planet. Doing what we want because we can. Doing what we want because we believe ourselves to be in control. I think back to Etna and the house buried to its bedroom. Could it be, far from being something to avoid at all costs, that living in a part of the world where the natural world can be violent and volatile, where it can swerve at any moment from passive to active, where human life is revealed as a precarious miracle, might be a good starting point for the life of a child? The illusion that we are in control, that the Earth is here for ever, gives us the arrogance to do what the hell we want. Perhaps living somewhere that shows you that you are not in control would have the opposite effect.

The traffic moves on but ahead I can see another jam, so at the next exit I leave the motorway. As we rise above the town and hit a junction the traffic snarls up once again. I sit leaning on the wheel, staring despondently out of the window at the steaming red and white striped chimneys of yet another oil refinery, flames flickering. 'Tempophagy', time-eating, a word created by climate change philosopher Tom Cohen to capture the idea that as we consume fuels made of millions-of-year-old fossils, we are eating (or burning) time. Oil, says Cohen, is a kind of compressed time, and of course he is right. But oil also brought money to Sicily, offering secure, salaried work for multinationals that meant ordinary, decent people could escape poverty, steer clear of the Mafia, avoid emigrating, buy houses, educate their kids and send them to university.

Izzy wakes up and clambers into the front seat.

'Where are we?'

I pick up the map. Izzy bends over to have a look.

'Somewhere along here,' I say, tracing my finger along the northern coast.

'And what are those?' She points out to sea. Beyond the chimneys of the oil refinery are the silhouettes of islands crisp against the pink sky.

I look at the map. Seven little islands, four of them no more than specks. 'The Aeolian Islands.' After Aeolus, Greek god of the winds.

'Mmm,' says Izzy.

I knew a little about the Aeolian islands but wasn't sure I could justify a trip there – upmarket holiday destinations with high prices. I'd always loved the name, the feel of all those vowels in the mouth, and had even played with the idea of calling one of the girls Aeolia. I liked the associations, too. That melancholic Aeolian mode (tone semitone tone tone semitone tone tone, or A B C D E F G A if you want to try it on a piano) and the Aeolian harp, played by the wind. I knew the islands were volcanic and I imagined them as bleak cones, shadeless and inhospitable like miniature Etnas, stinking of sulphur. Some of the more decadent of my rich Roman friends would go to the islands in summer, to live without electricity, swim and sunbathe nude, and catch fish which they would roast on volcanic coals. Positively ascetic – if I hadn't seen the amount of drugs they packed. Well, I figured, stoned trustafarians living under a volcano would be better than macho *mattanza* men.

Still stationary in the traffic, I pull out the *Rough Guide* and skim through the introduction to the islands. They are not, it seems, black, infertile places of exile, but lush, green islands of abundant vegetation and sweet grapes, sought out by writers, artists, fashion designers and filmmakers. I bin my image of cave-dwelling hippie families with waist-length dreadlocks and all-over tans and replace it with scenes of a white linen-clad intelligentsia wafting around vineyards sipping glasses of iced Malvasia as they look out to sea and quote Pirandello. Oh dear. I'm wearing New Look viscose. I may be a bit out of my league.

I read on. Only two of the islands have active volcanoes and the patron saint of the islands is Bartholomew, Bartolo, who is credited with having, so far at least, protected the islands from serious earthquakes. Even the earthquake that destroyed Messina caused no serious damage to the islands ... We can catch a hydrofoil from the next town, Milazzo.

Early the next morning, we are in the queue for the first hydrofoil of the day. I've read the guidebook twice but still haven't decided which island to head for. I dig out a pen. I need to anchor myself. Stick to the facts.

Lipari, the main island, has a proper town and pumice mines. *Boring*, I scribble. Vulcano is a smouldering volcano with bubbling mud baths and a town that looks like an unfinished spaghetti western set. *Ugly.* I write. *Stinks of rotten eggs,* I underline. Panarea is frequented by the fashion set, A-list heavyweights. *No way.* Stromboli is the most active volcano in Europe and caused a minor tsunami two years ago when an eruption triggered a submarine landslide. *A little too exciting.*

I turn the page. Alicudi. Population of eighty, electricity a recent innovation, the only land transport, donkey. A widespread belief in ghosts and witches, and in the power of individuals to control cyclones. Mmm. Possibly not the best place in which to raise calm, well-balanced children with open minds and the capacity to deal with all the twenty-first century might throw at them. Filicudi. Terraced hills criss-crossed by mule tracks and scattered with little whitewashed villages; a remote, abandoned village where an Afghan princess has reconstructed a house; another village on a beach of seashells where you can sit and watch the sun set while a retired banker from Catania serves you with swordfish cooked with orange zest and burgers made with tuna, capers, raisins and caramelised onion. Sounds like paradise and my mouth is watering, but then I remember a friend who had gone there for Christmas telling me that in winter the island gets cut off for weeks and depression spreads like the plague.

We have reached the front of the queue.

'*Si?*' says the man in the ticket booth, tapping the counter.

'Umm.' I turn the page of the guidebook.

'Salina is the greenest island in the archipelago...'

'Salina?' I ask.

The guy smiles. 'Salina? Sicura?' Are you sure?

'*Salina è bella?*'

'*Salina è bellissima.*'

'Umm. Serve the next person first.' I stand aside and read some more ...

The greenest of the islands, says the book, twin peaked, a population of under 2,000 dispersed in six little villages ... beaches, footpaths and rocky bays ... famous for capers, sweet wine and small tomatoes, fresh fruit granita ... the island where *Il Postino* was shot ...

And then I remember being in Rome in the 1990s, interviewing two food critics, Susan and Danilo, husband and wife, Italian and American, as they introduced me to *burrata*, served with a sundried tomato jam I have tried and failed many times to reproduce. Talk about tomatoes led us to talk about the south of Italy, and Susan told me Salina was her favourite place to be. The place that kept her sane.

'Salina,' I say.

Part II

SALINA

MIRANDA SYNDROME

'*Santa Marina Salina! Scalo di Santa Marina Salina!*' the crewman hollers. I stand at the open door of the hydrofoil, hanging on tight as the boat rocks, with an overpowering urge to sing 'O Little Town of Bethlehem' out loud. I can see nothing ugly anywhere. A green mountain, with a frill of amber-leaved vineyards, rises high above the little village of Santa Marina, spilling down to the sea around a comfortably proportioned church as yellow as butter. Its huge dome reminds me of a pregnant belly. *How still we see thee lie.*

We clatter off the hydrofoil and along the quay. The sky is the blue of copper sulphate, the sea cobalt. The houses are white, the lava-stone pavements black, and everywhere are great splodges of pink bougainvillea. The girls stop to stroke a sleek Siamese cat, well fed, dozing on a bench, and it yawns and stretches, regarding them with speedwell-blue eyes. The poor kitten Michel adopted died, though I didn't tell the girls.

Two *ormeggiatore,* dock hands, one white-haired, one dark, release the mooring ropes and the hydrofoil pulls away in a cloud of grey smoke. Lighting cigarettes, they head down a flight of steps to a small gravel beach where two small fishing boats are pulled up. They take a battered chair apiece and sit either side of a black plastic vat with hundreds of nasty-looking fish hooks hanging from its rim. The younger man – tall, rugged and dressed in a cable-knit sweater that has begun to unravel – cuts lengths of fishing twine which the older man attaches to the hooks with deft fingers.

The older one – crinkle-skinned, with curly white hair and a large belly – catches our shadows and looks up. Even from this distance, I can spot the twinkle of an old roué.

'*Totani*,' he says, looking up. 'We're going for *totani*.'

'*Totani*?' I ask, 'What are *totani*?'

'*Totani*,' says the other, with an impudent glint in his eye, 'like big calamari.'

'But meatier.'

'Much meatier.'

'Longer.'

'Thicker.'

'Than calamari.'

I can't help laughing. You can tell they've worked together for years. They're a double act, slick and deadpan, yet they somehow imbue the tired old double entendres with charm. Or is it just that I am beguiled by the first impression of the island and seeing everything through rose-tinted glass?

As Izzy asks me what *totano* is and what's funny about it, we walk off along the quayside to a bus stop where a tiny bright blue bus is waiting. Adding to my sense of having landed in utopia, the strains of a Mozart Flute Concerto are pouring through the open door. The driver leans out and asks where we want to go.

'Anywhere,' I say, 'everywhere.' Then, realising that this is an utterly nutty thing to say, I add, 'Wherever the bus goes,' in the hope that it might make me sound more normal. But I am not acting normal. Usually, for God's sake, I don't stand on a quayside exchanging double entrendres with dockers. On Favignana, I had held myself apart, repelled by the men, frightened, even. And now here I am, not only ready to let destiny take over, but revealing the fact to a bus driver, just because he listens to Mozart.

He jumps out and helps me get children, pushchair and suitcase on board. Tall, slim, silver hair, faded jeans and a black t-shirt. He looks more like a graphic designer than a bus driver.

'Anywhere and everywhere,' he says, turning the key in the ignition. 'Well, let's start with somewhere.'

As we pull out of the village, the Flute Concerto's final

movement begins. In the years I spent as a backpacker travelling Italy by bus, all I ever heard was RTL Europop. Is he a musician, perhaps, seeking exile from the concert circuit? A composer with writer's block? A philosopher undergoing an existential crisis? We swing up a road, high above the port, winding past citrus trees heavy with oranges and lemons, tiny vineyards, neat vegetable plots. All we saw on Favignana were arid fields run wild. We are the only passengers. At the crest of a hill, the driver stops, turns to us and points up a sheer-walled gully of indigo rock, where a bird of prey hangs motionless in the sky. Sweet, anise-scented air fills the bus. The girls fall silent and we watch, holding our breath, unable to believe that a bird can defy gravity for so long, just hang there, in the midst of nothing, moving, so it seems, not a muscle. It seems it must fall but then, with a twitch of a wing, it is off, higher and higher into the mountains until we can see it no more.

The driver starts the engine again and we carve across steep slopes dense with maquis, the colours intense as an acid trip: lime green, sherbet lemon, sea glass, copper, verdigris, coral and the decadent flesh-pink of naughty Parisian underwear. Olive leaves flicker silver-to-green in the wind, and above a black and crimson cliff with the texture of grog blossom, light gleams on the oval discs of cacti. The sea is not the turquoise we have become accustomed to but a deep cobalt blue, and where the mountain meets the water there are dark pebble beaches. The cliffs of the island of Lipari across the water seem close enough to touch, and further away is a conical island with a plume of smoke dispersing in the breeze. 'Stromboli,' says the driver, pointing. 'Watch tonight and you'll see the lava. And that,' he says, pointing to a smaller island a little to the east, 'is Panarea.'

'The VIP island?' I ask.

'Exactly. But now, in October, there's no one. Nothing. Paradise.'

'We want to live on one of these islands,' I say. 'I was thinking about Salina, but do you think I should look at the other islands too?'

'You could look at them. Of course, you could look at them. But I think Salina has found you already.'

Salina has found me? I repeat what he has said, double checking to see if I have understood the grammar. *Salina ti ha già trovato.* Yes, that is what he is saying. Not that I have found Salina, but that Salina has found me.

He stops the bus again. We are at the lip of another hill. Down below is a small, white village on a tongue of land tipped by a scuffed lighthouse that seems on the verge of toppling over.

'That is Lingua,' he says, 'you must go to Da Alfredo, they make the best granita in Italy.' And he kisses his fingers in the gesture of Italian TV chefs.

The bus driver drops us at the beginning of the village and suggests he leaves our suitcase somewhere he refers to as La Fontana.

'There's no one here, no one will take it.'

The sun is hot and the air invigoratingly scented with jasmine, capers, aniseed. All the houses are white, flat roofed, with stripes of blue, pink or yellow around doors and windows. Some have been meticulously renovated, others are in dire need of a lick of paint, and there is still the occasional ruin. All have roofed terraces in front of them looking out to sea, and it is these I love most, as someone who would always rather be outside than in. I spot sofas, dining tables, even outdoor kitchens with sinks and washing machines. One house in particular makes me stop in my tracks and drool. Sparkling, sugar-cube white, with stripes of pale blue around door and windows, and plumbago, jasmine and bougainvillea tumbling over a terrace. I lean over the wall for a better look. Tiny niches in the walls hold exquisite pieces of driftwood and on a table paved with antique tiles there is a creamy candle with the diameter of a dinner plate. Hanging at the door is a curtain made of lozenges of sea glass. Steps of pale, biscuity terracotta lead down to the sea. I feel like Persephone returning from Hades. *If I were a rich man...* I sing to the girls. Izzy joins in, and we dance down a side road to the sea.

We walk along a neat lava-stone promenade to a small piazza where a tiny bar with *Da Alfredo* painted on an old boat rudder above the door, has a few tables and chairs outside. A young, elfin-like man wearing a bellboy cap is sitting at one of the tables reading with a large husky dog sleeping at his feet. As we approach, the dog lifts its head lazily and opens its eyes. One of them is brown, the other blue.

'Hello,' says the man, clearly at ease in English, laying down his magazine. 'I'm Piero.' He stands up and smiles at the girls. 'Now, what can I get you?'

The dog has a little sniff at Juno's bare feet.

'Ice cream?'

'I'm afraid we don't have ice cream but we do have granita – icy fruit. If you come inside, I'll show you what it is and you can try to see if you like it.'

Juno beams at Piero. Izzy looks at me. 'Oh, can we Mum, please?'

I have just discovered Juno's shoes are not in the pram.

'Where are your shoes?'

'Don't know.'

'Did you throw them out?'

'Don't know,' she says, looking guilty, then turns to Piero and beams.

'We'll have to go and find them before you have icy fruit.'

'No. No shoes. Icy fruit.' She looks down and wiggles her toes.

'They can stay here if they want, while you go and look,' says Piero.

Would I normally leave my kids with a man I had never met? Would they normally agree to stay with a stranger, even if he was giving them all the ices they could dream of? I'm starting to feel like Miranda, spellbound on her enchanted island, able to see only Ariel, not Caliban. Is there such a thing as a Miranda syndrome, I wonder, whereby you shut out reality and live with the fairies? I hesitate a moment. What am I doing, importing bogeymen to this place? It's tiny. There are people all over, pottering in gardens and sweeping terraces. He couldn't do anything without at least half a dozen people knowing about it. And even if he did, there would be nowhere to go.

'Are you sure?' I ask Piero.

'Of course I am.' He bows to the girls. 'Now, follow me to the land of icy fruit.'

I walk back along the seafront but there is no sign of the shoes. Still not quite believing I have done the right thing leaving the girls alone with a stranger, I turn round. I don't really see anyone wanting to steal a pair of sea-stained Clarks. I'll walk back through the village later, looking into all the gardens. Back at the bar, the girls are perched on the zinc counter, watching Piero spoon pink and orange granita into a glass.

'Watermelon and melon,' says Izzy. I try it. Ambrosial.

We go outside to sit down. There's a light breeze ruffling the sea, rattling through the leaves of the palms shading the bar.

'Excuse me, but are these yours?' Laughing Home Counties English. I look up.

A young woman with glossy brown hair, dressed for comfort in baggy trousers and a roll-neck jumper, is walking towards us, holding up Juno's shoes. A small blond head peers out from behind her knees.

'I'm Emma and this is Max.' Max's head promptly disappears. Izzy gets up and tiptoes up to Emma, and peers around her back. Then she darts to the other side. Max's head appears, this time with his hands over his eyes, draws back again, then appears again on the other side of Emma, this time giggling. Juno laughs, spattering the table with granita.

'OK, Max, I'm going to sit down now.' She rubs her sacrum and sinks into a chair. 'Now, Max, why don't you take the girls to the beach?'

Max leads the way down the beach, and Emma and I watch the children play on the pebbles. Emma tells me she is married to a fisherman and has been living on the island for four years. She met Gaetano on holiday, fourteen years ago, when she was nineteen, he sixteen. She went back home, did a degree, had a career and almost married a PhD student. When life was difficult, she'd think of the island, remember Gaetano and in the end, she left the PhD student, did an Italian course in Tuscany, then came back to Salina. At second sight it was still love, and after a couple of years of commuting between London and Salina, she married Gaetano and moved to the island for good. Max is three, his sister Ilana a baby.

As the conversation moves to the Italian art of disciplining kids through candy, a squarish, heftily built woman wearing a hot-house-flower-printed housecoat and pushing a pram with zeal bursts onto the piazza and makes straight for Emma. Inside the pram, a miniature version of Max is fast asleep.

'*Cavolo di San Bartolo*, Emma,' the woman crosses herself, '*che dobbiamo fare?*'

Saint Bartholomew's cabbage?

'My mother-in-law,' says Emma softly.

'*Madonna mia.*' She turns to me, gesticulating wildly with mightily muscled arms. '*Che dobbiamo fare?*' What can we do? She runs her hand through her hair, thick, springy, and dyed one of those shades of pinkish orange that can only come from a bottle.

'I don't know,' I say. 'Um. *Ciao.*'

'Meet Ros, Izzy and Juno,' says Emma.

'*Ciao, cara, ciao.* Rose, Easy, Juno. All my olives, you understand, all my olives. Lost, lost, doomed to be lost.' She hesitates, then her eyes light up. 'Do you drive?'

'Well, yes ...'

Giuseppina crosses herself again. '*Padre, fighiu e spiritu santu*, Father, son and holy ghost, thank you. Holy mother, full of grace, pray for us sinners now ...'

'But only an automatic,' I say.

'Boh! It's fifteen kilometres, you can drive that. You can drive, you can drive anything.'

'Giuseppina, she can't drive the Lapa.'

'And why not?'

'She can only drive an automatic car,' Emma says with the tone of patient impatience one adopts for a particularly trying child.

'Nonsense. Come on ... you can drive, you can drive anything. What is an automatic car, anyway? One of those electric things they have on Panarea?' She takes a hop and a skip. 'Wheeee.' She makes a peculiar wheezing sound. 'Eh Max?' she calls down to the beach. 'Wheeee?' Max, Izzy and Juno glance up. Max shrugs and turns back to gouging a road out along a patch of sand. Izzy and Juno stare at Giuseppina.

'Giuseppina,' says Emma firmly, 'an automatic car is not an electric golf car and she still can't drive the Lapa. Now. Start at the beginning.'

It takes us a good half hour to establish that Giuseppina's husband Rodolfo has been informed by the Carabinieri that driving regulations in Italy have changed, and that a licence is now required to drive the Piaggio three-wheeled pickups with a 50cc scooter engine known in the rest of Italy as an Ape and in Sicily as a Lapa. Giuseppina and Rodolfo have 300 kilograms of olives picked and ready to take to the olive press on the other side of the island, and no way of getting them there. Giuseppina has rung everyone they know who has a car, but no one is answering.

'They all have caller ID,' murmurs Emma, 'so they know when not to answer.'

'Well,' says Giuseppina, bristling suddenly, 'some of us don't have time to sit on walls all day. *Ciao* Max! *Ciao bimbe!*' and she stomps off out of the piazza.

Emma sighs, stands up and takes the brake off Ilana's pram. 'I better go and help, or I'll never hear the end of it. I don't suppose you'd want to come too?'

OLIVES AND CHANEL

Izzy, Juno and Max decide to squeeze into our pram, and we head along the shore of a small salt lagoon where six ducks are swimming watched from a distance by a white egret with a magnificently curled crest.

'We think it came from Africa but got left behind,' says Emma.

Max sits up and disentangles himself from the girls. 'And,' he says, with a serious little sigh, 'there were eight ducks, but Willy ate them.'

'Willy?'

'Piero's dog,' says Emma.

Max gives a little we-are-all-victims-of-fate shrug. 'And he ate Nonna's sheep.'

Juno giggles and starts rolling around.

'No, Juno,' says Max, 'that is not funny. A dead sheep is *grave*.'

'Gravy?' says Izzy, eyes wide open. 'A dead sheep is gravy?'

'*Grave*,' repeats Max.

'Serious,' I say, 'not funny.'

'Well, it did have its funny side, in retrospect,' says Emma quietly. 'Giuseppina went on the rampage at midnight with an iron bar. I'm not sure if she was going after Piero or Willy.'

We turn the corner up a little alleyway and arrive at an immaculate black wrought-iron gate set in a white wall. The gate is locked. Through it we see several huge pumpkins balanced on a wall, a pile of plastic seed trays and the end of a hosepipe dribbling water onto the bare concrete.

119

'Giuseppina!' Emma shouts.

'Nonna!' shouts Max.

'Nonna!' bellows Juno and they all collapse into giggles.

'*Arrivo arrivo. Madò, pazienza pazienza*, anyone would think that all I had to do was answer the door all day. No patience, no patience at all ... *Mannaggia*, where did I put that key?'

And she comes round the corner, digging into the pockets of a different housecoat, faded, patched and printed with daisies, which she has tucked into her knickers. The yard is full of huge baskets of olives and hemmed in behind them on a plastic chair is a slight, hunched old woman wearing thick, black-rimmed glasses. Some of her hair is dyed the same colour as Giuseppina's, the rest is white.

'They share a bottle,' says Emma, 'and there is never quite enough left for Maria.'

Maria is deaf, dumb and, despite the glasses, now virtually blind. Sensing me pass, she shouts *Pa Paa, Pa Pa Pa Paaa*! smiling, excited, hands searching the air. I bend down to kiss her, and she moves her hands over my face, touches my hair. They are cool and soft. *Pa pa pa paaaa*! She runs her hands down my back, and pulls my t-shirt down, smoothing it so that it covers my midriff, then gives me two smacking great kisses.

Giuseppina is leaning on a table, trying to write their surname, Zangari, on coffee sacks. The sacks have clearly done years of service, for they have been patched, hemmed, re-hemmed, washed, folded and (I would swear) ironed. The writing is not proceeding well, for the marker pen has dried up.

'Here, unscrew it and add some alcohol.' Giuseppina passes me the pen and a bottle of white spirit.

I look at the pen. Her frugality is admirable but there is absolutely no way the pen unscrews.

'You'll have to buy another,' says Emma.

'What? Buy another? I've only had it for four years! Throw money away?'

'Well, how else are you going to mark the sacks?' says Emma. 'Or are you just not going to bother and let some cowboy from Pollara steal your oil?'

A short man of about seventy with white hair cut neatly around a burnished bald pate enters the yard with a chin jerk. Izzy returns it. Juno copies her and Max collapses in giggles on the floor at the man's feet.

'*Ciao, Nonno!*' he manages through the giggles.

'Hm,' grunts Nonno. Then he lights a cigarette, watching the kids play, face softening.

'Hang on,' I say. 'Izzy, can we lend Giuseppina the felt pens?' There's a pack of chubby Woolworths toddler's pens in my bag. Just the thing.

'Can I do the writing?' Izzy asks. I pass her the pens.

'Well,' says Nonno, drawing deeply on his cigarette as Izzy laboriously copies ZANGARI onto every sack, 'no one else is going to have their names written like a rainbow.'

Nonno finishes his cigarette and starts to pace the yard. The latest regulations dictate that to maintain fish stocks, all fishermen have to spend one month a year on dry land. It is Rodolfo's third day in exile. He can't sit still, says Emma, can't think of anything to do and hates everyone. Gaetano's worse. Sounds like PMT to me. To make things even more difficult, it's the olive season and Giuseppina keeps pressganging the men into assisting with the harvest. On Sunday, she made Rodolfo and Gaetano climb the mountain to pick olives. Fishermen hate the land, says Emma, they think of cultivating it as women's work, so Gaetano has taken off to sea on someone else's boat. It's not legal, but he'd rather face the ire and fines of the marine authorities than be near Giuseppina during the olive harvest. Nonno, however, is trapped. He can't find anyone who'll take him on their boat. He's not allowed to drive the Lapa. He can't go anywhere.

Izzy has finished labelling the first sack and Emma and I hold it open while Giuseppina hauls a mighty basket of olives onto a table and tips it in.

'*Eh. Oue,*' snaps Nonno. 'Don't fill the sacks too full or we won't be able to move them.'

'Hmmf. Nonsense, they weigh nothing,' grunts Giuseppina,

demonstrating her strength by swinging the sack, which must weigh a good fifty pounds onto her shoulder.

It takes another hour to fill the olive sacks and tie them up with string. As soon as the last knot is tied, Nonno evaporates, as if into thin air.

'Let's go find Nonno!' Max shouts.

'Will he want them to? Doesn't he want a bit of peace?' I say.

'No. If he can't be at sea, he's happiest with kids. Let them go!'

'Is that safe?' Two three-year-olds and a five-year-old alone?

'They'll be fine, don't worry. Max has been going down to the piazza alone since he was eighteen months old.'

Giuseppina invites us inside into a small, low-ceilinged, rectangular room with a fireplace piled high with boxes of *panettone* and bottles of sweet spumante, which, she informs me proudly, she bulk-bought when they were on offer last January. There's a pile of stale bread on the table, which she has been grating into a big plastic bowl. Seeing me looking at it, she nods dismissively at Emma.

'She,' she says, '*buys* breadcrumbs. Can you imagine it? Makes me the laughing stock of the village. Who buys breadcrumbs for the love of the Madonna?' And she swings out of the room, unhitching her housecoat from her knickers.

When Giuseppina comes back into the room, she is wearing a turquoise shirtwaister with crossed tennis rackets appliquéd to the chest, wafting clouds of Chanel No. 5.

'*Che profumo!*' I say. What a perfume!

'She cleans the house of a lady from Palermo with a perfume shop,' says Emma, 'who saves her all the spare samples.'

Giuseppina switches on the TV and dives into a cupboard, tossing packets and bags of biscuits, cakes, brioches, tarts and pastries onto the table.

'But who needs breadcrumbs when we have cake?' she cries, disappearing into the kitchen for Fanta, Coke and fizzy wine. 'And who needs water when we have wine?' She pops the cork of the wine, and pours me a plastic cup of sweet, lukewarm, pink foam. It is quite disgusting.

Giuseppina has fallen silent, transfixed by the TV adverts.

'I've got that,' she announces proudly, as an ad for Vileda mops comes on the screen. I dispense with the fizz in a nearby plant. 'And those,' she says, as a skinny blonde woman demonstrates the efficacy of disposable dusters, 'they are marvellous, a miracle, they should have me telling the world about them. Look at her nails. You can tell she never dusted a room in her life. What does she know about anything?'

I excuse myself to go to the loo. Giuseppina looks at Emma, alarmed.

'But she can't. I haven't done the washing up! There wasn't time, with the olives.'

'Don't worry, I won't look at the kitchen,' I say. 'I just need to go to the toilet.'

'I know,' says Emma, 'but the washing up is in the bathroom sink.' And she explains Giuseppina has no running water in the kitchen, no hot water anywhere and a toilet you flush with a bucket.

'This house may be simple,' says Giuseppina, when I come back from the bathroom, 'but it's mine. Look at that sister of mine in Australia, all airs and graces with her central heating, swimming pool and three bathrooms. Avocado, aubergine and wheat, I ask you. But does she own the house? No, does she hell. The bank owns it. And does she sleep at night, for worrying about whether she's going to be able to pay the bank? Well, I very much doubt it. And what will happen to them, I say, if Christmas trees go out of fashion?'

I look at Emma for an explanation.

'Her sister and brother-in-law, who left the island for Melbourne thirty years ago, have a Christmas tree plantation. Giuseppina's worst nightmare is that they will turn up unannounced and make the humiliating discovery she has no running water in the kitchen.' Emma is on her feet and halfway out the door before Giuseppina can get going on the evils of Christmas trees.

Back in the piazza, Emma fixes us up with a room above one of the restaurants on the seafront. It has a tiny terrace, like the crow's nest on a boat, with unhindered views of Stromboli and Panarea, and that first night, after the girls have fallen asleep, I sit there and watch the red glow of lava on Stromboli. Favignana and the past days travelling through Sicily – the depression, the uncertainty, the oil refineries and trashed beaches – feel like a nightmare journey taken by another me in another place, both so distant that it is hard to believe that either exists any more. A day with Emma and I realised how lonely I have been. Her extended family, too. I'm in awe of the robust, rollicking, downright rude melodrama of afternoon tea with the Zangaris. After an English childhood of Saturday afternoons with aged relatives, during which my parents managed to remain polite no matter what was said, it's like going to the opera after a lifetime of string quartets. I find it exhilarating, astonishing even, to be with a family where differences of opinion are clashed with the panache of cymbals.

I call Mum and tell her about Salina, Emma and Giuseppina, the cultural differences between family life in Sicily and Yorkshire. 'True,' she says, 'although if I'd had to share our lives with Auntie Elsie and Uncle Albert instead of seeing them for an hour every two weeks, things in Far Headingley might have become very Sicilian indeed.'

As I finish the call, I tell myself that nowhere, not even Salina, can be paradise. There will be plastic bottles on the beach, macho men, intimidated wives, wicked gossip, petty jealousies, a thousand imperfections. But this is my reason talking, not my heart, and anyway, I think, watching the moon rise above the sea, it's OK to be happy, even if the world is imperfect.

WORMERY

'Ahh, Eeengleesch,' hisses Ettore, inching his wheeled office chair a few inches closer to mine. 'I need *private* Eeengleesch lesson.' Ettore is one of the island's estate agents. A creep fit for a seventies sitcom with dyed amber hair and scheming eyes, he oozes aftershave and self-satisfaction. After one day on Salina, I had woken with my mind made up. I didn't even have to make a decision, because our lives on Salina had already begun. But as we were having breakfast on the piazza, Emma and Max came to join us, and I realised there was one thing I hadn't thought of.

'You have to promise to tell me the truth, Emma.' I said, 'If we moved to the island would it feel like we were stepping on your toes?'

'No! What rubbish! I can't think of anything better!' she said laughing. 'But you'd better start house hunting right away because the estate agents usually close for the season at the end of October.'

Ettore tells me he has the perfect house to show me, big, he says, and beautiful, with a garden and sea view. I ask if we can go to see it now.

'At sunset is better,' he leers, 'more romantic.' He wheels another inch closer, bends towards me and gives my knee a squeeze with a hairy hand. I can read the name on his gold ID bracelet and wish I'd had the girls to sit on my lap for safety. I shoot up out of my chair, banging my shins on his desk, and whip over to a large map of the island on the wall.

'Where is it?'

As he walks over to join me, I dart back to the chair to retrieve my bag.

'Here,' he says, 'come closer, then you can see properly.'

'That's fine. I can see from over here,' I say, clamping my bag against my torso like a shield. 'Can we go and look at it now?'

Ettore insists that it is too far to walk and that we have to take his Vespa. I place my bag on my lap, shuffle as far away from him as I can, hooking my legs backwards around the petrol tank, and grip the seat-rest behind me. It is agony but I manage to avoid body contact for the entire two minutes it takes us to shudder up a steep hill to a road that runs high above the back of the town. The air is clear and crisp. The islands I now know as Lipari, Panarea and Stromboli seem close enough to touch, and, beyond them, to the south and east, I can see hills, pale, blue and distant.

'Calabria,' says Ettore, putting a hand on my shoulder, and pointing to the east.

I slither off the bike and point to the south. 'And over there?'

'Sicilia and Etna.'

Etna? Etna must be a hundred miles away or more.

Far away, an oil tanker slides across the sea and, rising behind it, I can see a range of hills, pick out pinnacles even, and white patches that must be villages. But I can't make out Etna and assume he must be having me on. Then I raise my eyes a bit and see the huge bulk of a mountain, high above the clouds, its upper slopes covered with snow. Ettore unlocks an iron gate and we walk up a rubble path, past pines and orange trees, to a house that resembles a large white shoebox. It is brand new, its floors covered with shiny white ceramic tiles, and it has all the charm of a mortuary.

'But this is too small,' I say. Which it is. A small kitchen, a living room and a bedroom.

'Aaaha!' says Ettore, grinning manically. 'But just you wait.'

And he walks over to a door and opens it theatrically.

I peer inside. It is a cupboard.

'Very nice,' I say, 'a very nice cupboard.'

'Step inside.' Ettore beams, like a diabolic conjuror.

'Actually, I'd rather not.' I take a step back.

'Well just watch then,' and he flicks a light on. Mops, buckets, brushes, a hoover.

'Lovely,' I say. 'Very nice. All new. Lots of mops.'

'Look,' he hisses, 'over there, in the corner.'

I look. Behind the buckets and mops is a door. Ettore moves the buckets and unlocks it. He switches a light on. A draught of damp, cold air, heavy with mould, slithers into the house up a steep narrow staircase.

'Come,' says Ettore, and I follow him down the stairs into a narrow white corridor illuminated with bare lightbulbs so bright they leave an image of filaments dancing on my retina. There are four doors, each leading to a room with floor-to-ceiling glass doors opening onto a wall of earth. It reminds me of a diagram showing the cross-section of a wormery in my primary school nature studies book.

'Um,' I say, 'it's not really what I had in mind, living underground, watching worms.'

'Cool,' says Ettore, 'cool, even in August.'

'No,' I say, and walk up the stairs. Being trapped underground with Ettore is not a pleasant sensation.

'But you don't understand,' says Ettore. 'It won't always be underground. Next year, they will dig the hillside away.'

'But why didn't they do that first, before they built the house?'

'Ahh.' He smiles, as at an ingenue who understands nothing. 'The local council, you know, and UNESCO, they make life impossible for poor innocent people who just need a roof over their heads for themselves and their families. If you buy a *rudere*, a ruin, you are only allowed to build a house that covers the exact same space as the ruin. Ridiculous. An insult. So poor, innocent, ordinary people are forced to build secret rooms underground. Then, after a couple of years, they pay a little money to the council. The council gives them permission to excavate the house, and *voila*! They have all they room they need, with a view God himself could not improve on.'

*

Back in Lingua, Emma and the kids are in Giuseppina's yard. Izzy is pouring salt into a blue plastic vat of water with a potato at the bottom, while Max and Juno stir it with wooden spoons.

'Stop, stop,' shouts Max. 'It's floating.'

They all bend over the vat and peer at the potato.

'No, it's not.'

'More, add more.'

She pours in more salt and slowly the potato bobs to the surface.

'What the hell are they doing?' I ask Emma.

'Getting the brine ready for soaking the olives. It has to be so salty that a potato floats in it.'

I leave the kids to their brinemaking and head off to my next house viewing. A man called Bartolino, Emma says, has a house to show me just above the lake. We're to meet at La Fontana. I spent half an hour searching for La Fontana yesterday when I went to retrieve my suitcase, scouring Lingua for a landmark fountain, imagining something Bernini-like, if on a scale befitting a small Sicilian island – a couple of water-spouting cherubs perhaps, or, more likely, a dolphin or triton. In the end, it turned out to be a tap.

There are three public taps in Lingua, each as basic, unadorned and tap-like as the other, but only one of them is known as La Fontana. They don't have water in them every day, Emma told me, just twice a week when the valves are opened to let water flow into the cisterns of the village houses. Although the island is green, she went on, there is no tappable water source and water is delivered every week by a tanker. For centuries, the islanders had to depend on rainwater, something several families still do, to avoid the high cost of water. But why this tap, rather than the other two, should figure so high in the collective consciousness of the islanders as to be graced with the name La Fontana Emma had no idea.

I sit on the wall, lost in thought in the shade of an almond tree, as I wonder whether we too might be able to live on rainwater alone, when a slight man with curly white hair appears beside me as if from nowhere.

'Jeez, I'm sorry, sweetheart, y'know wha' I mean? I'm sorry

I'm late? But what with one thing and another? Olives to pick, garden to clean?' He has quick, blue eyes, dimples like commas in each cheek, and is speaking rapid English with a heavy Australian accent, making every sentence he utters a question. 'So, sweetheart, we'll go see the house shall we, though I don't think it'll suit you? Basic, y' know wha' I mean? Old fashioned-like?'

Bartolino trips along the road, quick and light as Mercury, chattering all the time, so that by the time we have got to the house I know he lived in Sydney where he worked at an uncle's fruit and vegetable shop, married another Aeolian exile, had children and then, after fifteen years, decided they'd had enough.

'*La vita della città*. City life, I don't know, Ros.' He sighs. 'Seems to me cities are full of false friendships, designed to hook good people in and divert them from their proper path.' Not only in big cities, I think, remembering poor Sebastiano and the Favignana estate agent. 'Real friendships, simple, true, reliable friendships just don't seem to exist. It's all, oh, this guy can get me this. Oh, this guy knows this important person ...' I wonder what happened to Bartolino in Sydney but don't dare ask more.

I try to imagine how bewildering life in Sydney must have been to an island emigré who had grown up in a small community where everybody knew everybody else and there was no need to navigate society in the way you have to in a city, where every day is full of encounters with strangers. In the 1970s, when Bartolino left the island for Australia, there was virtually no tourism to Salina, so it must have been rare for islanders to see anyone for the first time. Everyone was already known to everyone else, generation after generation, and when a new child was born, their identity would already have been established by what people knew – or the stories they had heard – of their parents, grandparents, extended family, even long-gone ancestors. How stifling would that be?

'Here, I am outside all day, working in this beautiful place surrounded by nature. Just look at that sea.' It is flat and silken, like a cloth of gold, shimmering with the pinks and golds of the sun setting on the other side of the mountain. Some trick of the light is making the cliffs of Panarea seem translucent.

The house we are going to see belonged to Bartolino's great-grandfather. He hadn't left a will, which meant there were now thirty-seven legal owners scattered between the island, Turin, Australia, America and Argentina. Bartolino tells me that no one could agree on what to do with the house, except for the fact no one wanted to spend a penny on it. Bartolino did the odd job of keeping walls and roof intact. 'But it's nothing, y' know? Nothing?'

The typical Aeolian house is a shoebox divided into several rooms, each with its own windowed door leading onto a terrace shaded with a roof of cane, and often a glorious, scented tangle of vibrant flowering shrubs. The houses are whitewashed, with a stripe of colour around the windows and doors. Around the terrace, there is a low wall, with a *bisuolo*, or long, tiled bench built into it, stone pillows in each corner, designed for siestas. The more Bartolino talks about the disgraceful, unmodernised state of his house, the more hopeful I become. Maybe it will turn out to be the very house in which *Il Postino* was shot.

It isn't. It's a hovel. Two dark, damp rooms with a tiny terrace covered with moss from which there is nothing to see but the dank, untempered wall of the house in front. There's an outside loo, a hosepipe for a shower and the kitchen comprises two rusty gas rings and a fridge patinaed with black mould.

'You were imagining the *Postino* house, weren't you?'

I nod.

'Well, even that's not paradise. But the owner rents it out, so you may as well go have a look.'

THE HOUSE OF *IL POSTINO*

'Did you know that Sicilian for penis is feminine, *la minchia*, and Sicilian for vagina is masculine, *lo sticchio*?'

'No, I didn't, and it's fascinating, but I don't think it's the kind of thing *National Geographic* will publish.' Pippo Cafarella, a mercurial figure, mischievous as Puck, looks instantly deflated. 'Though,' I hesitate, for some reason feeling responsible for restoring his bounce, 'the psycho-socio-sexual implications are quite extraordinary, aren't they? For how men and women relate to their own sexuality as well as to each other.'

'Yes, and as I said before, look the way the waves penetrate the shore, the way the water moves through the algae like the ripples of an orgasm...'

'Tosh, you were just trying to shock me, see how I reacted.'

I am with artist Giuseppe Cafarella, known as Pippo, and his Swiss psychiatrist wife, Anna, picking our way across a ledge of rough, powdery volcanic tuff white in the high afternoon sun, on the coast below the village of Pollara. Pippo and Anna are the owners of the house where *Il Postino* was filmed. When I told the travel editor at *National Geographic* that I was thinking of renting the *Il Postino* house, she asked me to write a few hundred words for a special edition on the world's surviving paradises. Pollara is a village of a few score Aeolian houses clustered high above the sea in what was originally the crater of a volcano. Half of the crater has been devoured by the sea, leaving a narrow crescent of black beach below a sheer amphitheatre of crumbling rock. We reach a tiny inlet backed by caves where the locals keep small boats and fishing tackle. It's easy to tell which boat is Pippo's. It is called *Minchia Pazza*. *Pazza* means crazy.

The article may supposed to be about paradise, but sitting on the bleached rock as Pippo describes his childhood is more like watching a Tim Burton film. 'It was schizophrenic,' he says. 'Term-times I spent in Messina living in a gloomy palazzo of many rooms inhabited by two ancient aunts, the goddesses of death, I called them, who had lost their loves in the earthquake of 1908 and spent their lives in mourning and madness. Imagine them, Ros, veiled, pallid, dressed in black, kneeling at *prie dieu*s in shuttered rooms before images of emaciated thorn-crowned Christs, present on Earth, but not of it.'

Listening to Pippo is like being taken by the hand and led through gloomy room after room after room, doors ajar, shutters closed, porcelain shuddering at the echoes of receding footsteps, the rustle of a whisper or rat. In Sicilian palaces, he tells me, there are no corridors, it's one room opening off another, and anterooms that appear secret are in fact designed to be eavesdropped upon from above or below. Summers Pippo spent barefoot, free, savage on Salina, in Pollara – a place, he said, where people would only talk about what they could see in front of their eyes, could only think of getting enough to eat.

This is not what *National Geographic Traveller*'s paradise-seekers will want to hear about, so I suggest we walk up to see the house and ask them to tell me how it happened that the 1994 Italian classic *Il Postino* was filmed in a house in the most inaccessible part of an already remote island.

'Well,' said Pippo, 'I got a phone call early one spring from some random guys in Rome who said they wanted to rent the house for a month or two. I was a bit surprised, asked how the hell they knew about the place, and they said they'd been in Pollara the year before, seen the house and were fascinated by it. I told them the place was completely basic but they didn't seem fazed, so we agreed on a rent, token, there wasn't even any electricity. I was curious to meet them, so the next time I was on the island

I came over and discovered a film crew. They told me they were just doing the exploratory shots for a film about Pablo Neruda. I was a bit pissed off of course, but the director, Radford, calmed me down, and then he told me that the film was to star Massimo Troisi. Troisi, you know, was an exceptional man. Humble. Understated. Sensitive. Vulnerable, an innocent, not at all a film star, and for years he'd been coming to Salina and had a deep affinity with the island. He was forty, he knew he had a heart condition and needed surgery, but he was determined to make this film first, and insisted on it being made on Salina. It was listening to Troisi talking about the island that persuaded me. So we agreed on a higher rent and started to work together. I got electricity laid on for them, advised them on the colours to use to repaint the house and found the furniture. The rest, as they say, is history.'

The house comes into view, weathered and apricot, surrounded by a forest of olive trees grown wild, mighty tortured branches creeping across the dry earth like a school of monstrous octopuses. Close up, Pippo shows me its walls are painted in impressionistic daubs of rose, coral, peach and pumpkin, to give *sfumatora* – shade, depth, subtlety – to the colours on film.

Pippo and I sit on the cool, cracked tiles of the *bisuolo*. Soaring above the village is the volcano's caldera, its rugged blood-red crags and pinnacles breaking through a thick cover of myrtle, juniper, wild fennel and prickly pear. Above us, a couple of men are building a drystone wall. As Anna joins us with a tray of lemonade, I see her clocking the men, then meeting Pippo's eyes. He seems about to say something, but she almost imperceptibly shakes her head and hands me a glass of lemonade.

'Tell me if you need more sugar.'

We take our drinks inside. The interior is gorgeous, though basic. Bare floors, bare walls, its rooms sparsely furnished with the austere rustic furniture that appeared in the film. A purple and orange bedroom that did not appear in the film, dating back to Pippo's hippy days. A canvas by Pippo, abstract, textured, crumpled, that he painted and then anchored on the beach for the sea to erode, another one scorched, its vibrant acrylics melted, that he had blasted with a kind of blowpipe. The solvents, he says, have destroyed his lungs.

We go back outside; the grounds are vast, stretching from the coast to the foot of the caldera, and Pippo and Anna's son, Federico, is camped out in a den he's made below the branches of a thousand-year-old olive tree. Pippo and Anna offer me the house at a very low rent. Of course I want to live here.

'I don't think you should,' says Anna. High above us, a blue bus teeters down the hair-pinning road cut into the amphitheatre of rock and scrub. 'You've just arrived on the island. It's too remote. That bus only comes four times a day.' Anna is tiny and quietly spoken. At first, I thought she was shy, but then realised that she's the kind of person who prefers to listen, observe and reflect before she speaks.

'You really think I shouldn't?'

'I think it's too extreme, the remotest outpost of a remote island. Until recently, until really recently, the women here would be left here for months while their husbands went to sea on merchant ships or abandoned for ever as brothers, sisters, sons, daughters emigrated. Look at that bus.' Anna points to the road, curling down the sheer slopes of the caldera, the blue bus inching along slowly as a caterpillar. 'When that was a mule track, it took two hours to get to Malfa, so no one went. The psychological impact of that kind of isolation is severe. Anthropologists have tracked the myths and the magical practices of the women of these islands with awe, as if the women here were the direct inheritors of a tradition that goes back to ancient Greece and beyond. But I see something else, something like the collective madness or hysteria or even trauma of women with no agency.'

'When I was a kid,' says Pippo, 'once a week, the ferry arrived from the mainland. There was no place to moor. People had to climb down a rope ladder into boats and be rowed to shore. They would throw a cow into the sea and it would swim to shore, and then it would be killed and butchered right there on the portside. Like an ancient Greek sacrifice.'

'Now,' says Anna, 'the biggest excitement of the week is when the ice man arrives.'

'Ice man?' I can't help but picture a giant frosted superhero with icicles for fingers striding down the mountain.

'Eissman,' says Anna, 'a refrigerated van full of frozen ready meals. The kind of crap we came here to get away from.'

Pippo's phone rings.

'*Sì, pronto.*' He laughs. 'Nicole Kidman?' He laughs again. 'OK, I'll tell her.'

Anna looks at him quizzically. 'What now?'

Pippo grins. 'Oh ... nothing.' He looks at me. 'There's another house for you to look at. In Lingua.'

Lingua? Perfect! We could be neighbours to Emma.

A car door slams, echoing like a bullet across the silent village. The drystone wallers pause as a man in an immaculate black suit and tie crosses the scrub towards them.

Pippo drives me to Santa Marina, and we stop for a coffee at a tiny blue kiosk on the main piazza.

'So,' I say, 'what about this house in Lingua, and how come anyone knew I was looking for one, anyway?'

Pippo pauses. 'Look over there.'

On the piazza, women stand in clusters, plastic carrier bags at their feet, chatting to each other; a young mother with an orange pram strolls up and down, talking on her mobile phone. Three old men sit on a wall by the hydrofoil office, and two girls with plump, brown midriffs and acid-washed jeans lean bored against a palm tree.

'How many days have you been on the island? One? Two? Well, let me tell you what I've learned about you already. You're the American bitch who married the baker's nephew in Brooklyn and took all his money. You're the Australian tourist who had twins with a fisherman from Lingua, and then buggered off. You're a German tour rep. An English heiress. The woman in the advert for Scottish smoked salmon. You are Nicole Kidman – and before that goes to your head, someone just saw your hair from the back! But whoever you might be, they all know by now that you are looking for a house. Some of them will ask about you because they really do have a house to rent. Others will just do it because they want to find out who you are.'

I laugh uncomfortably. 'You're exaggerating.'

'No.' Pippo juts his chin out. I give him a sceptical smile. 'Well, just a bit.' He grins like a cheeky boy. 'But seriously, do you think there is any one of those people who hasn't noticed that I am sitting on the sea wall chatting to a pretty tourist? I bet you anything someone will have called Anna already. It's a small place, with few people. There isn't a lot going on and so everyone knows everything. Gossip controls these people, affects their every action, because everyone knows that if they transgress, someone will know about it. The people who've always lived here, they don't know any different. But people like me, who've been away, we need to be anonymous sometimes. That's why I get off the island every now and again. Life without anonymity can drive you mad.' He pauses, and looks back at the piazza, where an old man in an electric wheelchair is rattling across the cobbles.

'Now, that guy I like. He doesn't listen to anyone. Literally. He goes around all day with headphones on listening to free jazz.'

'But this house, Pippo, what do you know?'

'Nothing. That was a friend of a friend whose cousin had heard from a cousin of Piero—'

'Piero? The guy who has the bar at Lingua?'

'Right. Anyway, this cousin of Piero knew you were looking for a house and apparently there's some American artist whose dad has a place. She's called Diana. Or something. Anyway, you've to meet this American at her house at six.'

We call Piero. The house is right on the sea, Piero explains, at the foot of the hill at the beginning of the village. It is white with a blue stripe.

The sun is low now, turning the sea opalescent, tinging the clouds pink. The kids insist we run down the hill into the village and I am still running when I spot the house. White, in fact, dazzling sugar-cube white, with stripes of pale blue, the exact shade of the plumbago tumbling over its terrace ...

I pull the pram to a stop. 'More Mummy, more!' the girls squeal.

Tiny niches in the walls hold exquisite pieces of driftwood, olive roots bleached white by sun and smoothed by sea. The terrace is paved with antique tiles and hanging at the door is a curtain made of lozenges of sea glass. Steps of pale biscuity terracotta lead down to the sea. Bingo. It is the house we saw when we got off the bus. With the creamy candle on the table.

A lone woman is sitting at a table in the shade of a palm tree, her head bent over an open book. She has blonde hair pulled rictus tight into a ponytail, splaying out from a broad black elastic like water from a tap under high pressure. She is wearing a white lab coat, the sleeves rolled in immaculate folds to the elbows, and is either deaf or deliberately ignoring us. I stand there, feeling about twelve, raking the hair back from my face, and sniffing in a vain attempt to stop my nose running.

'More, Mummy, we said more. More MORE MORE!!'

'Shhh,' I say, fumbling in my bag for a tissue. The woman glances out to sea, then draws in her sketchbook with quick, deft strokes.

'But Mum, I'm thirsty,' whines Izzy.

Something bristles about the set of the woman's shoulders. I could swear it is a shudder.

I wipe my nose quickly on the back of my hand.

I open the gate gently. 'Excuse me,' I say, 'are you Diana?'

'Dinah, actually.' Her East Coast American is just perceptible below cut-glass, lady-in-waiting vowels. The woman nods, without looking up, carries on working. I take a step onto the terrace. Her fingers are long and white, her nails long, but cut square in a pink and white French manicure. Looking down, I notice mine are incrusted with dirt and curl them up, out of sight.

'Sorry ... I didn't mean to interrupt,' I sniff.

'But you did anyway.'

'Well,' I hesitate, 'Piero said I had to meet you here at six about a house.'

Without warning, one of Juno's battered pink shoes flies through the air and lands less than an inch from the woman's immaculate white-Birkenstocked left foot. She looks down, distastefully.

'About the house?' She raises a perfectly shaped dark eyebrow. 'Well,' she says, stretching her lips into the semblance of a smile, 'I don't really think you'd be suitable, do you?' I run over and pick up the shoe. Her damn toenails are perfect too and she smells of Jo Malone. I can't think of anything to say, so I walk back to the road in silence.

ROOM WITH A VIEW

Back at the bar, Piero is sitting talking to a large lady with soft curls, a pretty face and a flowing kaftan.

'Hey, Rosie, come here. Maria Rosa here has a place, up there on the hill above the lake.'

'But, Piero, I can't show her it. It'll be filthy. I haven't been up there since August.'

'Please,' I say, 'I'll see through the dirt. Please.'

'Piero? What do you think? Shouldn't I just clean it first and let her come tomorrow?'

'Show her it, Maria Rosa. She's OK. She's not like a stranger.' I beam at Piero, feeling as if I am walking on sun-kissed clouds.

I drop the girls off at Emma's and Maria Rosa leads me past the lagoon and up a flight of lava-stone steps that wind through a fruit orchard to a wrought-iron gate. She twists a key back and forth in a rust-pocked padlock, trying to get the lock to turn. She eases the key out of the lock, takes a nail file out of her handbag and runs its point down the grooves of the key. Then she tries again. Looking down the hill, between the walls of this house and the next, I can see the lake, deep blue now, the wind gently scudding the clouds reflected on its surface. I glance back at the gate. This time there is a click and the key turns. Maria Rosa pushes the gate open and frowns at the terracotta tiles covered with a film of black sand, dust, rotting leaves and flakes of white paint.

'God, what a mess,' she says. 'I'm sorry. This is really embarrassing.' There is a heap of rusty cutlery on a long table covered in an oilcloth decorated with faded lemons. She picks up a fork, walks over to a sink half full of brown water and prods it. 'Oh God, it's blocked with leaves. We've just been so busy …'

'But I'd be the same,' I say, 'if I had a house that wasn't going to be used all winter. Piero says you're on the island council.'

'Yes, and it's hard work because I'm the only one from the left. They want to build a heliport down there, right by the lagoon. Can you imagine? They claim it would be for medical emergencies, but if there's an emergency, the helicopter can land there anyway. No, they want it so that rich tourists can fly straight in. This may seem like paradise but this island is a microcosm of Italy, not just Sicily, and the islanders have their heads in the sand. But the heliport won't happen. Not over my dead body.'

I walk onto the terrace. The surface of the tiles is sticky and snags at my flip-flops.

'Oh dear,' says Maria Rosa, poking at the sink with a skewer now. 'Just look at this.'

But I am not looking.

'But the view!' is all that I can say. 'The view! Just imagine living with this.'

Sea, lake and clouds catch the early evening pink, distant islands glow translucent in the rich light, trees hang heavy with lemons and oranges. A view for postcards.

'I'll take it,' I say.

'You haven't even seen inside the house yet.'

'I don't care. I'll clean it up. I want to live with this view.'

'But you've got two children. I really don't think you can live here, *gioia*. There's no heating.'

'It'll be fine. They'll love it.'

'But look here.' She squats down and points to a little heap of damp gritty dust in the corner of a wall. 'D'you know what this is?'

'No,' I laugh, 'but I hardly think it looks life threatening.'

'Ants. The walls are infested with ants. They are eating up the house. Look.'

'But they're not the kind that bite, are they? Maria Rosa, don't worry, just let me see inside.'

The house is far from beautiful. It was built in the 1980s, I imagine, over the ruins of an older house, but nothing about it is particularly Aeolian. No lovely old beams, no little niches, no ancient majolica tiles, but the cistern with upturned zinc bucket and a neatly coiled rope lend a certain touch of romance. Best of all, it has a view to lift the soul on the rainiest of days, and there's nothing the kids can destroy or damage. It's in Lingua, a five-minute walk from Emma and Max, and who could want a nicer landlady than Maria Rosa? We agree a rent and settle on a moving-in date. Ten days' time, to give her time to get the house in order.

MR TANGERINE MAN

While Maria Rosa is getting the house ready, we go back to the UK. The night before we are due to leave, I toss and turn, afraid that once we are back in London, something will happen to prevent us from returning to Salina. That stupid fear of destiny again, of the world arranging itself to teach me a lesson. Even though I know I am being ridiculous, I can't throw the fear off, not quite. I tell Maria Rosa I want to give her three months' rent in advance and she tells me not to worry, that no one else is going to want the house in winter.

'I need to be sure. And ...' I hesitate, 'would it be OK if I leave a few things while we are in London?' I know I need to leave things here I could never abandon.

I sit in the little room above the restaurant packing a suitcase with items to leave behind. Sheets, blankets, clothes, books, toys. But are these enough to ensure that we have to come back? No, so I add to the suitcase my notebooks, precious letters, photographs and rose petals from a Brixton garden. My amulets.

Back in England I discover that there are times when, to be true to yourself, you have to accept that other people may hate you. And instead of rushing to soothe and placate, to compromise and 'be reasonable', if you believe the path you have chosen is the one you need to stick to, you have to be ice cold and resolute. Even if that means you have to watch other people hurt because of what you are doing.

One evening when I come to pick the children up from their father's house, I finally have the conversation I had been dreading. He comes to the door, holding a girl in each hand, pink ribbons in his hair. Izzy: 'Doesn't Daddy look lovely? I painted his nails too. And Daddy has brought us coats from Shanghai Tang, velvet. Come on Juno let's show Mummy ...' As they scamper upstairs, I tell him that living on a small island in Sicily is not a whim and that we are staying. He is furious and out the words tumble like possessions from a window as he tries every trick in his armoury of put-downs to derail me. I glance up and spot the girls peeping through the railings at the top of the stairs.

He follows my gaze, and lowering his voice, directs me into the kitchen. It's warm and cosy and smells of cinnamon. Two Elmer the Elephant plates sticky with maple syrup. He switches off a pan, then leans against the cooker, head bowed, taking a deep breath, as he always does to still himself after an eruption. One of Izzy's ribbons has come untied. How can I leave a man who lets his children tie ribbons in his hair? Because he may be kind and lovely to them, but he is not kind or lovely to me. The months away have given me the detachment I needed to recognise his derision and scorn for exactly what they are: shabby strategies in a well-worn repertoire. The pain behind his anger is tangible, and although I no longer hate him, there are some things I cannot forgive. Maybe things that no woman should ever feel she has to forgive. So even though I can see his point of view, even though I know I would be outraged too, were I in his place, and even though I acknowledge he has a point – the journey from London to Salina can take fourteen hours – I do not budge. I know with a fervour that burns gem-like hard that only with this distance and on that island can I breathe easy.

Standing the next day at the bus stop in Notting Hill – shelter glass now repaired – I wonder if I would have the strength to be a single mother if compelled to stay in London? A daily drudge of rain, buses, school, playgrounds, supermarkets, with charity shop coups as the highlight? I suspect not. On Salina, I'll be doing the same as every mother – school-run, dinner, parenting, housework – but at least I'll be sweeping floors in paradise. We'll walk to school along a road that curls around mountains high above a lapis sea, we'll help Giuseppina with the next olive harvest, plant violet cauliflowers, make friends with people who have orange trees. And when the girls are at school, I can run down from the terrace and forget the drudgery of house-cleaning as I lose myself swimming or in the pink bloom of bougainvillea. I will be woken by the beauty of moments and discard passing depressions and pesky anxieties as self-absorbed ingratitude in the face of the abundant beauties of the island.

Throughout the long journey back from England to Salina, I still can't quite believe it. Can't believe I made it happen. We have agreed on access. I can't believe he has accepted it. Can't quite believe I deserve it.

It's late by the time we arrive back on the island. Maria Rosa and her partner are away on a cruise to Egypt but have left instructions for the taxi driver to pick us up and take us home. The driver – amber-tanned, dressed in tight, white trousers and a Hawaiian shirt – is newly returned from an all-inclusive resort in the Dominican Republic (*cocktails, so many cocktails...paradiso, pa-RA-diso*) and finds it hard to understand why anyone would *choose* to live on Salina (*What do we have? Stones, even the beaches are stones ...*). He stops the car halfway up a hill I don't recognise, picks up the suitcases and heads up an overgrown flight of stone steps lit by a flickering streetlamp. I clamp Juno to my hip, take hold of Izzy's hand and follow.

It turns out to be a back way to the house. The steps lead to a harshly lit lava-stone path squeezed between the walls of smart summer houses shut up for the season. Dazzling whitewashed walls, cascades of plumbago and bougainvillea, the heady scent of jasmine and charmed lives. Then a one-storey hovel with paint-flaked doors, a collapsed bread oven and rusty gas cannisters heaped in a corner. As we pass, I hear a groan. Izzy screams '*FANTASMA!*' and tries to jump into my arms, almost knocking me over. The taxi driver laughs.

'*Tranquilla tranquilla, è la vecchietta.*' It's just an old lady.

Inside the hovel a light goes on, shredded by the shutters.

The gate to our house has been painted, a proper lock installed, and we step onto the terrace. The moon gleams weakly through grey veils of cloud and the sea below shimmers like ink. The taxi driver shakes his head, muttering *stones, stones, nothing but stones* and heads back along the path to his car, singing 'Macarena' to himself. I switch on the light, open the doors. The house is immaculate. It's been swept, scrubbed, mopped, given a lick of whitewash; the air is scented with cleaning products and even the ants have gone. The beds have been made – flowery polyester sheets with hospital corners – and there is a vase of wild flowers on the dining table.

I open a window to get rid of the smell of lemon Cif and a door slams shut, brittle echoes vibrating through the house like a dentist's drill. And within an hour, I have learned how empty rooms with ceramic-tiled floors amplify every sound: the children's voices, footsteps, the flush of the toilet, the whine of the electric pump every time we use water, the clatter of pans as I make pasta and pesto, of plates and cutlery as I lay the table for dinner.

The girls 'unpack' the suitcases, strewing the floor with bedding, books, toys, and miscellaneous English groceries. I rescue a battered box of Yorkshire teabags and a squashed loaf of Warburton's white sliced, then explore the cupboards. There's no hoover, but there is a battery of pans and brushes, mops and buckets, and a shelf of candles, matches, torches and packets of batteries. It is cold in the house, so after dinner I join two single beds so that we can all sleep together, and we huddle under several strata of duvets, throws and eiderdowns as I read the bedtime stories: *The Gruffalo* for Juno, then a chapter of *Ballet Shoes*, which puts Juno to sleep but has Izzy wriggling out of bed to practise saying *'Bonjour, Madame'* with a curtsy, then squealing that the floor is icy. We need rugs but in the meantime, I cover the floor with blankets and wonder what I need to do to turn this *tabula rasa* into a home.

I am woken early the next morning by Juno shaking me vigorously, her huge eyes shining with excitement, pulling off the covers, trying to drag me out of bed. She scampers out onto the terrace and I run after her to find my tiny girl in yellow pyjamas standing on the terrace wall shouting, 'Look, look, look, Mummy,' laughing and pointing astonished and incredulous at the sunrise. The sky is afire, coral, violet, tangerine; the islands of Stromboli and Panarea glowing semi-translucent, as if melting from within. I wrap Juno in my arms, empty my mind of thought and gaze, nuzzling her soft skin and breathing in the scent of sleepy child. She is so quiet, just staring at the spectacle in wonder, and I do the same, following tiny shifts in light and colour, the way the choppy sea stirs and scatters reflections, until Juno wriggles down and back into the house. A squeal from Izzy, giggles. *Let's make a tent*, then, after a while, silence. The girls have fallen asleep again, and so do I. The day can wait a little longer.

We are woken again a couple of hours later, this time by the sound of 'Mr Tambourine Man'. It's a blue-sky morning as zingy as a Matisse canvas, the leaves of the lemon and orange trees flickering in the breeze, sea and lagoon lapped with little white waves. Down on the road below the house, there's a big red lorry with a cluster of people gathered alongside. The girls spot Max and before I know it are out of the gate and running down the steps to the road, barefoot and in pyjamas. I throw on a dress and follow.

The source of the music is the red lorry, a mobile greengrocer's shop, its side open to reveal shelves of fruit and veg. I have come out without money but the fruit man, dark-haired and bearded with liquid chocolate eyes and the air of a 1960s dreamer, tells me to take what I want and pay tomorrow, so I choose big oranges and a bundle of broccoli, a great armful tied up in its leaves with string. Max is sitting on the wall with Emma, wearing a pale blue nylon checked school smock with a Peter Pan collar, holding a bundle of fishing net, waiting for the bus to school. Annoyed to discover that Max can't stay and play, Izzy announces that she, too, is going to school.

'Not in your pyjamas,' I say.

Max giggles. 'Definitely *not* in your pyjamas.'

'Well, *you're* wearing a nightie.'

'No, I'm not, it's a *grembiulino*.'

'Ah,' says Izzy, 'like the girls in Favignana. They had pink ones.'

'Seriously?' I say to Emma, 'Blue for boys, pink for girls?'

'Seriously,' says Emma, flagging the bus down. 'And that's only the start of it.'

'Do they make them in rainbow?' asks Izzy.

'Not yet,' says Emma. 'But there's a revolutionary idea if I ever heard one.'

Max climbs onto the bus, handing her the fishing net. The bus pulls away and Izzy begins to finger the fishing net, curiously.

'Gaetano gave it to Max, so after school you can go fishing.'

As we are about to walk off, the fruit man gestures to the girls. '*Aspettate*.' Wait. He peels two tangerines and gives them one apiece.

'*Grazie*,' says Izzy. Then skips off along the road. 'I like Mr Tangerine Man, Mummy, and isn't he ever so clever to write his own song?'

We are sitting on the terrace breakfasting on oranges and half a packet of crushed Hobnobs left over from the journey when there is a polite rattle at the gate. I answer it to a slight, dishevelled man in glasses wearing a red Telecom Italia sweatshirt and carrying a toolbox.

'Bartolino,' he says, shaking my hand. Our second Bartolino. Not surprising on an island where San Bartolo – protector of earthquakes – is the patron saint, but definitely confusing. In my head I decide to call him Bartolino Telecom.

'*Bonjour*,' says Izzy, curtsying.

'*Buongior – no*,' says Bartolino Telecom. 'I thought Maria Rosa said you were English?'

'We are. She just, well, it's too complicated to explain, but how can I help you?'

'Internet.'

Internet. Maria Rosa only put in the order last week. Well, I guess there's not a great deal of competition for internet installation on one small island.

'Internet!' shrieks Izzy, grabs Juno's hand and drags her dancing across the terrace. '*Oh happy day, oh happy day*,' she sings, as they skip around in circles (they spent three rainy afternoons with my mum in Leeds watching a *Sister Act* video I picked up from a charity shop). '*Oh happy day, oh happy day*.' They wiggle their behinds and make rabbit ears. '*When Jesus brought, when Jesus brought, my internet, my internet*.'

'They happy to have internet?' Bartolino Telecom puts down his toolbox and watches in bewilderment as the girls twirl around and end up in a heap on the floor. 'Why?'

'They have stories and cartoons for children, like TV but on the computer.'

'In England only, I think.'

As I take Bartolino inside, wondering if he genuinely has not grasped the worldwide bit of www, Izzy puts her hands on Juno's shoulders and stares into her eyes. 'Although, actually Juno, we don't believe in Jesus, but you must never tell anyone except Mummy.'

While Bartolino is busy upstairs, I turn to settling in. Organising does not take long as most of our luggage is English children's books – the girls' old favourites plus a small fortune in new acquisitions, almost forty kilograms of them, snuck in for free in our three cabin bags thanks to Easyjet's glorious policy of assessing by volume not weight.

Buying these books was my commitment to living here long term. I had to be sure that I had all I needed to compensate for the likely shortcomings of a Sicilian island school, and the lack of bookshops, libraries and museums. Salina might have nature in abundance, but even with two active volcanoes visible from the kitchen sink, observation would only take us so far. Yes, I can help the girls make up poems and stories and paint pictures, but I am sorely aware that, as far as science is concerned, I am a beginner. So back in London, I tried to imagine every question a curious child might ask about the world and made lists, which I took with me on long afternoons in Waterstones. The children's section became my sanctuary – a gorgeous, vividly coloured affirmation that the world is an astonishing, beautiful and endlessly fascinating place, proof that whatever life throws at you, there could always be compensation not simply *in* nature itself, but in the intrigue and challenge of learning about it. As I sat on a beanbag in the bookshop, entranced with a volcano cross-sectioned to reveal its 'plumbing' system, or a Mason Cash mixing bowl filled with the 'ingredients' needed to make a human, I felt a wonder in the world I'd not experienced since I was a child.

I arrange the books on the floor along the walls of the girls' bedroom. There are books on the ocean, volcanoes, rocks, minerals, weather, trees, animals, genetics, plants, flowers, the human body, chemistry and evolution, along with a children's gardening book, a cookbook, and books of arts and crafts projects. There are at least thirty picture books, a set of phonic learn-to-read books, Hans Christian Anderson, the Brothers Grimm and my childhood collection of battered Puffins – *Ballet Shoes*, *The Railway Children*, *The Saturdays* and *Tom's Midnight Garden*. Completing the suitcase library is a charity shop cassette player and a boxset of *Just William* tapes, read by Martin Jarvis.

I have barely finished organising the books when Bartolino calls down to tell me the internet is working. I run up to the office to find him sitting at my laptop, gazing at the screen with the rapture of a believer witnessing the appearance of the Madonna.

'Look,' he says, 'look, it's my bank account today, now, it's a miracle. Look, you can even see the fifty euros I took out of the Bancomat last week!'

'Isn't it like this every time you install the internet?'

'I've not it done before. Just the training course. I tell you, it's a miracle! Oh, I wish I'd brought my wife!'

'But there must be other places with internet on the island?'

He frowns. 'The hydrofoil office, the Carabinieri, the coastguard' – he counts them off on his fingers – 'the internet point, some hotels, yes, and some other foreigners, rich people, but Telecom Italia sent an expert from Palermo to install those.'

I wonder if I should invite Bartolino to come over one afternoon with Mrs Telecom so that she can see his handiwork and wonder at the miracle of online banking. He writes down his mobile number.

'Anything you need, any problem, please call.' He beams, singing, 'O Happy Day,' and he walks off down the hill, swinging his toolbox with a skip in his step.

Downstairs, Izzy is lying on the bed puzzling over a diagram illustrating the evolution of man. I bring the laptop down and leave her watching an animation featuring an orange plasticine chimpanzee while I get Juno dressed.

BUBBLES IN THE OCTOPUS'S GARDEN

By afternoon, the wind has picked up and the sea is crashing over the breakwaters, sending pebbles skittering across the beach. Max sighs, Izzy stomps furiously up and down the piazza and Juno sits on a step, watching the waves. Gaetano had told them they could cast down the small net in the shallow waters between the breakwaters and the beach. But the sea is too rough. When I decided it was a good idea for the girls to learn that human beings cannot always be in control of their lives, I hadn't considered that it would be me dealing with the grumpy fall-out when Izzy's plans are thwarted.

'Oh *Mamma Mia*, it's not a day for fishing, is it?' A rose-cheeked young woman in paint-smeared jeans, ancient boat-shoes and a huge man's shirt walks over. She sits on the wall next to the rolled-up net, trying to stop her curly hair slithering from a dishevelled topknot.

'They were planning to catch fish for dinner,' I say, 'but with this wind ...'

'*Grecale*.' Max sighs and shrugs. I have already discovered that, aged three and a half, he knows all the winds.

'*Grecale?*' asks Izzy, scrunching up her nose.

'This wind,' says the lady, speaking English now, 'from the north-east. You can tell by my hair. Look.' She stands up, pulls the scrunchie out of her hair and lets the wind whip curls across her face. Regarding the woman with scepticism, Izzy tentatively turns

151

her back to the sea, screwing her face up as the wind funnels her hair across her eyes.

'And now, turn around, and look at that island there. You see, the one like a rhinoceros? That is Panarea. If the wind whisks your hair off your face when you look at Panarea, then it's *Grecale*.' As the kids whirl around finding out what the *Grecale* can do to their hair, the woman and I squat down behind the wall seeking shelter.

'I'm Elettra,' she says, gathering her hair back into its ponytail. Her fingers are long and capable, with dirty nails and a smear of toffee-coloured varnish across the knuckles. I introduce myself, then point to the girls. 'That is Juno and this is Izzy.' Izzy runs up to us and performs a solemn and wobbly pirouette.

'*Buongiorno.*'

'*Bonjour.*' She curtsies.

'You're French?'

'English. She's just reading a book about some kids who do ballet and speak French.'

'Ah, and her name is Easy?'

'*I*-zzy, short for Ismene.'

'Ah, Izzy. The good thing about the *Grecale*, Izzy,' she says, 'is that the mountains stop it reaching the other side of the island. The sea at Rinella will be like glass. I'm on my way over there to look for octopus if you want to come, but you'll need masks and snorkels.'

Max runs home to get his swimming stuff. Then we drive to the chandlers in Santa Marina, where a barefoot man in sun-bleached shorts and a cotton cap is measuring out metres of rope. He fits us out with masks and snorkels, and gets the kids to practise by holding their noses and blowing out and breathing in through the tubes.

'This is fun,' says Izzy. 'I can feel the words in my nose. Why don't we always do this?'

'You look silly,' says Max.

Izzy checks her reflection in the mirror and sighs. 'True.'

We drive out of the village and along a corniche road cut into the rock of the volcano, now red, now grey, now crumbling fudge, then spilled-wine purple, high above the sea, hair-pinning in and out and up and down and around gullies gouged by rivers of lava. As we round a corner, we are so close to a cliff of basalt that I can see little holes where bubbles of gas popped once upon a time. The kids are quiet, concentrating on blowing through the snorkel tubes in their mouths, and I begin to fantasise about other occasions when snorkel tubes could be life-changing – at *aperitivo* hour, for example, or when I've a good book to read – until one of them blows a raspberry and they collapse into snorts and giggles.

Far below the road, the wind is whisking the sea into soft white peaks and on the horizon, the cone of Stromboli sits like an Alessi kettle on the boil, white plumes of smoke emerging precisely at the spot where the spout would be. Elettra drives easily, as if every bend, dive and ascent is as familiar as the inner working of her psyche. Born on Salina thirty-five years ago, she has lived here all her life, except for a few months studying in Turin. She is a carpenter, which explains the varnish on her knuckles and the sawdust that has snuck into every cranny of her ancient black Fiat.

As we drive, Elettra tells me how it was exciting but also unnerving to live in a city where she knew no one, after being brought up on a tiny island where she had known everyone for all of her life. 'Every mistake you have made, remembered, ready to be pulled out for a joke whenever it's needed.' I wonder if it will be like that for Izzy and Juno. Will a childhood on Salina leave them unprepared for life beyond, unequipped for life in a city, living with strangers?

The road emerges at the head of a plump valley in full autumn, cradled between the volcanoes, striped with vineyards, yellow, pink and cornflake brown, around a bell-towered convent. Here, volcanic happenstance created the most fertile and benign valley in the archipelago.

We drive on. As the road begins its descent to the other coast of the island, Elettra opens the windows, filling the car with the smells of turned earth, yesterday's bonfires, the honey of wild alyssum and the aniseed of the fennel growing high along the roadside. The sea spills out like a lake on a Swiss postcard from Salina to Lipari, and beyond to the island of Filicudi – three neat bumps, like the head, breast and belly of a pregnant woman floating.

Elettra parks the car below a church with a stripey façade as jaunty as a woolly jumper. I load our stuff on the pram and follow her and the kids along crazy-paved alleyways twisting past tiny white and blue houses, shutters closed. One cube up, one cube down, linked by an outside staircase, Elettra tells me she remembers when they were hovels for the poorest of the island's fishermen – 'Now they are summer houses for the rich, closed for the winter.' The sole sign of life is a very whiskery old chap, fast asleep and snoring on the *bisuolo* of a tiny piazza. *Shh* mouths Elettra, and the kids put their snorkel tubes back in their mouths and tiptoe past.

'I think,' Izzy removes her snorkel and whispers, 'he is probably a very dangerous ogre.'

'I know,' whispers Elettra, 'that he used to be the bus driver but now he makes very good pizza in that bar over there.'

The beach is black, but it's the first sand the kids have seen since leaving Favignana and they set about dripping and drizzling wet sand to make castles at the water's edge. Elettra and I sit on a basalt boulder, pocked with bubbles like risen dough, warm from the sun. There is not a breath of wind. The surface of the sea is viscous, barely oscillating, and I half-believe I could carry on and walk across to Lipari.

I pull my dress over my head and wonder if I could slip into the sea for a snorkel in silence without the kids noticing. Fat chance.

No, no, no

me too,

me too,

me too,

me too.

At least an hour it takes to:

get them into their masks and snorkels

make sure the straps are neither too tight nor too slack

teach them to put their faces in the water and to bubble through the pipes

get Juno and Max into armbands

take Izzy's mask and snorkel off again to wipe her tears when she accidentally sucks instead of blows

give her a smidge of half-melted chocolate to take away the taste of salt

let Juno and Max lick the chocolate wrapper because they can taste salt too, and it's not fair that Izzy got chocolate.

Finally, I take a very deep breath and turn to Elettra.

'*Andiamo?*' Shall we go?

Elettra folds a plastic carrier bag and sticks it in her bikini top.

'What's that for?' asks Izzy.

'I put it over my hand like a glove so I don't have to touch the octopus when I grab it out of its nest.'

'I see,' says Izzy.

'Come on! Let's go. Follow me, *ragazzi!*'

'Follow me, *ragazzi!*' shouts Izzy.

'*Ragazzi!*' shouts Max.

'*Ragazzi!*' echoes Juno.

And we are off, Elettra in front of them, me behind, watching six little legs kicking through the water. Below us, the sun casts a rippling caul of light and shadow on the black sand. Elettra leads the way along the coast to a small rocky headland, drenched in sunlight, and stops in the shallows, shallow enough for the children to stand up and rest, and removes her snorkel to say:

'Now we have to look for an octopus's garden. They collect pretty shells and coloured stones and bits of coral, and put them around the entrance to their nests.' The kids nod and off we go again, slowly now, in what feels like a sunlit aquarium, swimming through a vast shoal of microscopic electric blue fish, glinting shards of lapis lazuli. Turquoise and yellow parrot fish dart further below, and the children follow them, all thoughts of octopus's gardens forgotten. And I do too, watching the kids mesmerised by the submarine world, pointing at sea tomatoes shiny as tumours, pink sea spaghetti fluctuating in the currents, cauliflower-like florets of acid yellow and cushions of sucked-out rhubarb like petrified pan scrubs. We float above forests of translucent miniature mushrooms gleaming like slivers of mother-of-pearl in the light, and I can't resist grabbing a handful, but the instant I lift my hand out of the water they metamorphose into lifeless debris as appealing as parsnip peelings. The surface ahead is suddenly pocked, tiny silver fish jumping then falling like rain.

Snorkelling in these shallows, something becomes obvious that should have been obvious before, but that I had never thought about. Simply that the land, the rock we live on, with its skin of earth where the wild scrub grows and vines and pomegranates and lemons and watermelons are cultivated, continues deep down to the seabed. It might be one of the more obvious, commonplaces of GCSE geography that volcanoes are formed from the crust and mantle of the planet, but seeing it with my own eyes as I swim over one is quite different.

I follow the children, following a shoal of silver fish. Then, rising from a wedge of sand caught between two rocks, I spot bubbles rising. The octopus must be in his nest, dozing perhaps. No sign of a carefully curated garden but maybe this octopus thought his surroundings pretty enough as they were. In less than a metre of water, it should be a cinch for Elettra to grab it. I wave to Elettra and tell the kids to keep back, keep quiet and watch the bubbles. But the bubbles have disappeared. I look more carefully. The octopus must have scarpered. But just then, the bubbles begin again. Out of the corner of my eye I see Elettra arrive and the kids pointing. The bubbles seem pulsed, not breathed, viscid, like aloe gel, and they oscillate as they rise slowly to the surface. They stop and start, absent for minutes, until I am sure the octopus must have wriggled off. But then they bubble again, quivering geometries of liquid aquamarine and opal rising in the light.

'That's not an octopus,' says Elettra. 'Those bubbles are volcanic.'

'How on Earth can you tell that?'

'Because they move differently and are kind of squarish. Strange, though, I've never seen them here before and I've swum here thousands of times. There are bubbles further along the coast, and over near Panarea there are bubbles that are truly spectacular, like something out of *The Little Mermaid*. But I've never heard anyone talk about bubbles here.'

And I thought Salina was inactive. This suggestion that the earth beneath my feet is in constant flux is more than a little disturbing. Was I mad, or just irresponsible, to decide to bring up the children here? I remember as a child, standing entranced among the fairy-lit stalactites and stalagmites of Stump Cross Cavern, staring at the dripping water, convinced that if I watched for long enough, I might see the stalactite grow. Until I got to Salina, that, for me, was the speed of geological time. I wonder how much the land where you were born can affect your mind. If a landscape seems unchanging and unchangeable, like the Yorkshire of my childhood, would it nurture certainty? And likewise, would living in a volatile landscape seed volatility?

I explain some of this to Elettra as we walk back along the beach, the sun low now and the light gold, our shadows long. And she says yes, there is fear on the island – though not of Salina suddenly erupting, but that a major eruption of Stromboli would trigger a submarine landslide and tsunami.

'And earthquakes?'

'Earthquakes, people worry less about because we've all experienced them, and even the most severe ones haven't caused much damage. Certainly, no one ever died. They say it's because we are protected by San Bartolo but it's probably more to do with the fact the buildings are so low. Remind me to introduce you to the Cucinotta family. There's a house on their land that was built in the 1700s and is still standing.'

'So it survived the Messina earthquake.'

'As far as I know, on Salina, no one died in the Messina quake. However, the fear is there, hidden, but ready to bubble up.'

Looking out across the sea, I try to imagine what might be below the surface. An ever-present fear, like a subterranean lake of magma.

'These bubbles here, what do you think they indicate? Is Salina active after all?'

'My friend knows a geologist,' says Elettra, 'Francesco. He's investigating the bubbles at Panarea. I'll get his email and you can ask him.'

Late that night, when the children are in bed, I email the geologist. He writes straight back. Must be a night owl. 'Yes, the bubbles are "volcanic" and caused by the venting of carbon dioxide and other gases. The venting off Salina is very weak, so weak that the gases can only escape when the tide and the water pressure are at their lowest at the time of the full moon.' I write back and tell him how now, when I look at the sea, I can't help wondering what lies beneath.

I sleep in my own bedroom for the first time that night. I sleep deep and dream of a little grey house with a long lawn that runs to the very edge of a cliff. I am a child, lying on my stomach on the grass, with the tang of crushed dandelions on my hands, inching forwards under a wooden fence, poking my head over the lip of the cliff and looking down at the beach way below. Then I am walking towards a car, a blue Anglia, and looking back at the little grey house. The fence has gone and there is a huge bite missing from the lawn, right where I had been lying, revealing a crumble of red earth.

When I wake up, I remember that when I was little, my parents took the lease on a holiday house on the cliffs of the Holderness Coast, but coastal erosion became so bad that they decided to holiday at Scarborough instead. I open my laptop. The Holderness coastline is formed of clay and marl deposited by glaciers during the last ice age and it is eroding at the rate of two metres per year. I find a map online showing the lost villages of the Holderness Coast – thirty-six at last count. Not all of England is ancient and unchanging.

BATHYMETRY

Iwake with the sunrise. Francesco the geologist has written to me again: 'Here are some maps to answer your question, what lies beneath the sea?' I wrap myself in a blanket, make a cup of builder's tea and take it and my laptop out onto the terrace. It's a different kind of sunrise today, hazy and diffused, the only clouds low and distant, clinging like miniature mountains to the coasts of Sicily and Calabria.

Francesco has sent me a series of bathymetric maps, ultrasound scans of the Aeolian seabed rendered in eerie metallic hues, vertiginous works of digital art that allow you to soar like a superhero over a wonderland where island-mountains plummet down to 1,500 metres below sea level and submarine gorges look as if they might be rents in the crust of the Earth itself. I play at shifting my focus from the bathymetric map on the screen to the view across the sea to Lipari, trying to match what I can see of the real world with its representation on the map. Leaning back on my chair, I eventually reach a point where I can hold both in focus, so that it seems the screen is a window cut into the membrane of reality, revealing a submarine world of shiny mountains and crumpled plains, from which copper-tinted islands break the surface of the sea to bare their summits like nipples in a cutaway bra. I shiver and pull the blanket tighter.

Which is more real, I wonder, the bathymetric scan or my view over the bougainvillea, orange trees and lighthouse? The truth, I suppose, is that both are real. This scant tip of dry land on which

I have chosen to weave a life for myself and the girls and the submerged mountains and valleys of the seabed are a continuum, formed of the same rock, born of the same geological processes. I am beginning to learn that in this volcanic land, what observation tells you is permanent, knowledge informs you is in flux; what is here on Earth was once there below, molten or semi-molten in the crust and mantle. I close the laptop. T S Eliot was right, 'mankind cannot bear very much reality' and I decide that a hearty, two-feet-on-the-ground breakfast is required, so make porridge and maple syrup, then tell the girls that we are going to have a look at Max's school.

It's a gentle morning, sky and sea milky, the now-familiar shapes of Lipari, Stromboli, Panarea shaded to grey. We pass Rodolfo, pacing along in salt-soaked Birkenstocks, lost in thought and a cigarette, planting each foot firmly on the road as if still checking the sway of the boat he was on all night. He chin jerks hello, then climbs into his Lapa and drives off. A couple of seconds later, a rich, resonant 'Rodolfo!' fills the air, followed by Giuseppina in a yellow overall and flip-flops, hair newly dyed a sombre burnt umber.

'You just missed him,' I say.

'Rodolfo!' Her voice booms deep through the village but the Lapa carries on.

'You could fill an opera house with that voice.'

Giuseppina laughs, throws her arms wide and sings 'Nessun Dorma! Nessun Dorma!'

'There will certainly be no one sleeping now.'

'We had to be able to do it, make our voices carry, all the wives of fishermen, to call them in. Otherwise, we'd have had to walk down to the harbour every time food was ready.' I had noticed that the islanders do not seem overly fond of walking. 'The men can't do it, don't have the lungs for it, so they use a conch shell, blow it like a trumpet to wake the fishermen who live high up the mountain.'

'They still do that?'

'No, they have mobile phones now.'

'Well, can't you phone Rodolfo?'

'Rodolfo? He doesn't have a phone. Why would he? He doesn't need one. He has a wife with a voice.' And she walks off down the alleyway singing '*Vincerò! Vincerò!*'.

We carry on through Lingua, greeted with a *buongiorno* by every person we pass – a lady with a neat bun mopping her already immaculate terrace, two Moroccan men building a drystone wall, a man in a baseball cap sweeping the paths of the cemetery. I push the pram uphill, looking down through citrus trees heavy with lemons and oranges at a figure, bearded and skinny as a Giacometti sculpture, scything a field above the sea with rhythmic precision. A familiar sight, from art, costume dramas and a bread advert, where man scythed to the accompaniment of *Carmina Burana*, but I've never seen anyone scything a field in real life before, and thinking that scything fields has been going on for millennia upon millennia is enough to dissolve the anxiety of early morning. The skin of Earth may be thin here but the volcano has made the soil rich.

'But where do they play out?'

A good question. The school is unprepossessing, dating back to the Fascist era, grubby ochre with splintering paintwork and windows placed high to avoid any distraction the outside world may bring. It is surrounded by a yard damp from a dripping gutter and carpeted in slime, which suggests that outdoor play may be rare. I ring the bell and the door is answered by a capable-looking woman in overalls. She looks the children in the eyes, smiles and asks if they are coming to join the school. Izzy nods and explains in halting Italian that she is called Ismene, that she is English, and that she would very much like to come to school because she is friends with Max. Then she turns to me.

'I think I should be called Ismene at school because Italians think my name is Easy, not Izzy.'

'My name is Carmela, Mela for short.' And she tells us that there are seventeen children in the school, but twelve of them are her nieces, nephews and grandchildren, so everyone calls her Za' Mela, which literally means Auntie Apple. 'Come in,' she says, 'I'll take you to meet Maestra Adelaide.'

We follow her into a corridor painted vomit-green, smelling of fresh coffee and echoing with the babble of kids, scraping chairs and the shrill voices of hectoring teachers. Three closed doors and one slightly ajar, bizarrely revealing a single bed with a bare mattress. On the wall are black-and-white photographs of an old man in uniform with a huge moustache. I look at the caption. Prince Umberto visiting Salina for a couple of hours in 1923.

Za' Mela walks ahead, moving with a heaviness that seems to come from deep down, then turns to Izzy, smiling with encouragement, and takes her hand. 'Come with me, Ismene, and we'll find Max.' My mother was a primary school teacher and over the years worked with many women – teaching assistants, cleaners, dinner ladies – and Za' Mela reminds me of them, good women who worked hard, unthinkably hard, worn down with worries and disappointments, who seemed to have lost hope in adults, but still found joy in children.

Za' Mela knocks softly on a door and we all troop inside. Five children, the boys in blue overalls, the girls in pink, are sitting at desks, rolling scraps of white tissue paper into tiny balls. There are no toys, no books, no paintings on the wall, just a wooden crucifix, a photo of the Pope and a poster of the evolution of man, torn around the edges. The teacher, tall, thin and hatchet-faced in a spotless white lab coat and surgical gloves, leans against the desk, glowering down at the children. Sicilians are usually small, rarely thin, and over the past months I've got used to being head and shoulders above both men and women. But Maestra Adelaide must be six foot at the very least. The two girls and Max are crouched over their tissue-rolling, barely daring to glance up, but the two other boys simmer, cross faces scrunched, and, as the teacher turns to look at us, one of them darts a resentful glance into the back of her head. If looks could kill, death would have been instant.

Max risks a finger wave at Izzy and Juno.

'Max!' beams Juno. The class laughs.

'*Silenzio*!' snaps the teacher.

Juno runs over to Max, throws her arms around him and glares at her.

'*Bambina!*' She really is quite scary, this Maestra Adelaide, her lips a gash of scarlet, eyelids iridescent acid green. But Juno carries on glaring. She doesn't speak much, Juno, so working her character out is a case of conjecture – or wishful maternal thinking – but fierce loyalty and a visceral sense of injustice do appear to be key. For a ludicrous moment, I feel very British, the theme from *Dambusters* – which I used to play on the trumpet with the school brass band – pumping through my mind, and I am overtaken by a desire to throw my arms wide and declaim 'We will fight them on the beaches.'

'*Signora*, can you please control your child?'

I scoop Juno up, give her a kiss and whisper *clever girl*.

'And so, *Signora?*'

'This is Ismene. She is five years old and ready to start school.'

'*Madame,*' Izzy says sombrely and then, to my horror, curtsies. *Ballet Shoes*.

The Maestra is lost for words; out of the corner of my eye, I see Za' Mela clasp a hand to her mouth and scoot out of sight.

Za' Mela is still giggling on the front steps of the school when Juno and I leave. '*Mai, mai, mai*, never ever, ever in all my born days have I seen anything like it! *Bonjour Madame! Che monnella*, what a scamp! *Geniale*, brilliant, *Bonjour Madame!*' and Za' Mela curtsies with a smirk. 'Well, that's done me good, I haven't laughed like that in years. To see that one lost for words, priceless, priceless, priceless. Thank you, Rosie, thank you. See you at lunchtime.'

'Well,' says Izzy, outside the school five hours later, holding onto the pram and doing a wobbly plié, 'it is a very weird school indeed. We spent hours and hours and hours making those little balls of paper, teeny, tiny, and every time Federico and Luca hid under a table or climbed on a chair, we all had to sit IN SILENZIO with our hands on our heads. THEN, we all had to sit in a circle and watch IN SILENZIO while Maestra Adelaide picked up the little paper balls with tweezers and glued them on a snowman.'

'Max!' shouts Juno, as Max walks past hand in hand and deep in conversation with Rodolfo. Something about them makes me want to cry – it's the tenderness I think, between this blond Christopher Robin in a sky-blue school tunic and his grandfather, craggy and weather-beaten as a rock, holding Max's soft hand between rough, nicotine-stained, black-nailed fingers. As they pass, Max gives the shy little finger wave again.

'THEN,' says Izzy, jumping into the pram next to Juno, 'we stopped for *recreazione*, which is playtime without anything to play with or anywhere to play.' She pauses for a second. '*Panini*. They all had *panini*. I have to take a *panino* tomorrow. Don't forget. Za' Mela bought me one from the shop and it was absolutely delicious. Nice ham, no fat, the best thing about school. Oh, and did you see the bedroom?' I push the pram up the hill. A workout with two of them on board, but I am too impatient to either wait for the bus or walk at Izzy's pace. 'At this school, Juno, they have a bedroom! Federico and Luca showed me it while Maestra Adelaide was in the playground that isn't a playground having a cigarette. If the sea is rough, the teachers can't go home and have to sleep in that bedroom.'

She takes a deep breath. 'Then, Juno, there was a lovely surprise. A lovely teacher called Maestra Angela who was lovely, just lovely, so lovely, so kind.' She kneels up to look at me. 'But, Mummy, it was sooo embarrassing and I just didn't know what to do, because she stood in FRONT of that poster about the evolution of man, you know, the one showing how people used to be monkeys, and told us God created the world in six days. Usually, I quite like telling grown-ups when they are wrong but she was SO nice, I just couldn't.'

'Monkey, monkey, monkey,' Juno sings.

Izzy sits down and I brace myself for 'I Went to the Animal Fair' all the way to Lingua. 'Shall I tell you a story about monkeys, Juno?'

Juno nods.

'Well, once upon a time there was a zoo, and in the zoo were lots and lots of monkeys, and every time the monkeys had babies, they were more and more intelligent and less and less hairy, until finally a beautiful Indian princess called Mira was born.'

Juno yawns.

'No, Juno, it's important,' she says. Fortunately for Juno, before Izzy can launch into a treatise on evolution versus the existence of God, a three-wheeler Lapa sputters up and stops alongside us.

Max pokes his head out of the window. 'Nonno says do you want a lift?'

So we lift the pram into the cargo bed, climb in next to it and rattle back to Lingua, the kids squealing all the way.

Giuseppina, dress tucked in her knickers, is grilling fish on a tiny barbeque in her yard, while inside, Emma lays the table with disposable plastic plates. 'I know,' she says, 'terrible, especially when she has enough dinner services to open a china shop, but to her plastic plates are the ultimate mod con, a demonstration of wealth, even if the main reason she uses them is that there's no running water in the kitchen, which is the opposite of anything either modern or convenient.'

We finish laying the table and call the children in to eat. There's delicious pasta with cheesy cauliflower and a huge crisp, grilled *cappone* fish, which Giuseppina bones at the table and serves with a jug of olive oil, lemon and oregano, which the kids love so much they dip their bread in it. Then there is tomato salad with capers and mint, followed by home-made biscuits, which the adults dip in dessert wine and the children in chocolate Nesquik.

'So, Izzy, how was school? Max never tells me anything.'

'Maestra Adelaide is horrible, but Za' Mela is lovely and so is Maestra Angela. Max is very good, but Federico and Luca are so naughty that Maestra Adelaide told us it was actually autumn, *autunno*, but because we were so slow and naughty, we had to start to get ready for Christmas NOW. As if it was a punishment. Can you imagine a teacher who can make Christmas boring? So that explains why we are making snowmen. Next week, we are making Christmas trees, getting lots of different colours of tissue paper and rolling them into tiny balls for Maestra Adelaide to glue onto Christmas trees, because Italian glue is TOO DANGEROUS for naughty children. THEN, the last thing that happened was that I got into trouble.'

'You?'

'We were doing the *corpo umano*, the human body, and Maestra Adelaide gave us these outlines, like gingerbread men to colour in. So, I turned mine into a girl, and did a face and long hair and rainbow sort of pyjamas, and I thought it was really pretty, but Maestra Adelaide was FURIOUS.'

'What?'

'And TORE my drawing up and THREW it in the bin.'

'She did what?'

'It was just that I didn't understand all the Italian, and we were supposed to make the *corpo umano* all pink. No face, no hair, no clothes, pink. Naked. But without a bottom. Or a tummy button or anything.'

'Did you cry?'

'No. Federico cried and she laughed at him. So I curtsied and said sorry in a really quiet voice, but inside my head I called her every single rude word that I know.'

'You curtsied, Izzy...?' Emma looks flabbergasted.

'It's amazing, it works really well, I got it from *Ballet Shoes*, but Maestra Adelaide just thinks it's a weird English thing. I think Za' Mela knows it's a joke because I saw her in the coffee room laughing uproariously. Thank you for a lovely lunch. Can we get down now?' The children run into the yard.

'Uproarious?' Emma laughs. 'Is that a new one?'

'She's been listening to *Just William*.'

Izzy pops her head back round the door.

'I just realised something. If it's autumn, it must be Halloween.'

Last Halloween, we were living in Massachusetts and Izzy was attending a Waldorf nursery school, where trick and treating – considered too close to extortion – was replaced with a treasure hunt for home-made spiderweb cookies, exquisitely wrapped in compostable cellophane. The kids learned the witches' song from *Macbeth*, danced to *A Night on the Bare Mountain*, and Izzy led a parade of children in handmade costumes, dressed as a Pippi

Longstocking Pumpkin Fairy Princess – because why dress up as one character when you can dress up as four? They made pumpkin lanterns with child-friendly pumpkin lantern kits of plastic saws and cutters, and pumpkin soup out of the leftovers.

Emma looks at the calendar on the wall. 'Two days to go.'

Izzy races back into the yard. 'Max, Juno, we've got to find a pumpkin.'

'Pumpkin, pumpkin, pumpkin,' chant the kids, jumping around the table.

'What's a pumpkin?' says Max.

'*Zucca*,' says Emma.

'*Zucca*? No problem,' says Giuseppina.

DEADMAN'S BONES

Giuseppina's pumpkins are duck egg blue, fabulous beasts crying out for a double-page spread in *Bon Appetit*, but Izzy is adamant that a Halloween pumpkin needs to be orange. Tangerine Man's pumpkins are brown and so are those in the village shop, so Elettra sets about calling her friends to see if anyone has an orange pumpkin. I'm embarrassed at the upheaval we are causing and wonder if I am pandering to Izzy, suspecting that it would be better parenting to teach her to make do with what we have and take it as a lesson in learning to improvise. But both Elettra and Emma say the same thing, that the season is over, winter is coming and it gives everyone a sense of purpose, tracking things down, making things.

Izzy's enthusiasm has worked up Max and Juno to fever pitch. We've invited the other kids from the school for a Halloween party in the piazza and Emma's kitchen has become a Halloween factory: orange peel halves filled with green jelly ready to be sliced into ghoulish grins, cupcakes and cookies waiting to be iced, a pack of hot dogs destined to be turned into severed fingers. In the fridge are several practice fingers with stomach-turning realistic niches cut out for fingernails and painted with ketchup.

Giuseppina has produced a magnificent Macbethian cauldron, copper bottomed and fire-blackened, which she uses every spring to make bean and pasta soup to feed the entire village for the festival of Saint Joseph. She makes versions of this soup at least once a week, using whatever pulses and pasta shapes she has to hand, and the kids love it, so we are planning a Halloween version, which she can carry down to the piazza for a spooky beach feast by a bonfire. Izzy is trying to remember what *Macbeth*'s witches put in their soup.

'Eye of newt,' says Izzy.

'Chickpeas?' I suggest.

'Fenny snake,' says Izzy.

'Spaghetti,' I say.

'Toe of frog and tongue of dog?' Izzy frowns.

'Pappardelle is a bit tongue-like,' says Emma.

'And slimy,' I say. 'Let's not.'

'Well, orecchiette are little ears, and vermicelli are little worms,' says Emma.

'And macaroni looks like chopped intestines,' I say.

'What about baboon's blood?' asks Izzy.

'*Cosa?*' asks Giuseppina.

'*Sangue di … un … babboono?*' I say.

'*Babuino*,' says Emma.

'*Strattu!*' says Giuseppina with relish, opening her store cupboard and bringing out a huge jar of thick, dark paste the exact shade and consistency as dried blood. '*Strattu di pomodoro.*'

'G-ross,' mock-squeals Izzy. 'Guys, Giuseppina has a jar of blood in her cupboard!' Juno and Max run in to see.

'And look at my new wig!' says Giuseppina, cackling like a manic witch, grabbing a huge bunch of wild fennel and holding it on either side of her head like wild green hair.

'Witch's hair!' screams Izzy and the kids run off into the yard. Then my phone rings. Elettra has found someone who has orange pumpkins.

Next morning, after dropping Izzy at school, I meet Elettra for breakfast in the village café. She's talking to a traffic policeman with a neat goatee, who introduces himself as Mariano. He tells us in rather elaborate Italian – Italian that sounds more written than spoken – that his passion, since the 'demise' of his wife, has been to dedicate his spare time to 'tracing and recording the history of Lingua'.

'Until now,' he says, 'our history – or, to be more accurate, our histor*ies*, both personal and collective – have been preserved only within oral culture, easily forgotten, prone to being ignored by the young, who are hungry to be subsumed in the modern world of telephone, television, commercial music, internet. And I believe that it is *imperative* that our unique patrimony is safeguarded, for I believe that on a small island, and especially in a place like Lingua, the trajectory, the intimate, personal trajectory of the individual is indissolubly intertwined with that of the community to which he belongs.'

I need coffee.

'But,' says Elettra, speaking rapidly. 'Mariano has just told me the most amazing story about the charnel house under the church in Lingua, and he's agreed to come and tell it to the children for Halloween.'

'Even though,' he says reprovingly, but with a little smile, 'this *Allo-een* has nothing whatsoever to do with island culture. Though we do have witches.'

'Thank you, Mariano,' says Elettra. 'Now we've got to go and pick up a pumpkin from the Cucinottas.'

'Aah.' Mariano's whole face is illuminated. 'They grow the best pumpkins, capers and oranges in the world. Well, if you're taking her to meet the Cucinottas, don't forget to ask about the witches.' He picks up his hat from the counter, nods and leaves.

'What did he mean, about the witches?' I say as I knock back a double espresso.

'You'll see.'

We set out up the hill to Lingua, taking turns to push Juno in the pram. It's a glorious day, chilly and bright, with the coast of Calabria crisp on the horizon, the sea wind-shimmered silk. I visualise the submarine-scape revealed by the bathymetric map and wonder if instead of finding it frightening, I should marvel that the most destructive forces nature knows could result in such incredible beauty. A fragment from Ovid's *Metamorphoses*, half-remembered from a classical studies module swims to the surface: 'I will love you until trees grow on the ocean bed and seaweed on the highest mountain.' I recall the professor saying that Ovid was right, although he didn't know it, because 5 million years ago the Mediterranean had indeed dried up.

'The fishermen say it's a bad sign when you can see Calabria,' says Elettra. 'It can mean a storm is coming.'

'Elettra.' I pause. 'Did you know the Mediterranean once dried up?' I was reading about it late into the night, the Messinian salinity crisis, 5 million years ago, when the Straits of Gibraltar and Pillars of Hercules silted up, turning the Mediterranean into a salty lake that eventually evaporated and became one vast, endless salt pan. They say it's why the Mediterranean is saltier than other seas.

'I was trying to imagine it,' I say. 'Watching the Atlantic pour back in like Niagara Falls, terrifying but beautiful too.'

'But there would have been no one.'

'Which is kind of hard to imagine, too.'

We walk on, both of us lost in thought.

'Do you think, Elettra, that living here means that in some way, you have to understand, or at least confront, your place, your infinitesimally small place, on the planet, in time?'

Elettra laughs. 'Do I think the island fosters humility? No. Or, at least, not generally. I mean, there are some special people, I would say, who live with a very simple kind of ... *grace*, you could call it, but I don't think they would ever think that is what they were doing. But most people, Ros, are like people anywhere, out to make as much money as possible and be better than their neighbours.'

Elettra's phone rings. 'OK.' She nods. '*Perfetto*.' And hangs up.

'That was Zaccaria's wife. She's given him some dead man's bones we can have for Halloween.'

'Dead man's bones?'

'*Ossa dei morti*. It's a biscuit.'

'And who's Zaccaria?'

'You must have seen him,' she says. 'A gardener, bearded, tall and *sicco sicco*.' *Sicco* literally means dry, but the way she sucks in her cheeks as she carves a skinny figure in the air suggests drawn, ascetic, gaunt.

The Giacometti man.

As we walk down the hill into Lingua, we can see him in his field, squatting on his haunches in front of a caper bush, smoking, studying the plant, Zen-like but for the cigarette. He waves at us and comes to meet us on the road, nodding with the shadow of a smile. Close up, he reminds me of a Byzantine hermit, the kind you see stylised on church walls, hollow-cheeked, hollow-eyed, ribcage ridging a pale torso. Except that Zaccaria is not the kind of man I can imagine ever removing his shirt, even in 40 degrees. He walks over to his bright red Lapa and comes back with a bag of small cookies that look like home-made ginger nuts, each crowned with what looks like a slice of bone but turns out to be a kind of petrified meringue, heavily spiced with cinnamon and cloves, hard as rock, and strangely addictive.

A whitewashed house, its terrace curtained with a magnificence of bougainvillea and plumbago, marks the entrance to the Cucinotta's world. We follow neat paths winding through lush gardens where citrus trees, hibiscus and jasmine mingle with lavender, rosemary and chillies. It smells wonderful and we follow hand-painted arrows saying 'capers' pointing the way to the main house. The Cucinottas are the last family in Lingua to live entirely off the land, growing olives, capers and vines. Three brothers and their sister, Nunzia, all of them single.

'Nunzia!' calls Elettra softly, 'Lorenzo! Gaetanino! Bartolino!' A third Bartolino. The islanders really were committed to keeping Saint Bartholomew onside.

'There's only me,' says a voice from amid the vines. 'The boys are getting the last of the olives.'

A woman in a lumberjack shirt stands up, chest-high in vines, which she is tying up with bendy twigs.

'Juniper,' she says. 'Nature's cable-ties. Now, Elettra said you wanted to see the old farmhouse.'

She leads us through the vineyard to an old house with a beaten earth terrace. The walls have lost their stucco and, above one of the doors, Nunzia shows us where the branches of an ancient olive have been embedded to form a lintel. We step inside. The Cucinottas use it as a warehouse and open sacks of salted capers perfume the air. The roof, Nunzia points out, has withstood 300 years of earthquakes and still doesn't leak.

'This was a luxury residence for the 1700s,' says Nunzia, 'it even had an inside WC.' She opens a door to show us a polished chestnut plank with two bottom-sized holes side by side. 'They had big families back then, so I guess it speeded things up in the mornings.' It brings to my mind immediately, and indelibly, one of those absurd German weather houses.

We head out onto the terrace. There, Nunzia draws back a wooden latch, hand-polished smooth, and a scarred wooden door swings slowly open. A smell of wine, raisins, damp wood and stone hangs heavy in the air, and the shaft of light from the open door falls on an immense beam hanging on loops of rope, thick as a fist, and a wooden corkscrew, two metres high or more, that makes me think of a torture chamber.

Juno grips my hand tight.

'This is the *palmento*, where we make the wine,' whispers Nunzia, squatting down to talk to Juno. 'Don't be scared, *tesoro*. Let me show you the big stone bath where we squash the grapes with our feet.' Curious now, Juno pulls me forward into the *palmento* and allows Nunzia to lift her up into a shallow stone tank. 'You see?' Nunzia is still whispering. 'We take our shoes and socks off and squidge the grapes with our feet. She carries Juno over to a faded colour photo on the wall of two men with trousers rolled up, ankle deep in what looks like sloppy plum jam. 'You can help us next year if you like?'

'Yes!' whoops Juno.

'But quiet now, we mustn't disturb the wine. Shhh. Can you hear it?' She carries Juno over to a wooden barrel stoppered with wine-soaked muslin, and we stand silent in the *palmento* listening to the faint pop and plip of wine fermenting.

STRANGE FRUIT

In the Cucinottas' kitchen, a man in old canvas fatigues and a tool belt hung with secateurs, sheath knife, penknife and a bundle of willow shoots is tucking sprigs of rosemary into a roasting tray of chicken and potatoes.

'*Ciao*,' he says. 'You must be the English mamma who needs a pumpkin!' His face, like Nunzia's, is defined by enviably arched eyebrows.

'This is Bartolino,' says Nunzia, prodding the chicken.

'Ciao. You are my third Bartolino!'

'Bartolino the Third, hey?' laughs Nunzia.

'Like a king? Or an American tycoon! Come to think of it I probably *am* at least the third Bartolino Cucinotta ... if not the fifth or sixth ... or even eighth like your King Enrico.' Bartolino grins.

'Before you get ideas, Bartò, can you find Juno a pumpkin?'

'A pumpkin for Allo-een?' asks Bartolino. 'A good, big, orange pumpkin?'

'That's right.'

'To make a kind of lantern, *vero*?'

'Yes, exactly! I thought no one knew about Halloween here.'

'We have cousins in New York,' says Nunzia.

'Though sadly not tycoon ones.'

'Juno,' says Nunzia, pulling a tray of golden bread slices out of the oven and drizzling them with thick green olive oil, 'do you want to help Bartolino choose a pumpkin? Here.' She sprinkles the

174

bread with salt and oregano and pops some in a brown paper bag. 'Take this for Juno, Bartolino, in case she gets hungry.'

Juno, who has not taken her eyes off Bartolino's tool belt, follows him out of the kitchen.

'It seems strange,' says Elettra, sitting down at the long kitchen table, 'to be in here without your Papà. It's the first time I've been here since he died. He was always here, Ros, Armandino, sitting in the corner in that dressing gown, topping and tailing beans or podding peas …'

'He couldn't sit idle.'

'That dressing gown! It was an English *Milord*'s dressing gown, Ros, he bought when he was working in Australia,' says Elettra. 'Burgundy silk, all padded and piped and corded. We were all in an amateur dramatic society and we were always doing these English country house murder mysteries, possibly because our main asset was Armandino's magnificent dressing gown!'

'Elettra,' says Nunzia reproachfully, 'we were also quite good.'

'I always suspected,' says Elettra, ignoring her, 'that islanders love country house murder mysteries because there are certain … *parallels*, shall we say, between being confined in a large house and being trapped on an island.'

'Elettra!'

'Think about it, Nunzia – a small community that can't move anywhere, generations of resentments and infighting, lashings of petty jealousies, mean gossip and little *dispetti*.'

'*Dispetti?*' I ask.

'Nasty tricks, always anonymous, to teach someone who has disrespected you a lesson. From emptying their water cistern or slashing tyres to putting superglue in a padlock.'

'Glue in a padlock?' I say. 'That'll just be kids! They do it in England too, for Halloween, though usually with syrup instead of glue.'

'Not in Sicily, Ros. In Sicily it's a message from the Mafia,' says Elettra flatly. 'To people who don't do as they are told.'

It feels like a cloud has passed over the sun. Nunzia is palpably disturbed by the turn the conversation has taken. Elettra takes her scrunchy off and runs her hand through her hair. It seems like a good moment to change the subject.

'Mariano said I should ask you about *streghe*.' Witches.

'*Streghe?*'

'*Majare,*' says Elettra.

'*Majare?*' It's not a word I know. Maybe it's dialect.

'Well,' says Elettra, '*majare* were magical women.'

'Ordinary women with magical powers …?'

'Yes, apparently ordinary women, living apparently ordinary lives, usually married and usually poor—'

'Always poor, because everyone was poor.'

'These women would steal out of bed in the middle of the night of a full moon, leaving their husbands sleeping. They'd strip naked, rub their bodies with an unguent as they chanted a magical spell, and then gather on the beach, where they'd borrow a boat and fly it to extraordinary banquets in the lands of their horizons. Sometimes they flew to another island or Calabria, but also to places far, far away.'

'America, Australia, Argentina.'

'Egypt, Tunisia, Spartivento.'

'And sometimes make love to handsome strangers – or, at least, that was what their husbands assumed. But mostly, they would fly naked to banquets and parties and eat incredible foods that no one on the island had ever tasted, that none of the stories describe because no one could imagine what you might eat if you were wealthy.'

'Except for the strange fruit.'

'Except for a strange fruit, discovered by a fisherman one morning in the bottom of his boat.'

'A strange fruit that no one had ever seen.'

'And his boat was wet, seawater wet, so he knew it had been used.'

'And the next night, he hid in his boat. The *majare* gathered aboard and cried …'

'How many are we tonight?' calls Elettra.

'Four!' calls Nunzia.

'*Vara vara vara per quattro*,' Elettra and Nunzia chant together.

'But nothing happened,' says Nunzia.

'*Vara vara vara per quattro* ...'

'Still nothing happened,' says Nunzia.

'There must be more of us, there must be five! Someone is pregnant!'

'*Vara vara vara per cinque* ...'

'And the boat began to fly ...'

'*Acqua sopracqua*'

'*Vento sopravento*'

'*Portami via a Spartivento*'

'And off they flew – or so the story goes.'

'But they never say what he saw.'

'They never do.'

'But when they came back to shore, the fisherman revealed himself to them.'

'And was killed? Maimed?' I ask. When people have seen the forbidden in fairy tales, the consequences are usually dire.

'No,' says Nunzia. 'He was fine, went happily back to his everyday life and the *majare* never used his boat again.'

'Which I have always thought a very ... disappointing ending,' says Elettra.

'But the whole myth is sad,' says Nunzia.

'The desperate longing of women to escape from drudgery and bitter poverty and maybe violence to a place of unimaginable plenty.' Elettra turns to me. 'Emigration had begun then, and stories arrived in letters from America and Australia of marvellous lives.'

Juno runs into the kitchen.

'Marvellous lives in Australia, with swimming pools,' says Bartolino, following with a magnificent orange pumpkin.

'And steaks as thick as your arm.'

'Three cars. Wardrobes bigger than rooms.'

'Lawns like carpets.'

'When we still had dirt floors.'

'And bathroom suites the colour of avocados,' I add.

'She's been talking to Giuseppina!' Bartolino lights a cigarette. 'But they miss Salina. They plant wild fennel and capers so it smells of home.'

'And they do not have,' says Bartolino, walking onto the terrace and coming back with a hollow ball of basalt, 'A lava-bomb ashtray.'

'Enjoy Halloween,' says Nunzia as we get ready to leave. 'But remember, Elettra, don't frighten them too much.'

'And it looks like bad weather,' says Bartolino, 'so make sure you have some candles.'

As we walk back through the Cucinottas' garden, I grill Elettra. Did she ever know anyone who admitted to being a *majara*? No. Had she ever met anyone who had seen one? No. Did people actually believe in *majare*?

'Difficult to say,' she says. 'Difficult to explain. It's almost as if the stories come from a place that is half myth, half gossip. Someone claims to have seen something and everyone else is *desperate* – no, not desperate – *suggestible*, *open* to seeing it too, even without knowing it. But the stories are strange. Insubstantial and somehow … unsatisfying. They are never quite *stories*. The fisherman sees the *majare* and flies away with them in his boat, and you are expecting something terrible or astonishing to happen to him – an *epiphany* – but it all just fizzles out. And as soon as you ask a question, like you did, the narrative begins to dissolve.'

Fragments overheard, hearsay repeated, events eavesdropped upon that can't stand up to the clear light of rationality. But for a myth to become a myth, for it to be repeated and repeated, handed on, handed down, believed in or semi-believed in, it must come from somewhere, must have a reason for being and a reason to be kept alive. Surely there is more to the myth than the food fantasies of hungry women? Indeed it all seems very Jungian. Is the *majara* an archetype of a disempowered woman's desperation to escape, or was it that the men were afraid of losing their women and that the myth was born of their guilt? Could it have been that men knew they were treating women badly but repressed the truth because to face it would mean their behaviour had to change? The *majare* wouldn't exist, or the idea of them wouldn't exist, if women hadn't been desperate to escape the drudgery of everyday life. I think back to Favignana, the woman I saw showing her bruised eye to a friend and the defeat of the 'such is life' shrugs that they shared.

As we walk back down to the village, Elettra tells me that until recently, right into this century, if a woman's husband died, her brother-in-law not only had the duty to look after her but automatic rights to her bed, no matter what the widow wanted, or his wife. The practice is dying out, but not quite. It is whispered too that incest was rife, *that mother, that grandmother, that woman over there, buying cheese at the back of the shop* too afraid or ashamed to report abusive relatives, though that is changing too, as is the idea that domestic violence is an inevitable part of married life. A friend, Elettra tells me, heard her neighbour being beaten up by her husband and knowing they were church-goers, she went to the priest. The priest just sighed and said, 'What can we do, what can we do, but pray?'

I am agitated. Unsettled. The *majare* come unbidden into my imagination as we walk through the village – women pausing as they sweep dirt floors to gaze out to sea, looking over to the horizon as they hang the washing, to the moon as they bring it in. A woman stirred by shutter-sliced moonlight, slipping out of bed, glancing back at the form of her sleeping husband; a woman looking at her reflection in moonlight on a bowl of water, silently mouthing an incantation of hope, of escape; women gathering on a beach, getting into a boat, chanting the spell that will lift the boat into the sky and fly them to the land their dreams have created from the letters of emigrants.

Until recently – indeed, in living memory – Elettra tells me women had no freedom, little privacy, no agency.

'Nunzia told me that when her mother married, back in the 1950s, almost as soon as the first baby was born, her husband, Armandino, went to work in Sydney. SIX years he was gone, leaving her stuck at home with her mother-in-law and grandmother-in-law who chaperoned her like shadows, *guardians not of my honour, but of Armandino's*, she'd say, because in their eyes she was his property.

'Men,' Elettra continues, 'had their spaces away from home – their boats, their boat sheds, the bar, the sea – but women were always visible. Teenage girls and young wives would go to gather wild greens up the mountain as an excuse to get away but everyone knew where they were. You couldn't go anywhere without someone seeing you pass by. Even now, once you know someone well enough to go beyond *ciao*, the first question is, *where are you going, what are you doing?*'

There's a myth, a commonplace, that Mediterranean women are the masters because they hold the purse strings, but living here, talking to Elettra and Nunzia and other women too, I suspect it isn't true. Women may organise the money, do the shopping, arrange bank loans even, but they don't have the power to make decisions. They may joke that their husband doesn't even know the price of a packet of cigarettes, but many wives have no say in how the money is spent. The man is the man, and his word is final. The woman's job is to make ends meet.

I need a swim.

The sea has whipped up like egg whites while we've been at the Cucinottas, so we leave Juno making Halloween cookies with Emma and drive over to the other side of the island. The sea here is like glass and Elettra shows me the way along a path to a secluded beach of smooth basalt boulders, where she lies in the sun and I dive and glide and somersault naked underwater thinking that swimming is the closest I can imagine to flying. The water is cold, exhilarating, thought-annulling.

Afterwards, I lie shivering on a hot boulder, sun beating down, soaking up the heat from above and below, gazing up at a tiny ruin perched high on a ridge of the beetling scrub-encrusted slope. I imagine a young woman tying a knotted rope around a rock and throwing it down the mountainside so that she can climb down to the sea. I close my eyes. Jungian dreams only happen because they involve universal archetypes.

I tell Elettra what I just imagined.

'Tell me about when you decided to escape.'

'Escape?'

'When you left your husband.'

'I was sweeping the staircase in the house in America because we had people coming for dinner. It was this big, open, wooden staircase and I loved it. I loved the house, the sun flooding in, the beach through the open windows, the light on the sea, even the way the sand and dust blew in. Anyway, as I was sweeping, daydreaming, watching the motes dancing in shafts of sun, I got to the top of the stairs and tripped over the dustpan, sending all the sand and dust I'd collected spilling down the steps. Then suddenly, I heard this laughter, mocking laughter, and I looked down and he was standing at the bottom of the steps, watching me. "I don't know why you bother," he sneered. A tiny thing. A thing that would not have mattered if it had been done with affection. But it was the latest of a thousand petty mockeries, and, Elettra, I suddenly saw that he was capable of destroying even the most fleeting moments of ordinary, everyday happiness. If you can feel happy sweeping the stairs, then why the hell not, and why the hell should anyone have the nerve to try to take that away from you? Anyway, something just snapped. It was as if there had been a rubber band inside me and it had been stretched so often that it had no more elasticity, no more resilience. And it broke. No more perceptible than a flutter. But as soon as it had broken, my mind felt calm, glassy calm, and these words came into my head, clear as clear as clear.'

'What words?'

'I am not spending the rest of my life with this man.'

'Like a *majara* in reverse, from the golden paved streets of America to the island. You longed for escape and flew to a place that you believed existed but had never seen. No spells, no magic, no flying boat. Just determination.'

'Not just determination. Also, the culture I came from, where I was born and when. Growing up as feminism erupted.' The fortune of having a strong mother and a good education; being surrounded by books, theatre, films and ideas; of having been exposed to single, independent women who defied the status quo, and to a culture that believed that women should not be tied to men.

'Sometimes – no, Elettra, every day – I think that one of the best things in life is not to be answerable to anyone.'

WITCHES AND CYCLONE CUTTERS

'My grandmother was a witch,' says Elettra. Juno stares, eyes like big round buttons, Max frowns and Izzy looks sceptical.

Elettra and I are sitting on the terrace, hands sore from scooping the flesh from the pumpkins with cheap aluminium dessert spoons. Max and Juno are making shadow-monsters with a torch and Izzy draws witches, pumpkins, spiders and ghosts for Emma to staple on fishing wire. Elettra sighs, puts down her pumpkin and rubs her hands, watching Izzy draw a hat for a green-faced witch.

'Not an evil witch, like in the fairytales, but a good witch, a woman people believed had magical powers. She knew special spells, incantations.'

Emma stops what she is doing and listens.

Elettra drops her voice a notch and meets the children's eyes.

'Have you ever heard speak of the *malocchio*?'

They shake their heads.

'Well, here on the island, and, in fact, in all the lands of the Mediterranean, if you are jealous or envious of someone because they are more beautiful or rich than you are, or if you simply resent them because they have something you want, well, this is the time you can give someone the *malocchio*, the evil eye.'

'Just imagine being able to do that to your enemies. Like an evil curse!' says Izzy.

'A little bit. But not exactly. You see, the thing about the evil eye is that it just happens. You can give it to someone without even being aware of it, without even knowing or noticing. The evil can just slip through.

'Anyway, my grandmother, Nonna Lina, knew the magic spells to take away the power of the evil eye, and so when people feared they had been given the evil eye, they would call her. When I was a child, she would take me with her after school on her visits, to carry her things and help her up and down the hills. There were many signs of the *malocchio* – like headaches, burning the dinner, losing the cat, a child getting a fever, especially after someone had had some good luck, like a huge catch of fish or they had bought something special, like a new car. The dangerous thing about being lucky is that other people get jealous.

'Well, Nonna Lina was getting old. So one day, when I was eight or nine, she told me it was time for me to be the one to take away the *malocchio*. "Me?" I said. "That's insane! I know nothing about the *malocchio*. I can't do magic. I can't do spells. I can't cure people like you do! I don't know the words."'

'And what did Nonna Lina say?'

'She said, "No problem, I've written the spell down for you. You can learn it after lunch."'

'But there was a problem. I couldn't read. I'm dyslexic. But nobody knew.'

'So what did you do?' asks Izzy.

'I did the only thing I could. Went round the houses looking ever so serious, listened to whatever problems people had, then made up the spells in an invented language – you know, chanting in a weird deep voice, making my eyes big and waving my arms around.'

'What happened? Did anyone find out?'

'Never. In fact, Nonna was thrilled because everyone remarked on how I had inherited her gift!'

Elettra and I start trying to hack out faces in the pumpkins with dinner knives.

'I was looking at a book I have about *majare* last night,' says Elettra. 'The author says that the islanders have a "complicated relationship" with reality. I think what she means is that even now, with internet and tourism and books and TV, with knowledge, science, *facts* available; even now, for many people, the most natural way to interpret the world is still through myth and superstition. They still believe that if there is an earthquake, it must be a punishment from God, because there is always, always, *always* going to be something that is bad, either in your own behaviour or another's.'

'It's just so sad,' says Emma. 'I mean, believing in witches is one thing but believing you were responsible for an earthquake ... that would drive you mad, wouldn't it?'

'Do you have internet?'

I give Elettra my laptop and carry on hacking out fangs from my pumpkin while she navigates.

'Listen. Pope John XXIII in 1958, on the fiftieth anniversary of the Messina earthquake: Keep away from sin, the principal cause of great punishments ... if you want to avoid your city succumbing to an immensely larger calamity than that wreaked by the earthquake.'

'Imagine, hearing the Pope say that, if you had lost people you loved.'

I think of Pippo's story of his aunts, driven mad with grief for their dead fiancés, as we put the final touches to lopsided pumpkin grins.

In the middle of the night, we are woken by a storm straight out of a horror movie. Lightning that cracks your skull like a migraine. Aeolian thunder that would make anyone believe in an angry God. Apocalyptic, shaking the house, vibrating through the rooms like nothing I have ever experienced before. As the girls run to me screaming, I remember my dad used to say that when God was in heaven, the angels played Bach, but when they were playing for pleasure, they played Mozart. This, Dad, is Mahler, Wagner, Bruckner, Shostakovich, Schoenberg played all together by the massed percussion of the universe and I can feel it from my teeth to my toenails. We scrunch up together in the bed, and I pull the covers over our heads. Make like it's a game. *Let's pretend we are in a tent.*

In the brief lulls between the skull-cracking light and thunder roars, I say, 'You can hear the sea, raging like a monster itself, a water monster. You know, the ancient Greeks believed the sea was a god, Poseidon, and they called him the Earth Shaker.'

'You can see why,' whispers Izzy.

'I don't like him,' says Juno.

'Did we make him angry?' asks Izzy.

'It's just a story,' I say.

The wind rips up too and rain begins to machine-gun the roof.

'Can we watch?' whispers Juno.

I flick the bedside lamp on. Nothing happens. I try the main light. Still nothing.

'I think the electricity is off,' I whisper, 'a power cut. Stay there while I go and check.'

'No, don't leave us.'

I grope my way to the door with the girls holding onto my pyjamas, through absolute black, and push it open.

Lightning sweeps the terrace, illuminating for a few seconds the frothing sea, the silhouette of Lipari. There are no lights anywhere in the village, just the lighthouse flashing weak pops in the dark. Miraculously, the terrace is so protected that the washing is still on the rack, the Halloween decorations barely rustled. The torch the kids were playing with must be somewhere, so I set the girls crawling over the terrace looking for it, while I feel my way into the kitchen for the cigarette lighter and light the pumpkin lanterns. Juno gives a whoop and switches the torch on, and we sit, wrapped in blankets, and watch the storm travel across the sky.

The sky is clear next morning, the sun bright, but the sea is still churning and the wind wailing, wrenching at the bougainvillea on the terrace and whipping spray high above the roof of the church. There is still no power. I ring Emma who tells me that a power line has come down. No ships are travelling and the winds are too strong for a helicopter to land, so the electricity company's technicians can't get here.

'Maria Rosa has left us a million torches and batteries and candles, so with the gas cooker, we'll be fine. I am sure we can still manage Halloween.'

'Have you checked your water?'

I walk into the kitchen and turn on the tap.

Nothing.

It's only then that it dawns on me: our water is pumped from the cistern and so if there's no electricity, there's no running water.

'Quite exciting really,' I say down the phone. 'Like stepping back in time.'

'Hmm,' says Emma. 'Just wait till you see how many buckets of water you need to flush a loo.'

I decide this is the perfect opportunity for the girls to learn that water is a scarce and precious commodity, though it takes vivid descriptions of unflushed toilets and unwashed dishes to convince Izzy that using Coke instead of water is not the solution.

I unlock the cistern and peer down with a little shudder, remembering the opening of an Orhan Pamuk book with a man in a well. Far below, my face is a pale smudge in inky water. I let the pail down on a rope. The first time I draw the bucket up it is only half full, but I soon get the knack, giving the pail time to fill so it sinks deep into the water, before hauling it up as smoothly as I can. I love it. I love the sound of water echoing, the challenge of drawing the pail up without spilling a drop, the sense of doing something people have been doing for thousands of years, that until today I had only seen in films. I know myself well enough, however, to know that the novelty will soon wear off, and as I fill every bucket, pan and jug I can find with water, I tell the girls we are only going to flush the loo twice a day.

The next question is how to go ahead with Halloween. The rain has stopped and there is none forecast, but when we walk down to meet Emma and Max, we discover that the wind is thrashing the piazza, bending the palm trees almost double. The beach where we had planned to have a fire is a-froth with waves. The sea has hurled seaweed and pebbles onto the pavement, and Piero is standing with a dustpan and brush outside the bar. He laughs as we come towards him.

'What are you doing down here in the middle of a storm?'

'Looking for somewhere to have the Halloween party,' says Izzy.

'*Questi inglesi*' – these English – 'most sane people would *postpone* a party if there was a storm, let alone a power cut as well.'

'Well, we can't,' says Izzy, 'because tomorrow is not Halloween and today is.'

'Well,' says Piero, 'if you're determined, there's the back terrace by the lagoon. It has a roof ...'

Piero's terrace is perfect. Tucked into a corner so sheltered that the wind merely whispers the strings of Halloween decorations and flickers the tea lights and candles we set along the low walls. There are emergency lights too, if we need them, but the candles are more atmospheric. In one corner, Giuseppina stands over her Macbethian cauldron of pasta and chickpeas, set above the roaring blue flame of a portable gas burner, and in another, we have laid a long table with Emma's Halloween baking, illuminated by the pumpkin lanterns and votive candles in red tubes stamped with images of the Madonna. Word about the party spread quickly and, on a night when nobody has any light or TV at home, people have begun to congregate. Another table fills with bottles of wine, beer and Coke, and huge bowls of salad. Someone arrives with a barbecue, the butcher turns up with three kilos of sausages, the baker with a bag of yesterday's bread to toast, and soon there are sausages grilling, then chicken too, and pork, as people bring down whatever they had in their slowly melting fridges.

I sit with Pippo and Anna drinking warm red wine from plastic cups. They ask me about Halloween traditions and I tell them about tricking and treating, flour bombs and putting treacle on people's doorknobs. Pippo seems about to say something but Anna glances at him to stay quiet. I've seen that look before. I guess being married to Pippo means she has become adept at limiting the number of inappropriate things he says in public. I bumped into him outside the school last week and he tried to persuade me to help him organise a sheep-shagging festival as a satirical comment on EC bureaucracy. Fearing a reprise, I look around for Elettra but can't see her, but fortunately Mariano, the traffic policeman, begins to tell a story and a hush slowly falls.

'*C'era una volta*'– once upon a time – 'the dead were thrown through a trap door into the pit beneath the church.'

'Shh, shh it's a good one this.' Silence falls.

'Well, one dark, dark night in the middle of winter, the curate and the sacristan heard someone knocking on the trap door. Because the last rites had been read, popular belief was that the poor soul who was knocking desperately on the door now belonged to the world of demons and devils. As such, he had necessarily to be eliminated. Consequently, the curate took his heavy metal crucifix, opened the trap door to the charnel house and ...' Mariano pauses. 'Let us say he used the cross to exorcise the demon and return it to the realm from which it came.'

'What does that mean?' says Izzy.

'He bashed him over the head with the cross and killed him.'

She screams.

All the kids scream.

In the distance two spectral figures appeared, white, semi-translucent.

Izzy buries her head in my skirt. Max and Juno grab each other.

An adult gasps.

O Dio Mio.

Giuseppina crosses herself.

Ave Maria, Piena di Grazie.

Slowly, laughter spreads. Izzy peeks out.

Minchia! One of the spectres trips over its sheet and swears.

The spectres make a final ooo-ing twirl, then throw their sheets over their heads.

It is Elettra and Piero with bedsheets and torches. Izzy and Juno climb onto my knee. Someone starts to sing and others join in, a beautiful, haunting song in Sicilian that I don't understand, but that sounds like a lullaby.

I watch Pippo and Anna wave goodbye, switch on their torches and walk towards their car. As Elettra and I are wiping down the table, someone taps us on the shoulder. 'Don't turn round.' I put a hand on Elettra's and we stand, frozen. 'Have you heard the rumours?' We shake our heads. 'They say the padlock to Pippo's gate was superglued, and inside his house he found a photo of his sons torn in two.'

I can't help glancing over my shoulder, but our informant has disappeared into the shadows.

'Oh, Ros,' says Elettra. 'Maybe the *malavita* has come after all.'

I shudder. *Malavita* means organised crime.

As we walk home, I notice the wind has dropped, the palm trees barely shivering in a light breeze, and, as I draw more supplies of water from the cistern, I see the distant lights of the midnight ferry. I blow out the candles and hope that the electricians are aboard. One day of living in the dark feels quite enough, especially if the *malavita* has arrived.

GLORIA, *TESORO*

'Santa Glawse is gumming do down,' sings Izzy.

'Santa Glawse is gumming do down,' echoes Juno.

'It's Santa Claus is coming to town, actually,' I say.

'No, it isn't,' says Juno, concentrating on stirring the paints on her plate to make murky khaki. 'It's do down.'

'No, Juno,' says Izzy, delicately adding pink polka dots to a lilac dress of an angel. 'Mummy's right, Do Down is just the Italian version.'

The Christmas repertory for the school concert also includes 'Lass Grease-mass I give you my art' and 'I'm dreaming of a wide Grease-mass'. When I suggested to Izzy that she help with the pronunciation, she refused, saying that if she did, people might laugh. Consequently, I smile politely when Za' Mela tells me how amazing it is that all the children sing with a 'perfect English accent, just like Ismene's', though I do feel a bit guilty. Next year, if they have a pleasanter *maestra*, I'll volunteer to help.

Izzy's daily reports from school suggest that Maestra Adelaide divides her time between chatting on the phone and looking at jewellery catalogues while the kids do colouring in, tissue-paper rolling and letter tracing. Izzy's Italian is, nevertheless, improving rapidly, as the only interesting thing she can find to do is to eavesdrop on Maestra Adelaide's phone conversations with a friend called Gloria, always referred to by Izzy with breathy melodrama as *Gloria, tesoro*, which means Gloria, treasure. She has gleaned that the Maestra hates the island, thinks the children are like savages and *the parents, Gloria,* tesoro, *don't even ask. They are worse than the children, positively Neanderthal.* That's really rude, isn't it, Mummy?

The centre of Maestra Adelaide's world is her son, known only as Il Piccolo, the little one, and Izzy has become an authority on Il Piccolo's daily life, diet, health and bowel movements. 'Il Piccolo is having pasta and beans today. I think he must be constipated, Mummy. Maestra Adelaide was telling Gloria all about it, whispering in one of those pretend whisper voices that grown-ups use when they need to say something embarrassing, that it would help him in the bathroom, so that must be what she meant.'

Izzy has also discovered that Il Piccolo is learning the clarinet, but never practises, and that Maestra is also spending a LOT of her HARD-EARNED MONEY on a private teacher to help with his English. *Il Piccolo,* says Maestra to Gloria, *does not know how lucky he is, living in Milazzo, in a beautiful apartment. The poor children here live in such DIFFICULT CIRCUMSTANCES and have NONE of the luxuries Il Piccolo is fortunate enough to be able to take for granted. They live in conditions that are not much better than cavemen.* Which is a downright lie, as every house we have visited has been beautifully kept, and we are the only people we know who don't have a TV and DVD player.

Every so often, Izzy reports, Maestra Adelaide pauses her conversation to yell at Luca and Federico, who, she says, get bored quickly – 'Not surprising, Mummy. I'd be bored if there weren't all those conversations to listen to.'

On one occasion, the maestra was so cross that she threw Federico's pencil case out of the window. This incident *shattered her nerves. Gloria,* tesoro, non c'è la faccio più, *I can't take this any more.*

'And THEN, the very BEST THING EVER happened. You will NOT BELIEVE IT, Mummy. Maestra Adelaide went out to have a cigarette and coffee for her nerves and Federico climbed up on a desk and out of the window and ran away. Luca tried to follow but he was halfway out when Maestra Adelaide walked back in and pulled him back in by his legs. Poor Luca. He's a bit naughty but ever so sweet.'

We are sitting on the terrace decorating cookie-cutter shapes made of flour and salt paste. The last thing I thought about packing when we left England were Christmas decorations, so with money tight until I finish updating the guidebook, we are making our own. I can't afford a Christmas tree either, so we have put fairy lights on the lemon tree and are making decorations to hang on the branch of a pine tree Elettra begged from a neighbour, and that we have put in a pot of pebbles and propped up wonkily against the wall.

As Juno switches her attention to glitter glue, I surreptitiously hide the khaki paint and squeeze her a plate of blues and pinks. The girls are spending Christmas and New Year in London with their father, but it feels important to do the build-up, to create a sense of anticipation and excitement, though I am not sure how much of this is for them and how much is to silence the whisper voice that makes me question if I really am capable of building a new life for us here.

Juno has no memory of any other Christmas but Izzy remembers everything – the spectacular Christmas lights of London and Boston, wrapping presents, decorating the tree, making Christmas cookies, going to midnight mass with her granny, counting Christmas trees in the windows of Far Headingley. On the island, there are few signs of Christmas. A tower of panettone boxes printed with snow scenes and a few balding strings of tinsel among the packets of pulses have appeared in the village shop; there's a horrible crib scene with cardboard cut-outs outside the church and a consignment of the skinniest capons I have ever seen is on sale at the butcher's.

On the last day of school, we pass the village's two refuse collectors hanging a single string of Christmas lights across the road. Emma tells me that it's only in the past couple of years that Christmas trees have been sold on the island at all, and even then, only to order. Traditional islanders mutter about the Johnny Come Latelys who, aspiring to a Hollywood Christmas, embrace them as a proclamation of prosperity and cosmopolitanism, and think, as

Giuseppina says, that sticking a fir tree on their terrace makes them better than everyone else. Stockings are traditional but come out at Epiphany, not on Christmas Eve, and are filled by the *Befana*, the Christmas witch, with sweets for good children and coal for bad – although, these days, the coal is honeycomb toffee dyed black.

The Nativity was a miracle, true, I think, as I sit on the terrace one evening poking fishing wire through the hole in a Christmas star, but from what I've read I get the sense that Sicilians believe that the real miracle was yet to come. Easter in Sicily seems to have a far deeper resonance than Christmas. Throughout the region Good Friday sees daily life suspended, as towns and villages are transformed into sombre theatres for the long, often silent, reenactments of Christ's walk up the hill of Calvary to the cross on which he was crucified. In some towns, life-sized statues depicting scenes from Jesus's Passion are carried, in others, characters and events along the Via Crucis are acted by locals. In many the faithful process barefoot, and the processions can last ten hours or more. Easter Sunday sees joyous celebrations – the most moving I have heard about, featuring a statue of the Virgin Mary being carried through town, searching for her dead son.

The meaning of the birth of Jesus, I think, as I hang the star atop the pine tree, is only truly resonant in retrospect. And that, I think, is the crux of the problem. You just can't understand the significance of what you are doing, of the micro and macro decisions you make, until way into the future, when their consequences are manifest.

Salina will have a different impact on Izzy and on Juno, leave diverging memories behind even of days they have shared. Already, I can see it. For Juno, aged three, Salina is her world. It forms her inner landscape and through it she makes sense of the world. She thinks of the other two places she remembers – London and Far Headingley – as islands. She's forgotten Favignana already and has made friends with cats, bushes, rocks, stones and trees, as well as Max. Izzy, at six, remembers more, and has more to miss. She is aware – and when grumpy or bored reminds me – that her life is without Waterstones, Starbucks, Portobello, the Oxfam shop, High Street Kensington, Holland Park, the V&A, red buses, the tube and, most important, Daddy. They Skype him several times a week. So far, we've ducked out of telling the girls we have split up. We tell ourselves it is a way of protecting them, though in my case, I know I am scared not only of causing their ire but facing it.

Why can't Daddy live on Salina too?

Because he has to travel all over the world to work.

Why can't we live in London?

Because it's too expensive.

Why can't we travel with Daddy?

Because you have to go to school.

I am only too aware that the answers I give do not bear scrutiny and that sooner or later, I am going to have to fess up. I try to imagine how the conversation might go and to think ahead of ways of explaining the break-up that are honest but reassuring. I guess every parent wants to be dignified, composed, articulate, generous, even about a partner they, in fact, loathe.

Izzy wanders out onto the terrace in her nightie, tells me that Juno has fallen asleep, then looks up at the pine branch, wound with fairy lights, hung with our decorations. Iridescent glitter glue has made even Juno's khaki angels catch the light.

'Daddy would love this tree. I wish we could take it to London.'

'He would love it but I don't think it will fit in your suitcase.'

'I wish.'

'But we've got lots of extra decorations you can take. Let's decorate a box and you can give it to Daddy as a present.'

'And some for Granny Mollie too?'

'Definitely.'

'And Grandy Colin and Granny Pat?'

'Well, you won't be going to Leeds this time. They'll come and see you in London after Christmas.'

'Why aren't we going to Leeds? Don't you want to see your Mummy and Daddy?'

'Of course I do, but I've got to stay here and work.' The only chance since we moved here to get on with the *Rough Guide*.

'What?' It's a cry that seems to come from a place where her world is collapsing. 'What? What? What?' She is rigid with shock, her cheeks flushed, and I see horror in her eyes, then tears. 'How can you not be there for Christmas?'

And holding her tight, I tell her I love her, Daddy loves her, but ...

Phrases clatter out

And absolutely everything I say sounds

Pathetic

Patronising

Euphemistic

You know how children fall out? Well it happens to grown-ups too ...

Sometimes, over the years, grown-ups change and realise they are too different to live together any more

But we both love you and Juno more than anything in the world

'But can't you just be friends for Christmas?'

I hold her tight, as tight as I can.

'Sometimes grown-ups are really stupid and can't stop being stupid, no matter how hard they try.'

At the Christmas concert, halfway through 'Lass Grease-mass', Maestra's phone rings. She answers, shoots a look at the keyboard player and rushes out of the room. The kids falter, some of the parents start to sing, then Za' Mela stands up, gives the kids a big grin, and a very merry singsong is had by all, parents calling out their favourite carol, and everyone joining in. Maestra does not reappear. Afterwards, as the adults drink warm spumante and kids warm Fanta in plastic cups, Za' Mela brings out a tray of the most intricately decorated pastries I have ever seen and tells me that the Maestra's son, Giorgio, has fallen playing rugby and broken his leg.

'Giorgio? Il Piccolo?'

Za' Mela roars with laughter. '*Che Piccolo?* He's seventeen years old and two metres tall.'

Gradually, everyone goes home, leaving a sea of plastic cups and plates and crumbs and spilled Fanta. Emma rushes off to pack because they are going to England tomorrow and Elettra is going to Venice for Christmas, so I walk her down to the hydrofoil and wave her off. For the first time since I arrived on Salina, I feel very alone.

Back in the hall, Izzy and Juno have made a den under a table with a couple of other kids. Za' Mela introduces me to their mother, her daughter Sara. With pale translucent skin, a beautiful mass of dark hair and sparkling blue-grey eyes, Sara looks like she walked straight out of an Irish myth and has the same capable, good-humoured energy as her mum. As we clean up together, we joke about Maestra, tentatively at first, then blunter and blunter, ruder and ruder, as the anecdotes pour out, each one more outrageous than the last. At one point, Sara is laughing so much she trips over the dustpan, and we end up all three of us bent over, helpless with giggles, unable to speak. I wait for them to recover, then start to sing 'Ding Dong! The Witch is Dead'.

Izzy joins in, then Sara and Mela, and Sara's kids, and we dance around the dustpan, then carry on singing, humming, la-la-la-ing, as we sweep, mop, lock the doors, swing the rubbish bags into the bin and cross over to the café for hot chocolate.

BARBIE BEHEADED

We meet outside Palermo station as agreed. The children run up to their father, are instantly in his arms, Juno climbing up onto his shoulders as she always did, as if he were her tree, Izzy showing him her wobbly tooth. Our words are polite, voices controlled. My ex raises a sardonic eyebrow as if to say, 'Ahh, so is this the game we are playing?' I am disoriented, the traffic fumes are making me sick. Seeing someone so familiar but from an emotionally unfamiliar place is as odd as seeing the face of a person you once knew deconstructed by Picasso.

I cannot imagine how I am coming across but catch Izzy watching me, face pinched, looking puzzled. The exchange seems to take for ever, in syrupy slow-motion, but looking at my watch as I prepare to say goodbye, I realise it has taken less than ten minutes. I have never taken anti-depressants but this is how I imagine life would feel if I had. Any longer would be to risk pain, anger, recriminations erupting through the viscous calm of phoney cordiality.

I think of the bathymetric maps.

I watch the traffic lights turn to green as the air is filled with the massed sound of angry klaxons.

Juno looks up and says, 'I didn't know we knew so many people in Palermo.'

My ex looks puzzled.

'The only time on the island anyone pips a horn is to say hello,' I say.

That evening, the gods be praised, I have work to do, exciting work, a Sicilian princess to interview in her eighteenth-century villa outside Palermo. I hire a car and drive to the coastal town of Bagheria, once an elegant summer retreat for the city's aristocracy, now a notorious Mafia stronghold. Where the Mafia rules supreme, there are no planning regulations and, sure enough, within two minutes, I am lost in a shambolic labyrinth of low-rise tenements larded with gaudy plastic signage. I stop outside a window display of flash ballgowns on bosomy mannequins and check the street name. This is where the palace is supposed to be. I am not convinced, but then spot some arabesques of wrought iron poking above a pickup piled with crates of blood oranges. The fruit vendor points me to a security gate half-hidden behind a semi-demolished skeleton of graffiti-covered concrete. I press the intercom, the gate slides open and I drive in to find myself within the arms of a magnificent, miniature version of St Peter's Square. Before me, the concave façade of the villa dances cream and gold in the evening sun, and vanilla statues peer down from the balustrade. The villa's butler appears and greets me with 'Buonasera, sono Filippo'. I feel like Alice newly arrived in Wonderland.

Filippo leads the way through a magnificence of gilt, stucco, frescoes, Pompeiian miniatures, statuary, majolica tiles, silk, brocade and velvet, one room opening on to another, and another, and another, and yet another, just as I remember Pippo conjuring up the palace of his childhood, a seeming infinity of rooms, all interconnected, some with alcoves in between – for afternoon tea, embroidery, letter writing, conversation, kisses and whispers. In some of the alcoves are beds, velvet curtains on either side, and I imagine trying to sleep without four solid walls between me and the rest of the household, with not a sketch of privacy, and wonder if the women of the aristocracy and the poor island women had that in common.

In the *Sala dello Zodiaco*, below a ceiling frescoed with a horoscope, sitting on a lush raspberry velvet sofa surrounded by a collection of Victorian telescopes, corals, fossils and shells, I meet Principessa Vittoria Alliata di Villafranca. She has wavy carmine hair and delicate features. She pours us glasses of chilled Sicilian white wine and begins to tell me her story.

She is an extraordinary woman. A rebel, a survivor, determined to sculpt her own life, drive her own future. She ran away as a fifteen-year-old to Rome and paid her own way through school by translating *The Lord of the Rings* for an Italian publishing house.

'I refused to meet the publishers. I did everything in writing, nothing by phone, and insisted on leaving the manuscript every Friday evening outside the office door after everyone had gone home so that they wouldn't find out I was a teenager.'

I try to imagine having the self-possession and chutzpah – let alone the intellectual ability – to do that as an adult, never mind as a teenager, and I wonder what such a woman might have done if she had been born on Salina. If Vittoria had been a *majara*, I suspect she'd have rejected magic, built a replica of Leonardo's flying boat and flown to Xanadu.

But something tells me it's not simply being an aristocrat that gave Vittoria her grit, curiosity, passion and sense of adventure. She could have been a different kind of aristocrat, a shy, compliant, conservative daughter who did what she was told. Instead, she has a depth of self-confidence I can't even dream of. I remember meeting a Northumbrian primary school headteacher taking a sabbatical on a remote Greek island who told me he believed the most important thing a parent or teacher could give a child was self-confidence. And self-confidence, I think, does not *have* to have anything to do with class or education or wealth, though they can all help.

Vittoria's story is one she must have told often, a story that could easily leave 'ordinary' people thinking well, it was OK for you, with your fifty-four titles, but over the evening with Vittoria, I realise it wasn't like that at all. As she was living it, she had no idea if things would work out. She just knew she was stubborn, had grit and passion, hated to be bored, and that she couldn't bear to have the direction of her life dictated by anyone. Robert Rauschenberg (OK, most of us wouldn't move in circles where we'd even meet Rauschenberg) painted her with a moustache because he said he had never met a woman with such balls.

Vittoria went on to travel across the Middle East, studying Islamic law with a focus on the rights of women, writing a book on harems, raising camels. Then in the 1990s, as a single mother with a three-year-old daughter, she came home to Villaguarnera to discover that the Mafia had sequestered it, installed a thug as guardian and built a red-brick villa with a pool in the grounds. Sheep and wild boar wandered at will through villa and gardens, and outside was a guard dog with a chain running through the gap between the tibia and fibula in his leg, so that the pain would drive him insane.

I ask Vittoria to stop. Ask her to repeat what she had said, so that I can be sure I have understood. I have never in my life met anyone who had had to confront such pure evil. I look at Vittoria, composed, regal, in sequined Arabic slippers and an embroidered cobalt-blue kaftan, and wonder where she found the courage to face out the Mafia. Most people would have given up the villa, run a thousand miles. Not Vittoria. She and her daughter moved in, Mafia thug notwithstanding.

'We didn't come across him often. Though in the mornings, I would sometimes find one of my daughter's Barbies had been beheaded.'

Was she not afraid to die? Or that they would kidnap or kill her daughter? As the mother of another three-year-old, I discover I simply cannot ask those questions. I can't find a way of asking, without appearing to accuse her of irresponsibility or suggesting that in some way she had protection. I know when I am out of my depth.

We have dinner with Filippo, in a small dining room off the kitchen, and she tells me that, after his arrest, they discovered that the red-brick villa in her garden had belonged to Mafia boss Bernardo Provenzano.

'Which explains why,' says Vittoria, 'when the first Google Earth image of Bagheria appeared, there was a cloud masking Villa Valguarnera.'

POPPY SYRUP

Even on a cold morning, with the children and all my friends away, Salina seems like paradise. On the way back from Palermo, I had stopped at Alicudi and discovered a stark volcanic cone scaled by steps designed for giants. There was no flat land. It is an island, I discovered, where you can only trudge, not walk. Walking and being able to think as you walk seems fundamental to sanity. Even in a prison, there is a yard for walking. As I pick my way along the beach at Lingua, I wonder which Greek deity I should thank for the volcanological happenstance that made Salina habitable, with sheltered harbours, fertile soil, and sufficient flat land for comfortable living and walking. Poseidon, Earth Shaker and God of the Sea, probably, for the god who seems to destroy can also create. Indeed, where volcanoes and even earthquakes are concerned, they are virtually the same thing. Or would be if the Earth was not inhabited.

The entire Aeolian archipelago is the result of chance. It is chance that transformed eruptions of liquid magma into featherweight pumice, rhino-hide basalt or obsidian – the razor-sharp black volcanic glass that made Stone Age Aeolians rich. Chance that made Salina lush, Alicudi a stark cone. If the Earth were not inhabited and we were gods, we could watch in awe as geological forces erupted, liquified, exploded, sculpted, eroded, flooded, burned, froze and endlessly metamorphosed the planet.

The beach is made of sea-smoothed pebbles that from a distance appear grey, but close up display infinite variety. Blood reds, beef reds, brick reds, rust reds, rose reds, fudge pinks, chocolate, purple, burgundy, dove-grey, the blue-grey of a bruise, colours that seem to belong more to flesh and feather than stone, each one's beauty born in the happenstance of eruption. I sit down and pick up a pebble, orange-red, tiny holes left behind by gases bubbling inside the molten rock. The skin of the Earth feels thin here.

On my way into Santa Marina to buy food for my solitary Christmas, I pass Zaccaria at work in the field by the cemetery. He beckons me over and shows me a rock on which he has arranged a row of slim clay pipes, each snapped in two, which he found buried at the edge of the field below the cemetery wall.

'Opium pipes,' he says.

'Opium?'

'The isle is full of opium poppies, you see them in spring, lilac poppies.'

'People smoked it?'

'Some did. More often, they made poppy syrup to give to children when they were agitated or filled pillows with poppy heads to help them sleep.'

'But the pipes,' I ask. 'Why are they snapped in two?'

'I was thinking maybe because they became addicted. And someone broke them to try to break their addiction.'

In the piazza by the port are a few people dressed in shades of sludge, stamping their feet against the cold north wind, woolly hats pulled low, lips and chins sagging into collars turned up. Islanders take it as a personal affront when the wind is too strong or cold. Talk to them of fresh air, and the benefits thereof, and they gaze at you as if you are insane. There is a hydrofoil arriving but none of them are going anywhere.

Suddenly, a swift movement. A blond man I have never seen before runs across the piazza, smiling, laughing, waving, and races along the dock to the hydrofoil, impetuously like a boy. As he lopes past, his eyes catch mine and I have the sense that something amazing has happened, of looking for a nanosecond into dark eyes sparkling with – what? Spirit? Energy? Mischievousness? Laughter? I feel as if I have seen my soul walk by.

In a dizzy mood of gratitude for being alive, I dismiss the notion of a frugal Christmas eating pasta and beans while I input museum opening times into the guidebook, and buy a capon, abundant veg and a couple of very nice bottles of wine. I head home, swinging my shopping, walking on clouds.

I am still in a daft rose-tinted haze as I set the capon to marinate in yogurt and herbs, and spend the afternoon sitting on the *bisuolo* listening to music, peeling vegetables and daydreaming. If this was a film, a romantic film, a glance such as that would be significant, life-changing, even. But then, I say out loud to myself, as I stuff the capon with lemon peel and thyme and wrap it in pancetta, in another kind of film, with a different soundtrack, a glance like that would have been the ruse of a con man. I put the capon on to roast and, as the evening closes in, I make bread sauce, mushroom stuffing, gravy, roast potatoes, caramelised fennel and carrots. Enough to feed an army. I fill the mountainside with good smells, sip red wine from Vulcano and eat on the terrace in lamplight, escaping into the magnificent Maggie O'Farrell novel Mum and Dad have given me for Christmas.

Christmas morning is still and sunny, so I send messages to the girls and swim. Then, walking home, I see the bus pass by. I never dreamed the buses would run on Christmas Day, but I check the timetable and they do, so I pack a lunch of leftovers and take the next bus over to the other side of the island. There's a path I want to try that cuts over the flank of Salina's second mountain, Monte dei Porri, or Leek Mountain, to Pollara, so I call Pippo and Anna as I set off walking, thinking it would be nice to share my provisions over a sunset *aperitivo*, but there is no reply.

The path is carved high into the flank of Monte dei Porri, with eyefuls of glories at every step. Venetian red and Payne's grey rockfaces embroidered with gold, lime, silver and verdigris lichens that glow brilliant in the sun; Lipari and Vulcano below me, green, pink and ochre; Filicudi and Alicudi touch-paper blue silhouettes against the sky. The only living thing I see is a falcon. I stop for water and oranges leaning against the wall of an abandoned lava-stone bothy set among triffiddy olive trees.

The sun is low by the time I zigzag down into Pollara, the caldera flooded and warm with golden pink light. I call Pippo and Anna again – I am sure they said they were here for Christmas – but there is no reply and when I walk past their house, I see the gate is locked. I walk down to the tiny port and clamber past the caves. There is a new and heavily padlocked iron gate across the entrance of Pippo's. I peer through the grid. *Minchia Pazza* has gone.

The shoreline is in shadow now, so I climb back up into the sun and find a flight of steps I had not noticed before, carved into the powdery tuff. At the top is a tiny viewpoint, a natural stone crow's nest, where I sit and watch the sun sink while gorging myself on Vulcano wine and cold chicken, mushroom stuffing and wild rocket in ciabatta. I try to conjure up the eyes of the laughing, smiling man, and decide he is a poet, maybe Norwegian, definitely Nordic, and imagine that we are lying against the warm rock, wild fennel heads above us incandescent in the setting sun, gazing down on a sea so dark and viscous that we conclude it must have been the kind of sea Homer described as wine-dark. We talk of the fear and enchantment that entered the imaginations of sailors at sea, of Nordic sagas and Greek myths, of gods and goddesses, monsters, sirens and mermaids. Sleepy with wine I close my eyes and by the time I wake up the sun has sunk below the horizon and the village is in shadow. High above, I can see the little blue bus winding down the crater.

Would I be happier here with a man?

No. Only an imaginary one, I say out loud to the crater.

IANCURA

'That enchanted crow's nest with the magical flight of steps you found on Christmas Day?' says Elettra, two days later. 'You have no idea! You don't know how lucky you were!'

'Well, I did, I do,' I say. 'I thought it was amazing, like something out of *Alice in Wonderland*. I half expected to see the White Rabbit.'

'White Rabbit, my foot. Red Queen more like. Or worse.'

'What?'

'Well. Listen to this. The rumour is that some dastardly property developer has been buying up the whole of Pollara, paying twice the market price or more, whatever people want, and that his heavies made that staircase in a single night, with a pneumatic drill, so that he could have his own private *belvedere*.'

'But it wasn't private, it was just carved into the cliff. No gate, no fence, no wall.'

'Exactly. That's the problem. The rumours are that, not content with buying property, he's appropriating the cliffside as well. And that everyone's too scared to say anything. Except Pippo. The rumour is that someone, a fisherman, agreed a price for a shed by the sea but when he went to finalise the sale, the owner told him he had just sold it for double the asking price.'

From what Elettra is saying, the rumour factory has gone into meltdown. *They say that the property developer is planning to build a luxury resort. A butterfly farm. A donkey sanctuary. A 'Jerusalem of High Finance'.*

A Davos on Salina? Talk about surreal.

It's New Year's Eve. Elettra is back from Venice and we are making lentil soup. Elettra tells me you are supposed to eat lentils at midnight to bring money and good fortune, along with a disgusting vacuum-packed sausage called *cotechino*, so I suggested lentil soup instead to use up the last of the broth I made from the capon carcass. To keep us going until midnight, we have a mountain of tiny prawns from Lipari, smoked tuna, anchovies in lemon and chilli, caper pesto, wild rocket salad and home-made rosemary focaccia. I've just poured glasses of dry Malvasia when my phone rings. According to the display it is Pippo but it sounds nothing like him. Instead of his usual quicksilver audacity, curveballs and good-natured joshing, a wavering voice says formally that he has received two calls from this number, didn't recognise it and wants to know who I am.

'It's Ros, Pippo! You sound weird. What's wrong? I was in Pollara on Christmas Day and the house was all shut up and the cave barricaded, and ...'

I put the phone on loudspeaker.

'They smashed *Minchia Pazza* to little pieces. They put an iron gate on my cave, just appropriated it.'

'*O Dio*, Ros.' Elettra sighs. 'I had hoped it was all just voices, rumours.'

'Oh Pippo,' I say. This does not feel like a good beginning to 2005.

'And when I challenged them, they beat me up.'

'Ros,' says Elettra, 'nothing like this has ever happened here before. We thought we'd somehow managed to avoid the kinds of thing that happen on the mainland, but I guess it was only time.'

Elettra and I are invited to a New Year's Day barbecue at the Cucinottas' mountain house, Paolo Noce. I've only reached chapter three of the Sicily guide and the girls are back the day after tomorrow, but I can't resist. It's a beautiful morning of what they call *iancura*, the still, silver sea and sky hazed, fused, the horizon imperceptible, and Lipari pale blue and flat as a paper cut-out.

Pippo's report of events in Pollara seem like they belong to another world. But of course they don't. Beauty can be transformed into a commodity, and beauty that can be appreciated from the luxury of an exclusive hotel commands high prices. Perhaps it was inevitable that eventually the speculators would arrive on Salina. Though maybe if we weren't in Sicily, we wouldn't have to worry. Salina is a protected nature reserve, a UNESCO world heritage site, and planning regulations are theoretically strict – you can only build in the footprint of existing ruins, nothing new can be created – but that is only in theory, as the house with the secret underground floor proved. Loopholes can be found, sweeteners palmed, threats implied, blind eyes bought.

As we walk along the path to Paolo Noce, Elettra tells me rumours are circulating that the local doctor refused to treat Pippo after he was beaten up. That the doctor was on the town council, or was friends with or related to someone who was, and that it was thought unwise to write a medical report that could cause 'problems' and give the island a bad name. I am not sure if this is true. Pippo was in no state when he phoned to be asked why he didn't just go to see Salvatore in the Carabinieri. After all, the very reason Carabinieri cannot serve in their place of birth is to keep them impartial. It's at times like this, I say to Elettra, that I feel most foreign.

'Me too,' she says, 'even though I was born here. But Salina has never been like this. A friend from some godforsaken village in the centre of Sicily told me she was brought up to never tell anyone anything because you never know who are talking to. She meant that information about someone could be valuable to the *malavita*. But Salina is different.'

I remember Michel saying exactly the same thing on Favignana.

The path to Paolo Noce is wide and crunchy, following a high stone terrace along the contour of the mountainside. The sea is so smooth it could be made of solid glass. Turning a corner, we get the first sight of the house, a white sugar cube perched on a ridge above a grove of olives as tightly packed as Calabrese broccoli. As we walk along a narrow track that has been beaten through the trees, we hear voices, laughter, smell wood smoke. Nunzia is on the terrace slicing bread. Bartolino is arranging a spiral of sausages on a grill. They point uphill to a white hat poking out of the top of an olive tree, a pair of orange-trousered legs protruding below. Gaetanino with the hat, Nunzia tells me, Lorenzo with the orange trousers.

The house is enchanting, straight lines and angles blurred below layers of lime and whitewash, chalky white and plumbago blue, with a bright blue door and two circular windows like panda eyes. A zinc bucket with rope coiled as neat as a charmed snake sits by the well, and next to it is a stone sink ridged for washing clothes. Nunzia shows us inside the house. We enter a large room with two iron bedsteads, a washstand, candlestick, a pair of slippers, a radio, binoculars and a bird book. Next door is a tiny kitchen with a miniature hand-built range comprising two whitewashed niches where pans can be set above hot coals or wood. If ever there was a house where people could live lightly on the planet, this is it. There is no power, no running water, but every aspect of the place is beautifully thought through and lovingly curated. There are candles and oil lamps, and by the small stone barbecue built into a sheltered corner, oregano, mint, rosemary and chillies have all been planted within an arm's reach.

I know it's not practical to live here, forty-five minutes' walk from the village, without electricity and running water – even the Cucinottas only live here when sleeping over for the olive harvest – but I can't resist going into pastoral dream mode. I picture us living at Paolo Noce, kids barefoot and schooled by nature, me writing a book, a *Walden* for the twenty-first century, until I realise that there would be no way we could be self-sufficient here and that carrying shopping and cajoling children up hundreds of steps from the village would be about as pleasurable as spending the rest of my days on Alicudi. And besides, I would miss my evenings with Emma and Elettra.

As we grill sausages, the Cucinottas tell me how as kids, they helped their father terrace the mountainside so that they could plant the olives – and that their father removed an entire strata of lava to get to the deep, rich earth below. The volcano has given such riches, says Nunzia. To those who are prepared to work, says Lorenzo. The mountain has to be respected, says Nunzia, you need to be careful. Even if it won't erupt again, the terrain is slippery, friable, says Bartolino, and you need to plant your feet well. How would it be on the mountain in an earthquake, I ask, would there be landslides? It is not earthquakes that kill people but buildings, says Lorenzo. Paolo Noce has survived many, Bartolino adds. Gaetanino fills our cups with wine and lights a cigarette.

THE INSECTS OF
SAN BIAGIO

Emma is feeding Ilana, Giuseppina is shelling fava beans, and the kids are eating toast with Marmite they brought back from London. They have returned full of the glories of the V&A (a treasure hunt for kids and you have your own rucksack), the Princess Diana playground (you can climb on a real pirate ship). Primark (the most beautiful clothes you have ever seen) and central heating. Red cars, says Juno. School uniform, says Izzy. Chocolate, says Juno. Brownies, says Izzy. Police cars, says Juno. Canopic jars, says Izzy. Canopic what? I ask. Her friend Edie is doing the Egyptians at school and her Christmas holiday homework is making canopic jars – 'Which is kind of gross because they put dead people's insides inside them, but kind of cool as well.'

'A real pirate ship.' Max sighs. 'I wish we had one.'

'There isn't even a climbing frame on Salina,' groans Izzy.

'Well, there are lots of other things to climb on,' I say brightly, racking my brains.

'Like?' says Izzy.

'Rocks,' I say, 'the wall, the lemon tree ...'

Izzy does not look impressed.

'Well,' I say, 'English children would be ever so jealous if they knew you rode in the back of Gaetano's Lapa.'

'Ah,' says, Izzy, smiling, 'now that gives me an idea. We could climb ON TOP of Gaetano's Lapa. While it's moving. Like circus children.'

'Well, maybe when it's NOT moving ... ?'

Emma gives me one of her looks.

In between mouthfuls of toast and Marmite, Izzy is teaching Max a clapping song about love, marriage and an alcoholic baby. Meanwhile, on the island, we have had the excellent news that the nursery school has moved into a freshly restored, purpose-built building and, even better, that Maestra Adelaide has left the island permanently to tend to the needs of Il Piccolo.

'Cause for celebration indeed,' I say, and wonder if there might be a nursery place for Juno.

Although, as Emma points out, we shouldn't celebrate until we know who her replacement will be.

Although, as I point out, it would be hard for anyone to be worse than Maestra Adelaide.

Juno and Max

Sitting in a tree

K-I-S-S-I-N-G

'What's K I blahdy blahdy blahdy blah?' asks Max, scratching his head.

Izzy splutters.

'Tell me ...' says Max warningly, waggling his finger.

'I might,' says Izzy, waggling her finger back and scratching her head.

Juno giggles. 'Kissing!' She laughs, scratching her head.

'Kissing! Yuk!'

'Um,' says Emma, 'do you think they are scratching their heads rather a lot?'

'Do you know what nits look like?'

'No.'

'What's Italian for nits?'

'Don't know.'

'Giuseppina, can you have a look and see if the kids have got insects in their hair?'

'Insects? *Pidocchi?* O, *Minchia di San Bartolo.*'

She stands up and starts examining Max's abundant blond curls.

'*Uova di pidocchi* [nit eggs], *minchia.*'

She moves onto Juno. '*Pidocchi. Minchia.*' And to Izzy, '*Pidocchi.*'

'*Minchia,*' says Juno. Her first Sicilian swearword.

'And me, Giuseppina?'

She comes over and tries to finger through my hair, which is its usual tangle.

'San Biagio, do you never comb your hair?'

'San Biagio, that's a new one,' says Emma.

'Shredded to death with a comb, patron saint of hairdressers.' I once had to compile a list of gory martyrdoms for *Time Out*.

'Did you know that, Giuseppina? San Biagio is the patron saint of hairdressers?'

'Of course I know that. But how come she does?' Giuseppina grunts. 'Doesn't look like she's been to a hairdresser's in her life. It's full of sand and salt. But no *pidocchi*. Because *pidocchi* like clean hair,' she says pointedly, hands on hips. She reflects a moment. 'Now, what you need to do is dye their hair. That'll kill the *pidocchi* off alright.'

'Yay!' squeals Izzy, who has been nagging me since Halloween to have her hair dyed orange.

'You never did.' Emma looks at Giuseppina. 'Tell me, you never did ...'

'Did what?'

'Dye Gaetano's hair?'

'Now, why would I ever have had to do that?' she says. 'He never had nits.'

'Well, what was all that about dyeing hair to kill *pidocchi* then?'

'Well, it's a chemical, isn't it.'

'Just not a nit-killing chemical.'

Giuseppina shrugs and turns back to shelling her beans.

We print off instructions from NHS Direct, buy a bottle of nit-killing shampoo and a lethal-looking metal-toothed nit comb, and set to work. According to NHS Direct, reads Emma, it is extremely important that every strand of hair passes through the comb, that the treatment is repeated every five days and that schools are informed.

'How do you spell *pidocchi*?' I ask Giuseppina.

'Why do you want to write a word like *pidocchi*?'

'We need to tell the school.'

'God in Heaven, my girl, you can't *tell* anyone.'

'But what if the other children get them?'

She shrugs. '*Che dobbiamo fare?* The only important thing is that nobody knows where they got them from.'

'What do you think?' I ask Emma.

'Let's tie their hair up tight and ask Za' Mela, she probably knows as much about nits than the NHS.'

'Or more.'

The stuff has such a horrendous stink that I feel dizzy, as if my legs are about to give way or the Earth has begun to float. Come to think of it, I've felt like that a few times recently. Low blood pressure, probably. I decide to get myself checked out next time I spot a doctor. The emergency clinic is next to the new nursery school and as emergencies are thin on the ground in winter, most of the doctors seem only too glad to pass the time treating a few non-urgent people.

'Especially pretty females,' says Emma.

'Better wash my hair then.'

LOOKING FOR A
TSUNAMI

For once, there is no doctor in sight when we arrive at Santa Marina for the first day of the new term, and as it is too early for school, we sit down to wait. Eventually, one of the doctors strolls out of the clinic, green tunic tucked into high visibility yellow trousers over an impressive paunch. As he heads past, a gust of wind rattles the branches and he looks up at the tree.

'It can be dangerous, you know, to sit under a pine tree. The cones might fall on your head.' He has a shiny bald pate, a naughty smile, and looks like a cross between a pizza chef and Federico da Montefeltro. He lights a cigarette.

'Actually, I was waiting for you. I wondered if you could check my blood pressure.'

'Why? What's wrong?' He clamps the cigarette between his lips and takes my wrist in his hand to feel my pulse.

'I have low blood pressure, always,' I say, trying not to breathe in his smoke. 'But over the last week, I keep feeling weird. Not exactly dizzy, but lightheaded, as if my legs are about to give way.' I hesitate. Knowing I'm asking for it. 'As if the Earth is moving.'

'That's probably because it is.'

'What?'

'Stromboli's in one of its phases of intense activity so there's been a series of earth tremors.'

'What?'

'Normal. If it rains there are puddles, if the wind blows,

215

pinecones might fall and hit you, if Stromboli gets agitated, the Earth moves. Normal.'

'It doesn't seem normal to me, coming from England.'

He takes a deep drag of his cigarette and shrugs.

'In England, doctors don't smoke, so that doesn't feel normal either.'

'If I were a doctor, I wouldn't smoke. But I'm a vet.' He grins impudently and reaches out to shake my hand. 'My name's Arcangelo.'

'Your parents clearly had great expectations.'

'Yes. To have a son who became the Pope.' He chucks his cigarette butt down and crushes it with his boot. 'But there's still time ...'

I decline Arcangelo's invitation to breakfast and walk over to the school. Za' Mela is standing outside. I go over and start telling her about the nits, then realise she is ashen faced, trembling.

'*Stromboli è in eruzione*.' She grasps my hands between hers, then points prayer-like to the sky. 'Oh, *Signore*,' she implores, gripping my hands tight. Her palms are cold and clammy, and I can feel her pulse racing. She points down the hill to the sea. 'How many metres above sea level are we, do you think?' She's talking fast, breathlessly, 'Do you think it's fifty? They say fifty metres is safe but I don't believe them. Look what happened in Thailand with the tsunami. Or, more to the point, what happened to Noah. Think about it. Just look at what happened to Noah. And are you telling me there aren't enough sins here on this island to make God want to teach us a lesson? We're in the hands of God, and if He willed it, the whole island could be swallowed up. Gone forever.' And she looks up at the top of the mountain. 'Just imagine it, the whole island drowned, water right up to the cross at the very top of the mountain. My son showed me, you know, that the sea here is full of drowned mountains. He had a map.'

'I know, I've seen it too,' I tell her, trying to imagine the impact of the bathymetric map on the mind of someone who believed in an avenging god. 'But let's think, let's try not to panic.' Za' Mela is scared and she has spent her entire life here. The doctor is not scared but I am not sure I would trust him.

'Oh *Signore*, oh *Signore*, Santa Maria, San Giuseppe, San Bartolo and all the angels ...'

'Mela.' I put an arm around her and walk her over to the wall to sit down, making sure that she has her back to the sea. Through the trees, I can see huge clouds of charcoal smoke above Stromboli. As I watch, another puff appears, soot-black and briefly glowing. It is like watching TV with the volume turned off.

'And the little ones haven't learned the earthquake drill yet.'

A helicopter appears from behind Lipari. 'You see, look?' Za' Mela stands up and points. 'It's the Civil Protection helicopter.'

'Mela, don't worry, it's there to protect us,' I say, aware even as I am speaking that it is a stupid thing to say. My instinct, too, is to take the girls as high up the mountain as possible, where at least we would be out of the way of a tsunami. Instead, I call Emma.

'*Stromboli è in eruzione*,' I say.

'I'm right here,' she says, 'behind you.'

And turning round, I see her and Max walking through the garden, deep in conversation with a middle-aged lady with curly brown hair, who smiles warmly at us all, then places a hand on Za' Mela's shoulder.

'Mela.'

'Stromboli. We haven't done the earthquake drill.'

'Don't worry,' she says, looking round at us all. She smiles from her eyes and sits on the wall, looking at each child in turn.

'*Buongiorno bambini*, I'm Maestra Giulia. The new teacher. Now, tell me who you are.'

'*Sono Ismene*,' says Izzy.

'*Sono Max*,' says Max.

'Juno,' says Juno.

'*Io sono Luca*.' Luca squeezes between Izzy and Max, grinning from ear to ear.

'Federico,' says Federico, scrutinising Giulia with a wary smile, and passing Za' Mela a Kinder egg, which she opens for him.

Giulia raises an eyebrow.

'His breakfast,' says Za' Mela, handing Federico the egg.

'Chocolate for breakfast? And a toy inside? Well, Federico, what a lucky boy you are. Now, let's go inside and start our new school together.'

She stands up. Juno slips her hand in hers and looks at me.

'She's only three and hasn't actually started school yet,' I say.

'Are you happy for her to start? She seems ready.'

I smile. 'Of course.'

'Bring her passport along and we can do the paperwork when you collect her. OK, children, let's go inside and see our new school.'

As they walk away, I hear her ask gently if anyone knows what an earthquake is.

'It's when the monsters under the earth begin to move,' says Federico.

'Not quite, but that is exactly what it feels like, isn't it? Wobbly.'

Za' Mela rises slowly to her feet. Emma gives her a hug. 'Try not to worry, Mela. Think about it, remember, the islands are protected by Saint Bartholomew.' Mela looks at us and sighs. There is suffering as well as kindness in her eyes, as if she has seen and knows too much.

'San Bartolo, yes, but they've sent the helicopter too, and the big coastguard ship. Did you see it in the harbour?'

'Mela,' says Emma, 'that's just come to annoy the fishermen, you know, the usual safety equipment check, net sizes, all that.'

Mela does not look convinced as she walks towards the school.

'Are you really not worried?' I ask Emma.

'A little, of course, but not much. There are minor earthquakes all the time – weirdly enough, usually in winter. But it happens every few years that Stromboli enters a phase of what they call "intense activity". In 2002, a huge chunk fell off and caused a minor tsunami. But Stromboli's very closely monitored and we don't get tsunamis like the Asian ones here. The sea is too deep. By the time a wave hits land here, most of its force has been diffused. Still, the best thing to do is to pack an earthquake bag with essentials and passports. It's probably better not to sleep naked just in case you have to suddenly leave the house at night, and to always have shoes and coats ready by the bed. And if you don't have time to get out, the safest place is under a doorway, because that is where houses are strongest. But most people gather on the main street – it's high enough above sea level. At least if there's time.'

Five hours later, Izzy dances out of school with a copy of *Pippi Calzelunghe* in Italian, and Juno scampers after her, beaming, kicks off her crocs, tears off her dress and shoves a crumpled page of wild red, orange and pink brushstrokes into my hand. 'Stromboli,' she says.

'Beautiful,' I say. Her first ever non-khaki painting. I thank Maestra Giulia, who tells me both girls were wonderful, but that as Izzy can read already she really should go to the more formal elementary school. 'The little ones won't leave her alone, they just want her to play with them and read to them.'

'I don't mind that,' I say. 'I'm just relieved to see her happy.'

'I know,' says Maestra Giulia, 'but she needs more stimulation.'

We have lunch in the café, then go home to pack earthquake bags. I explain to the girls that we need to pack only extremely important things, and Juno weeps when I tell her she can't take every single one of her cuddly toys, though stops when I suggest she makes an earthquake shelter for her menagerie and gives them Dairy Milk to cheer them up. I pack the rucksack with essentials, leave it by the gate, then look out to sea. It's like molten glass, oscillating in the breeze. The sky is a clear petrol blue. Stromboli is puffing dense cauliflowers of volcanic smoke, drawn slowly along the horizon, in thick stripes of white and grey. You'd need acrylics today and coarse broad brushes if you were trying to paint it.

I call Emma. We've two hours left of daylight, and the kids are manic on Dairy Milk and my anxiety. There have been no alerts from Civil Protection, no sirens, no guidelines as to what or what not to do, and no locals' examples to follow, as on a cold, sunny afternoon in January, all sane islanders are at home watching telly. We know the safest place to go would be up the mountain, but neither of us feel like cajoling the kids up steep crumbly paths, so we settle on the beach.

'As long as we keep an eye out for tidal waves.'

'Listen to us! "We're going to the beach but no swimming, and we need to watch out for a tsunami".'

'Surreal.'

'Absurd.'

'Let's take the binoculars.'

We sit on the beach with a flask of tea, scrutinising the sea, while Emma feeds Ilana and the other kids clamber over the rocks.

'Weird wave!' shouts Izzy.

'Weird wave!' shouts Juno.

'Tsunami!' shouts Max and topples into the water, fully clothed.

Izzy laughs, Juno jumps in after him and two speedboats come into view, as their wake rolls towards shore.

'Phew,' I say.

'Speedboats in January, though?' says Emma, passing me the binoculars.

'Dark blue and white,' I say.

'Red writing?'

'Yup.'

'Carabinieri.'

'More tea?'

'Please.'

As I am pouring tea, every molecule of air between Salina and Lipari begins to pulsate.

'Earthquake?'

'Helicopter.'

As Emma points, a helicopter flies low over Lipari, then begins tracking back and forward above the sea. As it passes over our heads, we can see the words *Protezione Civile* on its gunmetal grey belly.

'It's looking for something.'

We call the kids out of the sea and up onto the piazza. They respond straight away without a query or fuss, which is unprecedented enough to suggest our anxiety is palpable.

Once in the piazza, I take Ilana in my arms while Emma phones Gaetano.

'What's happening?'

Gaetano says something.

'What?' she says. 'What should we do?' She finishes the call. 'He says go up onto the main road. Someone has seen smoke rising from the sea, above a point off Capo Faro where there's a submerged volcano.'

An underwater eruption. As we walk up to the road, I remember a small, square hardback of photographs my parents had, documenting the birth of the Icelandic island of Surtsey. I loved that book, spent hours wondering at the images of rivers of lava staining the sea gold, pillows of basalt, lava extrusions like giant *churros*, volcanic gas billowing violet, green and white above a livid sea. They were the most incredible photographs I had ever seen.

The eruption of Surtsey was first spotted in the early hours of a November morning in 1963 by fishermen aboard a trawler, who noticed a horrible smell. At first, they thought it was coming from the bilges, but then the boat began to roll as if it were in a whirlpool, and the cook noticed dark smoke on the horizon. Thinking that it must be a ship on fire, he went to wake the captain, who called the local radio station and asked if any SOS signals had been received. There had been none. The fishermen went back on deck and looked again, this time through binoculars, to see dark columns of smoke rising high above the sea. They went closer. The black columns were getting higher and higher, ejecting stones. There were occasional flashes of fire. The water around the boat was hot.

By 10.30am, the fishermen, still at sea, reported that the columns had grown to 11,500 feet. At 3pm, a huge explosion created a column of smoke four miles high that could be seen in Reykjavík, seventy miles away. Looking down from a helicopter, scientists could see waves breaking over rock where before there had been nothing, as the new island began to emerge. A story fit for an Icelandic saga or Homer's Odyssey. If the eruption had happened thousands of years ago, the fishermen would have told the story and, as it was passed on from sailor to sailor, and from port to port, a new myth – a new angry god – would have been born.

The sun drops behind the mountain and I remember that the only photograph in the book to include people showed a mother and two children standing on a beach at sunset watching clouds of volcanic gas over an eerily opalescent sea. Izzy, Juno and Max, shivering in damp sandy clothes, suddenly look fragile. It didn't occur to either me or Emma to bring spare clothes, let alone the earthquake bags. We go up the hill to our house, Ilana crying as Emma bumps the pram up the steps, the other kids moaning that they are cold, wet, sandy, sticky, hungry, that their legs hurt, that they are *too tired* to walk. We cajole them along with promises of a hot bath, bubbles, hot chocolate, *The Gruffalo*, CBeebies, and I give in to Juno and haul her up onto my back. As we deal with the niggles and banalities of everyday life with kids, I see the images of Surtsey superimposed over it all like a gaudy apocalypse.

'Maybe what happened in Iceland could never happen here,' I say to Emma, once the kids are in the bathtub, Ilana contentedly breastfeeding. 'Maybe the volcanoes here are different.'

'Google Vulcanello.'

I go into the bedroom and turn on the laptop. 183 BC. *Not far from Sicily a new island issued from the sea which had not before existed.* So wrote the Roman historian Livy after the emergence of the island of Vulcanello, a miniature volcanic cone attached by a sandy isthmus to the island of Vulcano, the tip of which I can see right now through the window. 183 BC, 2,000 years or so, a blink in geological time. I think of the scores of submerged volcanoes and seamounts on the bathymetric map.

In the archaeological museum of Lipari, Emma tells me, there is a room containing hundreds of amphorae, storage jars, lost from Greek and Roman cargo ships wrecked during the storms that can whip up out of nowhere in the archipelago.

'It always blows my mind,' she says, 'that the amphorae are older than Vulcanello.'

'It blows my mind that I have existed for longer than Surtsey.'

Commonsense turns somersaults, geology spins cartwheels. Emma's phone rings.

'What?' says Emma. 'Hang on, let me put the phone on loudspeaker.'

'It's not a new volcano. It's Damiano,' says Gaetano.

'Damiano? Damiano the fisherman?'

'He saw the big coastguard boat was in port and thought they'd come to do a safety check. His flares were out of date so he set them all off at sea at once to get rid of them.'

Two days later, just as I am making dinner, it happens. The kitchen shakes and rattles. Not quite believing this is really it, a real live earthquake, I grab the girls, the earthquake bag and the pram and bump down the steps to the road. Giuseppina is sitting on the wall clutching the contract for her house wrapped in copious cling film, while Rodolfo nonchalantly munches through a plate of pasta.

Izzy and Juno sprawl in the pram, watching Rodolfo eat and Giuseppina muttering saints' names.

'What's Rodolfo eating?' asks Juno.

'Pasta with cauliflower.'

Juno sighs. 'I don't know why, but I always feel hungry when I come to your house.'

'Oh *carusa*.' Giuseppina glows, ducking down behind the wall and retrieving a battered aluminium pan.

The kids eat huge amounts of cauliflower pasta, all the emergency earthquake snacks, and then fall asleep.

Conversation runs out. I am hungry but the kids have eaten all the pasta. I would kill for the glass of wine I left on the kitchen table. We keep looking around, as if expecting to see houses wobble, but nothing happens. There's not even any wind. Rodolfo lights a cigarette and I consider asking for one. I am so bored. It feels like one of those awkward New Year's Eve drink parties where everyone wants to go home but no one dares to be the first to say so. What the hell is the etiquette here? Can I really just say, 'Well, it doesn't look like the earthquake is happening tonight...'

Eventually, Rodolfo stands up and announces he is going to bed. Giuseppina shrugs and follows him with her empty pan, saying, as she always does, '*Che dobbiamo fare?*' What can we do? I go home too, bumping the girls as softly as I can up the steps in the pram and carrying them into my bed. I decide it's better if we all sleep together, fully clothed, with the earthquake bag by our side.

I don't sleep that night, nor the night after, alert to any noise, every vibration. Eventually, in desperation, I get up and sit on the terrace, looking at the bathymetric maps, trying to imagine what might be happening a kilometre or so beneath my feet. In the mornings, I work at the café across the road from the school to be close at hand, just in case. In the afternoons, we keep away from the beach but by the third day I am exhausted. The weather is glorious. Stromboli appears to be steaming gently like a kettle again and there have been no more appearances by the Protezione Civile helicopters.

'I guess life has to go on, doesn't it?' I say to Emma over lunch at Giuseppina's.

'*Che dobbiamo fare?*' says Giuseppina.

'Also,' says Emma, 'it's five days since we did the nit treatment.'

'OK, then,' I say. 'Nit treatment then beach. The only thing is, I've been looking for the nit comb for days and I can't find it anywhere.'

'Oh,' says Izzy, 'I put it in the earthquake bag. You said we had to pack everything important.'

GHOST VILLAGE

It is February, it is *Carnevale*, the festival of transgression, masquerade, misrule, excess. The men are outside the village hall shooting the breeze over beer and cigarettes, watching flames licking through an immense iron grill, which looks exactly like the one Saint Lawrence is roasted on in Titian's *Martyrdom of San Lorenzo*. The women are sitting inside on metal chairs, assassinating characters *sotto voce* behind their hands and darting the occasional dagger-glance at their victims.

'Is that what you meant by giving the evil eye?' I ask Elettra.

'No. That's just, how do you say it in English? *Bitching.*'

Kids in crinolines and superhero Lycra scream around, throwing streamers and spraying each other with coloured foam. Having discovered that the costumes cost fifty euros each from the big supermarket on Lipari, I persuaded Izzy, Juno and Max to choose something from the dressing-up box. Izzy is a Posy Fossil Ballerina Pirate Princess (tutu, tiara and skull and crossbones jacket); Juno and Max are pirate twins. The racket is terrible, rattles, screams and Europop, and the tedium is broken only when someone gets foam in their eyes. In my pocket, I have the afternoon's email delivery – a copy of the developer's proposal for Pollara and letter of objection from Legambiente, the Italian Greenpeace. I want to show them to Elettra. We grab a plastic beaker of red wine each, go outside and perch on the wall below a streetlamp. I unfold the developer's proposal and begin to read it to Elettra:

Thirty per cent of Italian children have never seen a live sheep.

225

For two children in ten, the only cows they will ever see are those in picture books, and 80 per cent of children have no idea what happens to food before it reaches the table. The plan is to build an educational farm, with stables for donkeys, a butterfly house, botanic garden, a series of footpaths and meditation points.

It sounds so innocent. A model of contemporary eco-tourism. If I hadn't had the phone call with Pippo, I'd probably have been backing the project myself, notwithstanding the rumours of glued-up padlocks and torn photographs. If this was rural England, I wouldn't give it a second thought, but I've been here long enough now to know that things are not always what they seem in Sicily. Or perhaps it's just that in England speculators are better at hiding their true motives.

'*Mamma mia*,' says Elettra.

'You couldn't make it up.'

'The rumour from Pollara is that someone has seen workmen *creating* ruins. This must be why.' Elettra points to a paragraph on the second page of the proposal.

The paper talks of 'reviving' a nineteenth-century fishing hamlet on the fringes of Pollara, but Elettra is adamant that there *is* no fishing hamlet. That there has never been a fishing hamlet on the edge of Pollara, she says, just a few tiny stone sheds, each too small to swing a rabbit. I suddenly remember the man in the suit walking over to the drystone wallers the day of the visit to the Il Postino house. The look that passed between Pippo and Anna.

'But why invent a village?' I ask.

'Because building regulations on Salina are that you can only build on the footprint of pre-existing buildings.'

'I see. So, you mean, if you wanted to build a luxury resort it would be extremely convenient if there happened to be the ruins of a fishing hamlet in exactly the place you'd earmarked for your hotel?'

Izzy runs past, chased by two boys, one tall and weedy with incipient acne, the other beefy, bullet-headed and crewcut, both armed with cans of pink foam. She swerves back to me, gives them a quick 'nuh nuh nuh nuh nuh' and buries her face in my lap. The weedy boy meets my eye and runs off. The other halts. Eyeballs me. Aims the can. He looks like he will grow into the kind of man who has a neck tattoo. I meet his eyes, dare a little shake of my head, when out of nowhere, there's a roar and his maxi-sized duplicate grabs his wrist, takes the can and slaps his head.

'Have they gone?' asks Izzy.

'Yes.'

She turns her head and glares at the boy's retreating back.

'Tell me please, what is the fun of a party if Michelangelo is here?'

'Ah. So that's Michelangelo?' I say.

'Elettra, is this how you give the evil eye?' She screws up her eyes, purses her lips and glowers.

'*Tesoro*, what happened?' asks Elettra.

'Elettra, Michelangelo has ruined my life.'

On Maestra Giulia's suggestion, Izzy has moved up from nursery to elementary school. By the end of the first week, she was best friends with one of Za' Mela's grandsons, a gentle and rather solemn little boy called Ivo. In week two, it became more serious, and on Valentine's Day he presented her with a blue velvet rabbit and a box of Baci. A week later, Michelangelo and his friend Leonardo told Ivo it was sissy to hang out with girls. Shy, sensitive and a third the size of the other lads, Ivo decided it judicious to break off the engagement. Ever since, Izzy has been listening non-stop to 'Positively 4th Street' and sings it in the bath every night with cathartic gusto.

'If the evil eye doesn't work, I might ask Daddy to send me some sweets from the joke shop on Kensington High Street. There are sweets that make you fart, sweets that taste like fish, sweets that taste like smelly feet and sweets that turn your mouth blue ...'

In the hope of taking her mind off revenge, we queue up for sausage sandwiches and go back into the hall.

We are back in the hall eating bread and sausages in paper napkins when the doors fly open. Icy cold air blasts through the room and in run three crazed, sexually ambiguous geriatrics, clad in stocking masks, mangy fur coats and sagging support tights, violently swinging vinyl handbags. They are men. Men in a weird kind of drag, who leap around the hall clasping gossiping *signoras* to their bosom, smacking kisses on the cheeks of the sourest old ladies, settling down, one after the other, on the lap of the plumpest, primmest lady of all, nuzzling her flushed cheeks like cats obsessed. There is silence, uneasy laughter, fear, even. Then two plucky lads of about thirteen leap on the last of the nuzzlers and tear off the stocking mask.

'Who is that?' I ask Elettra.

'That,' she says, raising her eyes heavenwards, 'is Onofrio, who is standing to be mayor.'

'But why?' I say. 'Is this a normal part of Carnevale celebrations?'

'No. Not at all! Onofrio probably just thought people would be more likely to vote for him if they think he'll be good fun.'

Out of nowhere, I hear an American voice say, 'Ros? Is that you?'

I turn round to see Susan Lord, the food critic from Rome who first spoke to me of Salina more than a decade ago. It's too noisy in the hall to talk, and too cold outside, so we arrange to meet the next morning while the children are at school.

We are in Susan's living room, the most urbane – and warm – room I have been in since arriving on Salina, sitting on a heavenly sofa surrounded by books, drinking Oolong tea from blue and white porcelain. The house is high above Lingua, Elastoplast pink, and reached up by 197 mossy steps. The views stretch from Stromboli to Mount Etna, and the only sound is birdsong. We have caught up on the last ten years, discovered that Izzy's nursery school in Massachusetts was in the town where Susan was born, and she tells me that a couple of years ago she and her husband published a book about the food and traditions of the Aeolian islands. She shows me. It's a marvellous book, full of photos of people I recognise, the recipes interwoven with interviews about island traditions, islanders' lives and memories.

I notice that Susan and Danilo have dedicated the book to

the late actor, Massimo Troisi, star of *Il Postino*, and as the conversation moves to the film, I realise Susan knows nothing about current events in Pollara.

'We were so exhausted after finishing the book. I mean, it was wonderful researching it and talking to so many people, but it got to the point where we couldn't go anywhere without people stopping to tell us how they cooked this or that. All we've wanted to do since finishing is to hide away here!'

I show her the speculator's proposal and Legambiente report and she calls her husband in from his study. He reads the papers. Nods gravely.

As I am walking to collect the girls from school, I get a text. The rumour is that when the Legambiente letter was presented to the relevant member of the council, they tore it up.

SEA NYMPHS POPPING SALMANAZARS OF CHAMPAGNE

Spring is in full swing. After months of broccoli, cauliflower and various leafy greens, seasonal eating has lost some of its charm, so the arrival of peas, mint, basil, datterino tomatoes and beautiful violet aubergines with flesh so sweet you can eat them raw is truly exhilarating. My kitchen table is as lush and colourful as the cover of an Italian cookery book. There are fresh hens' eggs too and Giuseppina has given me a huge bunch of wild asparagus. We have the first of the year's strawberries and on the island there are trees full of *nespole*, early season stone fruit with a vanilla-scented flesh that you pop out of its skin and let slide into the mouth off smooth shiny stones.

I make *pasta alla Norma* with fresh tomato and basil sauce, scattered with cubes of fried aubergine and caramel-crusted baked ricotta, a wild asparagus risotto and a mint and pea frittata. When we are invited to the festival of San Giuseppe on the other side of the island, I bake a Victoria sponge and fill it with strawberries and the first fresh cream I have been able to buy since we arrived on Salina. For it is not only the fruits of the land filling the shelves and fridges of the village shops, but the gastronomic luxuries the island shopkeepers know tourists will expect. There is fresh milk instead of the long-life stuff, which is all we've been able to get through the winter; Greek yogurt, artisan cheeses and salamis; bags of Sicilian pistachios, almonds and hazelnuts; and jars and jars of 'typical Sicilian' pestos, olives, anchovies, tuna, sundried tomatoes and capers, with chic labels and eye-watering prices.

The festival of San Giuseppe, Saint Joseph, on 19 March, featured a kind of Last Supper with villagers dressed up as Jesus, Joseph, Mary and the apostles at a long table, while the rest of us, queueing for pasta and chickpeas, watched them eat. Jesus, as Izzy pointed out at the top of her voice, ate with his mouth open.

A week later and islanders are dressing up as biblical characters once again, as Good Friday is marked with a re-enactment of the Passion of Christ by Santa Marina's am-dram group, moving through the village from piazza to piazza. It is dramatic and harrowing. Onofrio, the future mayor, has exchanged his creepy Carnevale stocking mask for red and gold robes, and is resplendent as Pontius Pilate; Christ is played by Calogero, the long-haired, bearded guitar teacher and lead vocalist in the local cover band. We stand on a wall looking down on the piazza, watching as Pilate condemns Jesus to death and four poker-faced Roman soldiers drag him inside the church. Long minutes later, Christ reappears, crying from pain, scored with scarily realistic weals and dripping blood.

A woman at the front screams, 'What have they done to Calogero?' and passes out.

A few minutes later, an ambulance siren echoes through the crowd.

'At last,' says Juno, 'the doctors are coming to help poor Jesus.'

Izzy declares she had never realised religion could be so exciting and runs off with Max, following the blooded trail of Jesus like hounds after a hare. Elettra and I decide we have had enough and take Juno to the café for ice cream. As we walk past, the paramedics are helping the woman who fainted into the ambulance.

Since we arrived in Salina, the café has never had more than a dozen people inside at a time. After a few months of seeing the same people every day, I know people from their backs, from their clothes, from the way they walk, even from the car they drive. Consequently, entering the café and finding the place heaving feels a bit like walking downstairs to find your living room full of strangers. Strangers, what's more, who look like the shiny, happy cast of a washing detergent advert. I am instantly aware of the mend in the skirt of my favourite dress and the crumbling soles of my sea-impregnated Birkenstocks. Elettra is adjusting her hoodie and hitching up her jogging pants. I catch sight of myself in the mirror behind the bar and see my hair is in its usual wild state. I try to rake it through with my fingers but am scuppered by knots. Juno has chocolate ice cream on her t-shirt and her hair has not yet recovered from a wet afternoon when she decided to cut it herself.

We get three *acqua sporcas* – fizzy water with a scoop of lemon granita – then scan the room for somewhere to sit.

'Elettra!'

Elettra looks around.

'Over there, Elettra, someone's waving.'

'Thank goodness,' says Elettra, walking over to a corner table where a man and a woman are sitting eating lemon granita. They squeeze up and make room for us.

Tanned, androgynous and athletic, with the features of Greek heroes on a red and black vase, Arturo and Ava Zavone could be twins but are brother and sister. Elettra tells me that Arturo runs the island's best bakery, and that his bread is wonderful, slow-risen and caramel-crusted, and reason enough for taking the bus to the village of Leni where he lives. The bakery is an old family business and Ava tells us that no grains are grown on the island any more, that only the oldest islanders can remember, or remember being told about, the days when the terraced mountainsides were green with grain. *Emerald green, they were in spring, green like you see in films about Ireland, golden in summer.* Ava has plans to change that, she says, to plant wheat in a field behind her house, to experiment with different indigenous Sicilian varieties to see which ones are most suited to conditions on Salina. She is opening a home restaurant, where people can come and sit on her terrace and eat simple, traditional Aeolian dishes, home-cooked and home-grown. They are just telling me about how their sister Simonetta makes cheese from goats her husband tends and honey from their own bees, when a slight man with curly brown hair and gentle eyes walks over to us and says, 'Is one of you Ros? I'm Francesco.'

'The geologist? Thank you so much for those bathymetric maps!'

'I'm not so sure she should be thanking you,' quips Elettra. 'They terrified her.'

'Not terrified, they just ... made me think a lot.'

Francesco pats my hand. 'Made you see things differently?'

'Exactly.'

'Andrea, over there, thought you might be you.' He points at a man in a faded cotton cap, shorts and t-shirt, who comes over with two more lemon granitas. He is deeply tanned, with spiky white hair, dimples, the grooved face of a smoker and the sinewy, muscled body of a fly-weight boxer.

'Andrea runs Amphibia, you know, the diving school here,' says Francesco. 'But in low season he also works as our diver and provides our boats.' He goes on to explain that he has been sent by the INGV, Italy's institute of geophysics and volcanology, to monitor emissions of volcanic gas on the seabed near Panarea.

'The *bollicini*, the bubbles!' says Elettra.

'The ones you told me about? *The Little Mermaid* bubbles?'

'I want to see *Little Mermaid* bubbles,' says Juno.

Andrea looks at Francesco. 'No reason why not? Are you free tomorrow?'

The next afternoon Andrea and Francesco pick us up in a magnificent grey and white RIB, and we speed over a glassy sea towards the cliffs of Panarea, glinting in the sun. The bubbles, Francesco tells us, appeared in November 2002. Fishermen spotted huge white plumes and when they were investigated, it was discovered they had been caused by massive columns of gas bubbles rising from the seabed. Until then, the scientific consensus was that Panarea was extinct. Which I take to mean that where volcanoes are concerned, nothing is certain.

As Andrea steers the RIB gently between pinnacles of fudge-gold rock that looks good enough to lick, it becomes clear that the

island's familiar rhino-shaped silhouette is an optical illusion and
that Panarea is formed of several islets. Below a rock called Lisca
Bianca, Andrea cuts the engine, Francesco throws down an anchor
and we put on masks and snorkels, while Andrea convinces me to
let Juno swim without armbands – 'I'll teach her how I taught my
kids.' Then, in we jump.

Below us, vast shoals of bubbles, iridescent in the sunlight,
rise up from a vent in the seabed, as if sea nymphs were popping
Salmanazars of champagne. Ahead of me, Juno is kicking through
the water alongside Andrea, a hand flat on his back. As I watch,
she glides away from him, following a school of tiny blue fish. He
swims beside her, keeping her in arm's reach, glances back to me
and gives me a thumbs-up. What a place to learn to swim.

MAESTRA GRADGRIND AND THE DOLPHINS

'Oh my God, I don't believe it!'

Izzy is sitting at a table outside Da Alfredo doing her Italian homework with a strawberry granita to help alleviate the boredom, while Juno and Max play on the rocks, and Emma and I sit on the wall. It is warm now, mid-April, every day longer than the last, and we've got into the habit of giving the children picnic lunches on the beach after school. Juno is loving school with Maestra Giulia, singing songs in Italian when she sits on the loo, asking for *acqua* instead of water and demanding a *caramella* (sweet) every time she falls over because that is what happens if they fall over at school.

Izzy is having less fun, her teacher an apparently dedicated follower of Gradgrindian pedagogy. There is no classroom library, no story time, no books in the school at all, as far as I can see. The children are taught to read not by reading, but by learning to write a different letter, one at a time – a hitherto unsuspected disadvantage of a phonetic language. Every few days, Izzy comes home with a page of a specified letter to copy out in her exercise book, written in upper-case and lower-case print and upper- and lower-case cursive. The next step is to circle which of several pictures begin with the letter of the day, on which she can expect to be 'interrogated' the next morning. Since the time I had to drag Piero from the kitchen to ask him what the hell the Italian for funnel was, I bring a pocket dictionary to the beach.

'Mummy, Mum, come and see! I really don't believe it!'

I roll off the warm wall and join her, wondering what lexicographical treat is in store for me. She has finished writing her page of ninety-six Qs and is pointing at a page towards the back of her Italian workbook.

'It's Pippi Longstocking! I don't believe it! Imagine finding Pippi Longstocking in the most boring book in the world, my *libro scolastico*. AND' – she points at a clumsy illustration of Pippi with scrubbing brushes on her feet – 'it's the bit where she scrubs the kitchen floor! Just WAIT till I tell Maestra Agata that we ACTUALLY did that at Ella's Pippi Longstocking party and that then we made cookies on the floor.'

I haven't yet met Izzy's teacher, just caught a glimpse of a wing of blue-black hair, a determined jaw, black anorak and jeans as she flees the school every lunchtime to catch the hydrofoil back to the mainland. Izzy reports that she doesn't smoke, look at jewellery catalogues or talk on the phone, but that the children are scared of her. From what Izzy has reported, she appears to consider the island much as a Victorian educator might have viewed the slums of Liverpool, frequently telling the kids to their faces that they have been born into a life of *social and economic disadvantage*, and consequently have to *work much harder than children with the fortune to have been born in the civilised world* in order to avoid a *life of savagery or destitution*. The notion of a child-centred education, or that an island from which you can see three active volcanoes has anything whatsoever to inspire a child, seems not to have crossed her mind. There has been no sign so far of any *joie di vivre* whatsoever, and I somehow doubt that Izzy's effervescent retelling of a wild kids' party in Massachusetts is going to be met with enthusiasm.

'I don't know, Izzy. She'll probably just make some devastating comment about how unhygienic it would be to make cookies on the floor,' says Emma.

'But Yoshi said her kitchen floor was ever so clean after we'd scrubbed it. When Pippi went to school, Emma, she lay down on the floor to draw because she said the paper wasn't big enough to draw her horse. I'd like to do that.'

'Probably better not to, at school anyway.'

Emma raises an eyebrow.

'Why don't you take your Pippi book instead?' Her prized possession is a beautiful hardback edition quirkily illustrated by Lauren Child, creator of *Charlie and Lola*. 'Surely we've got to do something about getting books into the school,' I say to Emma. 'And surely that would be the perfect start, the book from which a reading extract comes?'

'I wouldn't be so sure. It's in English for a start.'

'Ah. So, it needs to be an Italian book? Well, we've got Pippi in Italian too.'

'But you'll need to find a watertight pretext for taking it in.'

'But this is crazy, insane, we're simply talking about taking a book to a school that doesn't have any.'

'I know, but sometimes things that would be absolutely normal in England – no, more than normal, taken for granted so much so that no one would even give the alternative a moment's thought – things like this, like the idea that having books in a school is a good thing, full stop, things like this are seen here as radical, bizarre or even incomprehensible.'

We are interrupted by an excited squealing from the beach and run over to the wall to see Juno and Max standing on the rocks, waving, shouting, pointing.

'Dolphins!'

'*Delfini!*' I shout over my shoulder.

'*Delfini!*' shouts Piero, running out of the bar followed by the rest of the kitchen staff.

It's a magical sight, the dolphins leaping, joyous, somersaulting.

'Perhaps,' says Emma, 'she should take Max's book on dolphins? Just in case Maestra Agata thinks Pippi too anarchic.'

'What does anarchic mean?' asks Izzy.

'Rebellious, questioning the way things are done or doing things differently.'

'Like Pippi?'

'Yes.'

'Like me on Favignana when I wore different coloured socks to school?'

'Exactly.'

But Emma is right. There can't be a teacher on the planet who could object to a book about dolphins.

I was wrong.

Izzy runs out of school, incandescent with injustice.

'I told Maestra Agata that we had seen dolphins, and looked at the photos in the book, and worked out they were bottlenose, and I showed her the book, and she said, 'THIS BOOK HAS NOTHING WHATSOEVER TO DO WITH THIS SCHOOL!'

'How dare you?' I say to the teacher.

'This is absurd,' I say.

'My daughter brought in an educational book.'

'How can you have a school with no books?'

'How can you expect children to love reading if they have no books?'

'How can you expand their world if they have no books?'

'Who do you think you are?' she asks.

'You are about to find out,' I say.

THE BATTLE OF
STONE SOUP

I do not lose my temper easily, cannot even remember the last time I did so. This inability to vent my anger is not an aspect of my character I am proud of because it comes from a place of weakness. I don't like losing my cool and I prefer to keep my stronger opinions hidden, for fear of them being demolished by people who are better at arguing than I am.

'But this was different,' says Emma. 'You were not only defending your child but standing up for something you believe in passionately.'

'It would have been better if I could have approached the issue with a bit of poise. That way, at least, I could have felt dignified and ...'

'Superior?' Emma smiles.

Oh my God, Emma knows me well. 'Exactly,' I admit. 'But I am right, she is wrong, and I am not giving in. Is it really arrogance if you actually DO know best? I mean, there can be no valid argument whatsoever against having books in school.'

'Well,' says Emma, 'a little diplomacy wouldn't come amiss.'

We begin to talk to other mothers about books and reading, and it soon becomes obvious that the first obstacle we need to demolish is the idea that books belong to an intellectual world the islanders feel excluded from. The idea of giving a child a book as a birthday present is met with horror, and the notion that books could be as fun, funny and entertaining as film and TV with scepticism.

The women we speak to are bright, able, loving mothers who want the best for their children, but their own schooling has left them with the idea that books are difficult, boring and irrelevant, to be suffered not enjoyed. We tell them about World Book Day, when children go to school dressed as a favourite book character, but they are just perplexed. I suspect that trying to introduce World Book Day here might reek of cultural colonialism.

It astonishes me, indeed appals me, that there is no sign of child-centred learning in the land that gave birth to Maria Montessori. I wonder if things are different off the island or beyond Sicily; here, the emphasis is on learning by rote and repetition, with little interest in the development of critical thinking, curiosity, originality or imagination. Teaching children to have obedient minds worries me. If they learn to simply accept all they are told, how will they ever be able to navigate the truths, lies and shadow plays of the digital world? So far, Izzy's internet experience is limited to CBBC but it won't be long before she can read and write enough to navigate the internet alone. I don't want her to believe that everything she sees, reads or hears is true.

'We can't take on the entire Italian education system.'

'OK,' I say, 'we are not going to revolutionise the entire Italian education system. Although we should. But we can make a start. Introduce at least something that is child-centred.'

'Not child-centred. Island-centred.'

Emma is a genius.

'Stone soup,' I say. 'Ingredients, three kilograms of pebbles, preferably covered with seaweed, four tablespoons of olive oil, two onions, 600g of tomatoes, 200g *pani caliatu*.'

Emma and I are sitting in the piazza reading Susan and Danilo's book about the gastronomic traditions of the Aeolian islands. The book is called *Pani Caliatu*, after the rings of hard, rusk-like barley bread that formed the islands' staple food for centuries. It was made every month in huge ovens, baked once at a high temperature, then dried out slowly overnight as the oven cooled. Rock hard, it lasted for ever. Sailors took it to sea strung together like giant beads on a necklace and it was most simply prepared by being softened in water and dressed with oil, anchovies, capers and oregano. Stone soup is a genuine recipe for a broth flavoured with sea pebbles; another is *ova a niputiddata*, a broth infused with nepitella, the wild mint that grows everywhere, garlic, a few tomatoes and, if you were lucky, a poached egg.

Pani Caliatu is as much about the islanders as about their food. Susan and Danilo travelled the archipelago for years, talking to locals and collecting life stories along with recipes. There are tales in the book that speak of a world where wheat flour and pasta were rare luxuries, of emigration and returns, of lives in Australia dreaming of Aeolian pomodorini, of frugality, dignity and change, and of the love story of Emma and Gaetano. The photos eschew postcard prettiness and instead celebrate the beauty of abandoned houses and forgotten corners and the dignity of everyday life. Tough, tanned hands pull in nets, weave lobster traps, prise shellfish off basalt; nimble white hands knead dough, twist pasta, create micro-embroideries of pastry for Christmas biscuits filled with dried figs, almonds, sweetened with syrups of wine must and prickly pear. The recipes speak eloquently of poverty and a certain spirited determination to find flavour – even complexity of flavour – in ingredients that cost little or nothing: wild fennel, capers, anchovies, tomatoes, olive oil.

We have decided that the best way to launch our campaign to promote the joy of reading would be a festival inspired by Susan and Danilo's book. We will celebrate the gastronomic traditions of Salina at the same time as showing the kids – and reminding parents – that the islanders and the islands are interesting enough to have a book written about them. I call Susan who is enthusiastic, but practical too.

'I don't really think we can make stone soup. A cauldron of boiling water, slimy sea pebbles and 127 children might be a literal recipe for disaster. And we can't do anything until you get permission from the new Preside.'

Now that, I think, could be the real problem. The Preside, who heads primary schools across the archipelago, has called an extraordinary meeting of all the Santa Marina school parents. She started work at Easter; no one knows anything about her and no one has ever met her. I fear the meeting may have been provoked by my tirade at the teacher, but we finish writing the proposal and send it to her anyway.

PANI CALIATU DAY

The parents of Santa Marina and Lingua are crammed into the nursery school, some of us sitting on miniature chairs, others leaning at the back. There is an unholy racket, which shows no sign of abating when a woman dressed in loose, raw linen in beautiful shades of burnt umber, cream and terracotta, walks in and sits on the desk. She smiles, meets eyes, and when still people go on talking, she stands up and claps her hands. Eventually a hush falls.

'Good afternoon, everyone.' She speaks gently but firmly. 'I am the Preside and I would like to begin by asking each of you something very important. The acoustics in here are terrible and if we all talk at once, we'll hear nothing and all go home with headaches. So, can I ask you to please stay quiet while I speak and then, if you have anything to say, I will give you time, one by one. I am afraid as I don't know your names, you will have to put your hands up.'

The Preside tells us she worked for many years with children in South America and is now really excited to have this new job on the islands. Then, after running through various notices and notifications, she looks up and says, 'Are Ros and Emma here?'

I stand up and brace myself for a reprimand.

'Now, these two English mothers have had a wonderful idea …'

As we leave, the Maestra stops me and says through a lipsticked rictus, 'I don't know why you are wasting your time. Your children have books. Why bother about the others?'

*

243

'Here is the courtyard,' says Antonio Brundù. 'There's running water and a sink, and we can put out a long table for preparing the tomatoes. If you want to show a video, then we can bring a screen in from the children's library.'

'There's a children's library?' I didn't even know there was an adult library.

'It's only small,' says Antonio, 'but come and see.'

The venue for *Pani Caliatu* Day is the island's small and under-used cultural centre, run by Antonio Brundù, a slight, bespectacled and carefully spoken intellectual who is thrilled about our project and the chance it gives not only to let the children celebrate island traditions but to meet an author. The children's library is small but its shelves are packed with Italian versions of the colourful contemporary information books that fill our house.

'It's such a shame,' says Antonio, 'that no one ever comes. I've tried to encourage the schools but to no avail.'

'But these are amazing,' I say, leafing through a beautifully illustrated book on cetaceans. 'Exactly what the kids need.' I pick up a brightly coloured book about volcanoes.

'Borrow as many as you like and take them to the school if you want.'

'Aah,' says Emma, 'I'm not sure that will go down too well.'

'Look at this,' I say. 'Instructions on how to make a volcano. Why don't we do that too? Show kids that books can be fun! That it's not just about sitting down and reading, but they can give you ideas about doing things?'

'With 127 children?' says Emma.

'Ingredients for a volcano!' shouts Izzy. 'Wait, what does that say? Bi-car-bona ...'

'Bicarbonate of soda!' shouts Ivo.

'Yes!' shout the other kids.

'Vinegar?' shouts Izzy.

'Yes!'

'Tomato ketchup?'

'Yes!'

'Washing up liquid?'

'Yes.'

'Red dye?'

'Yup.'

'Funnel, water, empty water bottle?'

'Yes, yes and yes.'

We are on a sandy patch of beach building a volcano. It's a sunny afternoon and over on the horizon we can see Stromboli smoking gently. We ditched the notion of getting all 127 of the island's children together to build a volcano, and instead have eight, including Ivo and his little sister, Maia, Luca, Federico and the Carabiniero's daughter, Gaia, who shares Juno and Max's love of climbing rocks. Afterwards, we are to have a beach barbecue to continue the theme of fire. Ivo and Izzy, as the only ones who can read, are organising the younger ones.

Emma videos us filling a plastic bottle with tomato ketchup, red food dye, washing up liquid and bicarbonate of soda, and burying it up to the lid in a cone of black sand. The kids add a 'village' of white pumice stones and trees of seagrass, then I remove the bottle top and pour in vinegar. The 'lava' shoots up high in a disgusting froth of pink, vinegary foam and slithers down the volcano.

'*Eruzione!*' shout the kids as the froth narrowly misses the village.

'Can we make a volcano with real fire now?' asks Luca.

'I'm afraid not,' says Emma. 'That might be a little bit too dangerous. But we are going to make a fire to cook food.'

I light the fire and let the kids, carefully supervised, take turns to fan the flames.

'Do you think that's how people first got fire? From volcanoes?' asks Ivo.

The same thing had occurred to me and indeed, a bit of research indicated that current archaeological thinking is that it is highly likely.

'I think people who lived near volcanoes would definitely have used the fire.'

'Maybe that's how cooking started,' says Izzy. 'Chickens getting roasted on a volcano and people finding out they were yummy.'

'I don't think they had chickens.'

'What did they have, then?' asks Ivo.

'From what I have read, there were giant dormice and tiny hairy elephants, or mammoths.'

'They ate roast elephant and roast mouse?'

'Yuk.'

'In the Second World War,' I say, 'when there wasn't much food, people in England were taught to make squirrel soup.'

'Really?' says Emma.

'Yuk,' says Izzy.

'Official advice from the Ministry of Food,' I say.

'What about roast dinosaurs?' snarls Federico, baring his teeth.

'When the dinosaurs were about, not only were there no people but the islands didn't exist at all.'

'It was just sea?' The kids look out to Stromboli. 'No islands at all?'

'No islands. And for hundreds and thousands of years, there wasn't even sea. It all dried up.'

'So we could have walked to Palermo?' says Izzy.

'We could have walked all the way to Africa,' I say. 'Except that human beings didn't exist yet.'

'And then it filled up again?'

'Like a giant waterfall?'

'Like a giant toilet?'

Having only read half a Wikipedia entry on the Messinian salinity crisis, I am not sure how well equipped I am to explain it to the children, so change the subject by laying thin slices of chicken on a plate for them to scatter with oregano and salt.

'If you had all just arrived on the island and there was nobody here, there had never been anybody, you were the first people ever to land on Salina, what would you eat?' asks Emma.

'Roast elephant.'

'But how would you catch one?'

'With a gun!' Federico shadow-machine-guns the beach.

'You have no guns, you have absolutely nothing, only what is on the island.'

'Throw stones!' shouts Luca.

'That's not that easy,' says Izzy. 'We might miss.'

'Catch fish,' says Max.

'What with? No nets, no twine ...'

'Soup!' says Ivo. 'My nonna says when they had nothing to eat, they used to collect *finocchietto* and *rapuddi* and make soup.'

'And my nonno says *his* nonna used to make soup out of stones,' says Luca.

'Stupid! You can't make soup out of stones,' says Federico.

'Well, actually,' I say, 'funny you should say that but Luca is right, people used to make soup out of sea pebbles. Anyone for stone soup?'

Emma gives me one of her looks.

To Emma's relief, not one of the kids wants to try making stone soup, so I watch the fire while they gather a bundle of the bamboo canes that wash up on the beach and start trying to make a tipi. Izzy considers ripping up her skirt to tie the canes together, but Emma persuades her to buy string from the shop then helps them tie the canes together to make a wonky tipi with just about enough space inside for Juno or Gaia, the smallest. Federico places himself on shadow machine-gun watch; Luca, Max, Gaia and Juno go down to the water to see if they can catch fish in their hands, and Izzy and Ivo begin gathering canes for a second shelter, when something flies through the air and hits Izzy's behind. Another projectile follows and then another. Izzy and Ivo shout *run!* and race to the shore. Whatever the missiles are, they seem to be coming from the direction of the piazza. I glance up just in time to see Michelangelo and his skinny friend holding a bucket from which they are pelting the beach with something gelatinous, before ducking down out of sight behind the wall.

'*Medusa!*' shouts Izzy.

Jellyfish.

Michelangelo hurls another jellyfish, this time narrowly missing Izzy's foot.

'Stop!' I shout, running towards them.

'I hate you!' Izzy shouts.

'*Vaffanculo!*' shouts Luca.

Then Izzy grabs a cane and runs towards the lads. They are laughing at her, taunting her.

'Come here, little girl!'

'Come here, little English girl.'

I start running across the pebbles but trip and fall.

Izzy is up in the piazza now, brandishing her cane.

'You wouldn't dare, little girl, you wouldn't ...'

I pull myself to my feet just in time to see Izzy whack Michelangelo across the cheek with all her force. Either by luck or by the power of the gods of vengeance, the cane strikes its target. Michelangelo yelps then scarpers.

'His cheek was red. Did you see, Mum? AND I am sure there were tears in his eyes.'

My proudest, if not my most politically correct, moment of parenting so far.

I am in Arturo's bakery with Ava, waiting to collect enough *pani caliatu* to feed 127 children. The kitchen door opens, filling the bakery with a wonderful aroma of rosemary focaccia, but as Arturo joins us I can see he is looking anxious.

'Those people who are wanting to build in Pollara?' he says to Ava, handing me a box full of *pani caliatu*, 'I just came across them, all dressed in suits and shades like movie gangsters, over in Valle Spina looking at that ruin.'

'But it's just a shed, it's tiny,' says Ava. 'What could they do with that?'

'Where's Valle Spina?' I ask.

'In the middle of nowhere, about forty minutes' walk from the village, just off the path that goes to Pollara.' I remember the bothy from my Christmas walk. 'With no danger of anyone seeing them, then, if they decide to create a few ruins,' I say.

'You're talking about the "didactic farm"?' A portly man with a moustache walks into the bakery. 'Well, I have my concerns about that. The farm opens, time passes and then, who knows, maybe the donkeys die, the plants dry out and all that remains will be the buildings ...'

Ready to be turned into a luxury hotel, I wonder.

As I am taking the bag of *pani caliatu* up to the library, a text arrives.

Word is that a journalist from *L'Espresso* is going to cover the story. *L'Espresso* is Italy's leading news magazine. Can it really be true?

Children at Susan's slide show of photographs from the book cry out with excitement when they recognise an auntie, a house, a boat, a kitchen, a garden. *My granny, my KITCHEN, in a book? I can't believe it!* Then they are up to their elbows in bowls of tomatoes, oil, oregano and *pani caliatu*, mixing with their fingers, most of them deep in concentration, chatting in that easy way people of any age do when cooking together. I spot Federico flicking tomato juice into Luca's hair but as Luca doesn't notice I decide to turn a blind eye. When the food is ready they squeeze in together along the *bisuoli* of the courtyard with plates of *pani caliatu* on their knees, eating, chattering, joking, laughing. I catch Michelangelo lifting Juno up so that she can reach a bowl.

We show the video we made of the volcano. Then Emma plays storytelling games with the younger children while the Preside helps the older kids write reportage. Every twenty minutes or so, I take a small group into the children's library. The Preside gave us funds for rugs and cushions, and we've laid out open the most beautifully illustrated books to catch the children's eyes, so that when they walk in they are surrounded by scenes of sea creatures, butterflies, birds, deserts, oceans, soldiers, mummies, Roman towns, Greek temples, Einstein, Cleopatra, cake recipes and chemical experiments. There is not one child who is not interested. We've decided that reading is less important than just wanting to look at the books, so we give them free rein and then tell them to choose their favourite pages to make a display for the next group. I have an actual lump in my throat when Michelangelo, beaming, comes up to show me a book on the most famous Roman villa in Sicily, at Piazza Armerina. The page is open at the mosaic of a lion killing a horse.

'Look,' he says, 'it's all made of tiny pieces. Imagine being able to do that.' He hesitates, blushing. 'I am sorry about throwing jellyfish. Next time you make a volcano, I can help?'

I was wrong about the neck tattoo.

SUMMERTIME

School does not officially finish until early June but by mid-May, the temperature is tipping into the high twenties and most of the children stay at home. As mothers begin their seasonal jobs in hotels, boutiques and restaurants, first thing every morning, grannies, great-aunties and grown-up siblings bring kids to the beach and set up camp, colonising their chosen patch with zingy new beach towels, sun umbrellas, loungers, chairs and kilos of food and drink in cool bags.

Izzy instantly notices that all the girls have new swimsuits – and not just one, but two or three, because Italians think it unhealthy not to change out of a costume as soon as it is wet. She also points out that the girls have sarongs, kaftans, wraps to match their costumes, and one pair of sandals to walk to the beach, another to wear on the beach and yet another to wear in the water. Izzy's and Juno's beachwear is faded, worn, and they have spent so much of the year barefoot that they run with insouciance over pebbles. I examine the soles of their feet, expecting them to be leathery and calloused, but the skin is as soft as ever, just, it seems, thicker, better padded.

Rough Guides pays me so we go on a shopping spree to Lipari. Izzy stands at the door of UPIM in amazement – 'You can buy anything here, everything in the world!' The girls dance to the hydrofoil, joyous with a rainbow each of new bikinis, crocs, sarongs and kaftans.

Summer afternoons are too hot to be outside, so after lunch, the girls sit inside painting volcanoes on pebbles and making bracelets to sell at a *bancarella*, the stall they set up on the piazza wall every evening, along with exotic shells and coral from a souvenir shop in Brighton, which Izzy claims to have dived for off the coast of Lingua.

One morning, we find a surfboard with its back end broken off washed up on the beach, which they rename the canoe. Gaetano digs out some oars, and they spend hours and hours paddling about the bay, pretending to be explorers, looking like the line drawings in *Swallows and Amazons*. My fears of tidal waves and earthquakes have melted with the heat, and, after all, I think, Emma said earthquakes happen in winter.

We come down to the beach a few days later to find a man in his late fifties wearing baggy shorts, wellies and a scarlet t-shirt with the word BAGNINO emblazoned across his back plodding along the water's edge picking up jellyfish with a fishing net. He tells us he is the council's official lifeguard. Having created a little mountain of jellyfish, he retires to a dining chair under a faded umbrella and watches the swimmers. Whether he would have the speed or agility to rush to the aid of a swimmer in difficulty seems unlikely. Fortunately, Izzy and Juno are good swimmers now, though we have made an armband-on-canoe rule for Juno and Max, just in case.

Every week brings more mothers and children – from Messina, Palermo, Milan, Naples, Florence, Rome – and my mind grows rich with the stories of other lives, the differences, resonances and parallels of woman- and parenthood intertwining as we lie on the beach, cool off in the water, drink Aperol spritzes and *acqua sporca*s, think out loud, worry out loud, laugh, cry and wonder at the absurdity and glory and tragedy of it all. Sonia, condemned to a summer of factor 50, long sleeves and a brimmed hat because she is in the middle of filming and continuity have begged her to not get a tan; Rosaria, with blood-chilling stories of being a medic for Mafiosi at a high-security jail in Naples; Elena, who is juggling writing a thriller with a job in finance and ailing parents to care for; Federica, who arrives with two children, a sailing boat and a blue

Amazonian parrot and discovers she is pregnant; Annamaria, who loves the remotest places on the island as much as I do; Giorgia with whom I can share my fragility. We rarely eat alone, but there's no fussing with dinner parties or preparations. It's all spur of the moment, spontaneous. We cook together, drink together, wash up together and the food is always delicious because Aeolian ingredients are so intense.

With husbands in the cities working, time is elastic, and these female-led families mix and mingle, sharing ways of doing things as easily as we mothers do our problems and worries. Boundaries melt. I am rarely alone, but never feel I need to be alone, and I wonder how I'll adjust to island life again once they have gone.

VALLE SPINA

'**Y**ou can't go hiking in flip-flops, Giuseppina,' says Emma.
     'If I can walk up the mountain, collect olives, climb the trees to get the olives AND then come back down carrying a sack of olives wearing flip-flops, I can stroll along to this Valle Spina for a picnic. In fact,' she says, kicking off the flip-flops, 'I could do it barefoot.'

'So could I,' says Juno, kicking off her crocs.

'And me,' says Max, kicking his off too.

'Shall we see what Arturo thinks?' I say.

'Yay!' says Juno.

'Not about you, Juno, about Giuseppina.'

There are about twenty of us, gathered outside a B&B in Leni, ready to walk to Valle Spina for a picnic. It's just before sunset and the sea is a turquoise lake, the golden light making outlines crisp, details precise, colours intense, finding pinks, corals and greens in the rocky terraces. You can see why photographers like early evening light.

The first ten days of September were days of departure, days of tears and hugs from mothers and children alike, of standing on the port waving at ferries and feeling the distinctive shape and silence of each absence. It was as if each family had its own unique colours, sounds, words, smiles, laughter. Izzy slept with a hand-me-down sarong given by her new best friend, Anna; I had a cardigan that still smelled of Annamaria's soap; the kitchen became a treasure chest of other peoples' leftover groceries and I discovered that a half-full jar of jam donated by Giorgia could make me want to cry. It was the same for Emma. I found her too, one day, in tears over a jar of miso left by Annamaria. For the first time in months my phone was silent, so when I heard the Nokia tune a few days ago, it took a while to realise it was for me.

It was Ava, sounding excited. 'Arturo swore me to secrecy, Rosie, but I can tell you now,' she said. 'Remember the men in suits he said he saw out at Valle Spina? Well, he did a bit of digging and found out they *were* working for that same property speculator. That guy's bought up half of Pollara, you know, a thousand square metres, people are saying, and ...'

'And Arturo?' I was fed up now of the rumours, the same ones going round and round, gathering embroideries and embellishments with each circuit. Island imaginations have now been let loose on who may lie behind the property speculator. A Hollywood film star? Dolce and Gabbana? A Mafia boss? A Mafia boss's lover? Or, as was whispered to me last week, the ghost of Massimo Troisi.

'Arturo found out who owned the land at Valle Spina, then formed a little consortium. He found a dozen or so villagers who had some savings they were willing to invest. We didn't have much, nothing like the amount the speculator had offered, but Arturo went to meet the landowner and by the end of the conversation he had completely come over to our point of view. He actually *dropped* the price to match what we had cobbled together! Unbelievable!'

We are all in Leni because the Valle Spina consortium have signed the contract on the bothy and twenty hectares of land. This evening, Arturo tells us, we are guinea pigs. In order to raise money to maintain the land, the consortium is planning to take hikers on guided walks at sunset, followed by a barbecue at the bothy and a walk back in the dark with head torches.

Softly spoken but resolute, with a decisive instinct for fair play, I am more than a bit in awe of Arturo. He didn't grumble and gossip, lose his temper, or rant and rage, he just decided to be practical, and other people trusted him enough to follow his lead. Ava thinks he should stand as mayor of Leni, though I suspect nothing would induce him to enter politics. For a start, he always thinks before he speaks.

We do not look anything like the little groups of Swiss, British and French hikers who pour into the island every spring and autumn to climb the mountain. There's no Rohan clothing, no walking poles, not a hiking boot in sight. Giuseppina is in her favourite dress, decorated with tennis rackets; Max and Juno are wearing pirate hats; Izzy has a tutu over her shorts and is admiring Tangerine Man's daughter's silver trainers. Half a dozen of us have rucksacks but the rest are carrying cool bags heavy with food. Elettra and I are swinging a five-litre flagon of wine between us in a tote bag and Giuseppina's carrying a pot of something that is still warm, wrapped up in a faded linen tea towel. Tangerine Man has his arms around a giant watermelon.

'Well Arturo? Can she go in her flip-flops or not?'

Arturo sighs and looks at Giuseppina's feet. 'If it's true, she climbs to her olive grove in flip-flops, there's not a lot I can say ...'

Giuseppina puffs her chest out like a proud chicken, gives Emma a hard stare worthy of Paddington and leads the way out of the village.

It is an extraordinary path, easy, following one of the terraces that wrap around the sheer slopes of the mountain high above the sea, whose turquoise has now been joined by a hint of opalescence. We can see Vulcano entirely for once, its sulphur-stained crater steaming, and I wonder why we never worry about this volcano, always about Stromboli. Francesco, the geologist, is here, so I hang back to ask him why and he says that for volcanologists, Vulcano is more worrying, less predictable, all those toxic gases trapped, and that the fear is one day it just might blow. We walk on and although for a moment, I think, I need to take that in, visualise it, the apocalypse of Vulcano, I realise that I don't want to, because everywhere my eyes rest there is beauty, and why imagine the end of beauty before you have enjoyed it.

The path itself changes colour with the bedrock, from purple to ochre to auburn to charcoal to soft putty grey, with a sticky grit that clings to shoes, feet and ankles. The colours of the rocks that wall the terraces intensify by the minute in the lowering sun, coral, violet and Van Gogh golds dancing with the lime green and orange of lichen. The artemisia is silver, the summer-dried fennel head-high, the skeletal geometries of seed heads irresistible to Tanino, Valle Spina's dedicated photographer. It is he who notices our shadows. 'Stop,' he says. 'Look. Our shadows are green.' And so they are, a pink- and violet-edged green, otherworldly as the Aurora Borealis. *A miracle*, says Giuseppina; *a trick of the light*, says Tanino; *magic*, says Izzy. Here we all are, I think, projected on the rock, children of the volcano. As the path rises to a rocky promontory, the procession halts, *shhhh* passed back in a Chinese whisper, followed by *listen* and then silence. We stand in a row along the path in silence. A bird singing. The sound of my breath. A cough. A sigh.

Then –

Voices.

Girls' voices. Ringing clear as bells from far below.

Shhh.

I lean on a warm slab of weathered andesite, where rainwater has gathered in an almost perfect semi-spherical hollow. It rained last week and I was glad, watched it turn the dry earth around my broccoli seedlings to chocolate mud. Below the rock is a tiny ruined homestead. The kind of place a young wife might tie the end of a knotted rope tight around the rock and let it cascade to the sea. Just in case.

Voices again. Laughter ringing.

Look.

A common intake of breath.

We are as one in disbelief at what we are seeing.

Two girls far below.

Walking *on* the water.

Sirens.

Sirens?

Not walking but floating, gliding, floating on their feet.

Not on the water. Above it. Just above it. *Can you see? There's a gap between their feet and the water.*

Gliding.

Long hair, long bodies. Slender and golden on opalescent water.

Arms. Their arms.

They move with their arms.

Magic.

Majare.

Mermaids.

Nereids.

A mirage.

Fata Morgana?

Fata Morgana!

Giuseppina crosses herself.

Fata Morgana!

'Fata Morgana mirages are upside down,' says Francesco the Geologist.

'They're just ladies standing on surfboards,' says Izzy.

The path ends on the brink of a precipitous drop, vertiginous scree in petrified flow squeezed between jags of rock. The shadowed sea laps far below. On the far side of the ravine, a cliff rises so high we have to lean our heads right back, crane our necks, arch back, back and back, to see red-gold pinnacles cathedral-like against the deep blue sky. A bleat, hollow against the rock, answered by another. 'Goats,' whispers Juno. White dots, two, three, no four, clinging to a cleft in the pinnacle. *Their ricotta must taste of stone.* The setting sun ignites the rock, russet and rose, apricot and gold, as if its molten beginnings were a whisper away. Something makes us all fall silent, and we stand and watch the cliff face, as people in the past might have gazed at a basilica, a temple or a henge.

Later that evening, after feasting on barbecued sausages and Giuseppina's cauldron of slow-simmered borlotti beans, we sit around the fire outside the bothy, sipping wine and nibbling watermelon in the starlight. We'd sung while Arturo played guitar

– the Beatles, Bob Dylan and old Sicilian folk songs – and now the conversation is flying, dialect words well-worn as a soft, old leather ball, handled and tossed from one person to another. Joke follows joke, laughter follows laughter, gasp trips over gasp, and I feel my repertoire of Sicilian dialect increase with every sally. It is like a circle dance, I think, where no one leads or dominates, and when I dare to make a joke too, everyone laughs. I look around. Faces flushed with wine, food, laughter, warmed by the fire and high on the euphoric daftness that follows when a group of people, children of the volcano all of us, born, bred and adopted, have experienced something extraordinary.

SALINA, SEPTEMBER 2023

There was certainly some kind of magic in the air that evening. Afterwards, those who believed in God spoke of a sense of feeling blessed, while those of a more pantheistic bent said they felt the volcano thanking us. I felt blessed too but in a more temporal way, blessed by the extraordinary beauty of an evening where geology and a sunset contrived to create something sublime.

But there was more to it than that. That night was the first time I had a real sense of belonging to a community. We were united by place not mindset, and living on an island only intensified our interdependency, especially when the tourists left and the storms came. It wasn't a matter of selfless public-spiritedness. If you didn't get on with your fellows, who could you ask for help if you ran out of water or needed a rat catching or to mend a broken window?

Apart from Emma and Elettra, I rarely arranged to meet up with an islander for a drink or dinner. All our conversations – gossipy, frothy, sad, outrageous, predictable or compelling – happened when we bumped into one another by chance. This did mean that popping out to buy sugar could take two hours, but it also meant that we kept track of each other's lives, not merely with births and deaths, illnesses and recoveries, marriages and divorces, but with our ups and downs, hopes and anxieties, reflections and perplexities.

Over the years I lived on Salina, I got to know all those people well. Some lost parents, siblings, loved ones, even children; some fell in then out of love, or had their hearts betrayed; there were those who realised their hopes and dreams and those whose dreams never came true. But none succumbed to bitterness or despair.

They were kind, they cared and we almost always found something to laugh about.

Above all, among these people I could simply be myself.

AFTERWORDS

Cambridge, 7 December 2023

On my kitchen wall there is a new painting. A birthday present. A magical realist self-portrait of Juno as a young woman, spinning on the beach at Lingua, a little orange fishing boat bobbing in the sea behind her. Her dress is whisked up and slowly it dawns on me that the petticoats beneath are frilled with sea waves. And then I notice that where the skirt flies open in the middle, there is a flow of lava, and that the hem is decorated with images of Lingua, the lighthouse, lampposts along the *lungomare*, crashing waves, Da Alfredo's and, once again, that little orange boat.

Juno was eight, Izzy eleven, when I decided we had to leave Salina so that they could go to a more normal school. We moved to the Sicilian mainland and lived in Ortigia, the old part of Siracusa, golden, crumbling, Baroque and surrounded by a turquoise sea. There was a Norman castle where you could stand in the bastions and hear the sea crashing overhead, and soft sandy beaches too, and walks through a nature reserve, a children's theatre and *capoeira*. We could get pizza delivered and Juno found a shop that sold nothing but cupcakes.

But Juno was lost among the Baroque stone of Siracusa. Kicked off her crocs and climbed a lamppost on her first day at school, glaring at anyone who dared look at her. Boys tried to emulate her but skiddered down; mothers frowned and tut-tutted. I smiled, gave a tiny shrug of *sorry* and watched her. I knew she needed to be there, displaying her difference, showing she was no ordinary child, that she could be slotted into no pigeonhole, would not be tamed.

Izzy longed for England. Papered her bedroom with quotes from Panic at the Disco and had a virtual life on the internet, more comfortable with the kids she found there than her classmates. She rarely played any more. But every school holiday, every long weekend we could squeeze, we went back to Salina. Juno would leap off the hydrofoil, barefoot, dancing, singing her Salina song. *I know this bush; I know this wall; I know that tree.*

In 2015, we moved back to England. High school for Juno, sixth form college for Izzy. At first, we had no money to travel back to Sicily, and then the girls preferred to spend holidays with their father by a river on a wild estate in Ireland, with deer and a garden in the toothy ruins of a Norman castle. Then there was the pandemic and suddenly it was 2022 and seven years since any of us had been back to Salina.

I look up at Juno's painting and realise that it was probably inevitable that it was Juno who led us back.

It seems only fair that Izzy and Juno get to have the last word. I have written a book about their childhood but the story is as much – if not more – theirs. Salina happened for me in the context of a life already half-lived, a life in which I had already seen and done much. I was aware that living on a tiny Sicilian island was a choice, a rather extraordinary choice, among many other potential choices. For Juno, Salina was all she knew of the world. For Izzy, it was different. She remembered Massachusetts, remembered London, and so Salina must have felt stranger, more provisional or even random.

They have written about what Salina means to them now, aged twenty-one and twenty-four. I imagine that the shape of their years on Salina will shift in their lives, shrink or expand, change meanings as they grow older. They are both painful and wonderful for me to read. For Juno, Salina is home, while Izzy is looking, as I was eighteen years ago, for hers.

Juno

It is if I had a string somewhere under my left ribs,
tightly knotted to a similar string in you situated in
the corresponding quarter of your little frame.
— Charlotte Bronte, *Jane Eyre*

When we left Salina, I was lost at sea. The world I knew was gone and I felt torn in two. If you live somewhere where the horizon is never out of sight, you can't help wondering what lies beyond it. I spent much of my childhood longing to leave, to explore, to see something new. Once I got to see past the horizon, all I wanted to do was turn back.

Whenever I'm away from Salina, I feel the string Charlotte Bronte describes in *Jane Eyre*, a string tied between myself and Salina, a cord that is fraying at the edges but that keeps pulling at me constantly until it hurts. Even now, back in England, all these years later, I feel that pull, that physical pain that comes from being far from home. I find myself staring out at the window, at the moon at night. Knowing the same light is currently illuminating the black sea that crashes against Lingua makes the pull hurt a little less, and I'm just waiting until I can go home.

Coming back is wonderful but Salina is so isolated from the rest of the world that after a while, I can't help but feel longing of a different kind whenever I look at the horizon or a plane flying overhead. It sparks that same old need to escape, to pack a bag and move, to keep moving and never stop. So then I leave again. But

266

that string is always there, pulling at my heartstrings. I'll follow the siren song into the sea but the golden string will always pull me back home, hopefully, before I drown.

I carried the freedom I learned in Salina to Hyde Park in London, through the hell of English secondary school, all the way to Cornwall, running along on a different beach in a different country with different friends, but with the same audacity-born freedom. That is what Salina gave me. Freedom to me is eating peaches while swimming in the sea, tasting sweet fruit and the salt water on your lips mix, not worrying about getting sticky because the waves will wash you; freedom tastes like sweet peaches and sea salt-crusted lips. Once you taste freedom, you can't go back.

A lot of my childhood was filled with bossy Sicilian ladies telling me what to do: teachers instructing me not to speak English to Max in school, old ladies telling me I would die of cold, should eat more, eat less, believe in God, trust in Jesus, put my shoes on. My parents, instead, both of them, taught me the power of will. They both paved their own paths and even though those paths diverged, they were both built in the name of freedom and the will to pursue it.

Most people on the island don't know the freedom that I did, especially the girls and women. When I was seven, I told a girl I didn't believe in God and she told me, in a very serious tone, that I was going to hell. I wasn't particularly worried since I didn't believe in hell. The thing about believing in a higher power is that you will always have to play a subservient role. If I had grown up in a less religious culture, I might have had a more positive opinion of the Christian God, but as it stands, I would rather burn in hell by force of my own will than languish in heaven as a reward for being obedient.

I've had a fondness for the Ancient Roman gods ever since I found out I was named after the queen of the gods herself. They felt more real to me than the God my teachers were always banging on about. I knew Neptune – I swam in his sea every day; I knew Jove – he rattled my bedroom shutters every night. I knew Juno. Being named after the queen of the gods made me feel strong (and boosted my ego). I still have a soft spot for the old gods and have kept up my relationship with them by studying them at university. There's something ancient and primal about Salina, and that is why many of the people who live here need to believe that San Bartolo will protect them from earthquakes, that prayer will banish the storm. I never saw the point ... but, then again, I've always liked storms.

There were things about growing up in Salina that I hated – the lack of Dairy Milk chocolate for one, the constant expectation within the island society of conformity, tradition and obedience. There was a relief that came with being foreign. We didn't have to fit in. Being considered strange means you make your own way. It broke me when we left the island but I don't know if I would have been as wilful as I am now if I had spent my teenage years in Salina. By the time I left the island I had learned you could never be the most powerful thing in a room to someone who believes in God; the most I could expect was to be a pretty little angel.

> *Nevertheless, I long – I pine, all my days –*
> *to travel home and see the dawn of my return.*
> *And if a god will wreck me yet again on the wine-*
> *dark sea,*
> *I can bear that too, with a spirit tempered to endure*
> – Homer, *The Odyssey*

August 2020 marked four years since I'd been back on the island. Those last four years, ages fifteen to nineteen, had been a typical teenage cocktail of depression, anxiety and dissociation. Mum, Izzy and I had been in lockdown together for months, and it was driving me insane. I was living like a nocturnal creature, waking up at 4pm and going to bed at 6am, so that under the cover of night I could have a few hours to myself, where I could roam freely, like a zoo animal pacing around its cage. I've always been restless. I could never sit still for anything. Lockdown was my worst nightmare. I longed to leave like I'd never longed for anything in my life. All I could do to satiate my longing was stare out of the window every day and escape into the pages of books. I was Penelope looking out, constantly waiting, or Odysseus clinging to driftwood in the middle of a wine-dark sea, lost and wishing to be home. I wanted to run again, to climb on the rocks, to be around people who knew me, because I felt like I had been losing myself.

When I was nine, we moved from Salina to Siracusa so Izzy could go to a better middle school; when I was thirteen, we moved to England so Izzy could go to a better high school; when I was sixteen, we moved to Cambridge because Izzy was at university there. I've never liked being told what to do. I didn't like that my mum got to choose where we lived, even if it was my home, even if I loved it. The tragedy of childhood is that we are set down a path we didn't choose. The beauty of adulthood is that we can walk the path of our choosing. The first time I felt like I had truly gone somewhere because *I* chose to was in February 2022. I got on a flight to Catania and made my way back to Salina. I sat on the hydrofoil with my nose pressed up against the glass and I cried as the *faro* of Lingua came into view.

The first thing I did when I finally got to Lingua again was swim. The moment I dived into that familiar sea, completely submerged, feeling the air in my lungs start to burn, I felt freer than I had in years. The second thing I did was sit down to lunch with the Zangaris. Everyone was older and we hadn't seen each other for a while. Max walked in complaining about how cold it was outside and touched his freezing hand to my cheek to prove his point and the room was full of the sound of Sicilian and English and Giuseppina's food was delicious and there was loads of it. It felt like I had never left. I'd forgotten what it was like to be around people who were brought up in the same culture as me. I'd forgotten what it was like to be in a place that feels like home.

Salina is my hometown. It's where I longed to escape from so I could explore the big, bad world and is where I retreat to when the world gets too big and bad. The island taught me what I loved about the world and when I set out towards the horizon far from Salina, I would search for any reminder of home, greeting the ocean like an old friend and thanking it for keeping me afloat before I learned to swim, for catching me when I slipped and for being here again when I was feeling homesick.

I love my island. My childhood wasn't idyllic. It was hard. Hot in the summer and freezing in the winter, tough and fun and ordinary. The magical thing about it is that out of all the sunny little islands my mum could have chosen, she chose the one where I had the best childhood friends anyone could hope for: a best friend in Max, a little sister in Ilana, followed by Chiara, Alex, Corallina and Ondina, who I have known since they were born and have had the privilege to watch grow up. I saw what a true life partnership is by watching my mum and Emma work, mostly, seamlessly together looking after us. I got to experience the world of art and oak trees and double-decker buses with my dad in London. I wasn't starved for knowledge, art or music, like many of the young denizens of the island. I am who I am because of Salina, and I wouldn't trade my childhood there, my childhood friends, for anything. The characters in this book, who I don't remember not knowing, helped make me into the person who I am.

Like the island of Salina, I am the result of chance.

> We could never have loved the earth so well if we had had no childhood in it.
> – George Eliot, *The Mill on the Floss*

It is May 2023. I'm sitting on the terrace of the little house my mum has rented for the summer. She came back with me for Easter and hasn't left yet. It's about five minutes up the mountain and you can see the whole of Lingua from here, even the *scogli*, the rocks that protect the piazza from winter storms. The terrace is overhung by olive trees, the branches twisting and bending like an old woman's back so the tips of the leaves scrape the ground and cast shadows on the surrounding walls. On an island where you always feel watched, this terrace is completely hidden. I can just about see a glimpse of the nearly full moon through the trees, and

I stretch out, cat-like, on the curved trunk of one of the olive trees, the dipped branch perfectly shaped, almost like a hammock.

The harmonies of 'True Blue' by boygenius fill the air around me as I type a message to my best friend.

> **Juno:** I've been thinking about the idea of Love lately ... the idea of it being a choice ... like the feeling of love isn't a choice but it's also easy. It's easy to love people but it's hard to choose to love them every day – the effort, the time and the development it takes to have a person in your life forever, as well as the trust to know a person will do the same for you. True love is waking up every day and choosing to do whatever it takes to maintain that love and partnership. I think it might be like that for places too because that's how I feel about Salina. My mum chose it, then I chose to come back, and I truly love it because I know when I'm here it's because I could be somewhere else, but there is nowhere else I would rather be. More than anything, that's what I think was unique about my childhood. Most people search their whole lives for true love but I've known it since I was three.

Izzy

I am contemplating a visit to America. It's a call I feel every few months, in a variety of guises. Last autumn, I went as far as writing an application to a master's course at Yale, before I realised I wouldn't be able to get funding without committing to a seven-year doctorate.

The call is loud, but not loud enough to drown out everything else. This time, I will be going for just a couple of weeks – a visit with my best friend, who I met online when we were teenagers and I still lived in Sicily. If I ever do that master's course, I want to write about psychogeography: an exploration of an environment which emphasises personal connections, emotions and attachments. Traditionally, psychogeographers take unmapped, arbitrary routes through cities – but I have lived on enough small islands to know that you can get lost and leave memories behind you, like breadcrumbs, just about anywhere.

The call comes loud from a bay in Cape Ann. We lived in a small seaside town called Gloucester for a year when I was four, before Sicily, before my parents stopped being in love with each other. In my memory, Cape Ann feels like wet rocks and cold, grey sand, jagged and sharp like the piece of agate I would pick up on another beach a few years later, a long volcanic beach caressed into being by very different waters.

But if I hear the word 'sea' it is always the sea I knew in Salina that comes to mind. It doesn't even feel like a memory – it is just what the word 'sea' means. Salty and clear and open-palmed, with a treasure trove of delights to be seen through a snorkel: purple-spiked sea urchins, evil-looking red *pomodori di mare*, shimmering rainbow fish and, once, a glimpse of a shockingly pink sea slug in the depths below, the kind of colour you think only exists in plastic. The Mediterranean washes and then returns wood and glass and volcanic rocks in various stages back onto the shores of Salina's beaches, presenting a thousand gifts to my feet, my eyes, my hand, my mother, to be examined, praised, and tucked away.

But Cape Ann is different because it exists in my head in quick, hazy bursts, which might as well be copied from photographs than from any real consciousness. The Tyrrhenian is blue and inviting, sometimes even too warm as it soaks up the sunshine in August, clear enough that life feels like it mostly happens in its depths. I remember eating vanilla-fleshed peaches in that sea, and crying, and laughing, and learning to swim, and playing pirates, and cutting my knees, and being stung by jellyfish, and catching tiny crabs. But for me, the sea in Cape Ann exists to observe and be observed, to play a part in your psyche as you detangle and untangle your thoughts. I think in patterns and call-and-responses: one sea for my childhood, one sea for my adulthood.

Everyone has the same response when you tell them you grew up in Sicily. I never understood their rapturous envy when I was an adolescent – my visits to London twice a year were the only moments in which I was roused from the listlessness of teenage girldom to something like the bright lust for life I'd had as a child. By then, everything you've read about Salina – that sea, which, come moonlight or sunshine, really does sparkle – was just a remnant of a childhood I never thought about.

The year I turned sixteen, I fought daily with Mum about moving to England for sixth form. We have never fought like that, before or since: there was a desperation on either side that metabolised, in our two bodies, into fury. Mum wanted me to stay in Sicily, carry on the way we always had – the three of us, the sunshine, the ease and pace of life. I wanted nothing more than to go back to what I saw as home. I moved and, apart from a year in the pandemic, the three of us – Mum, Juno and me – would never live together again.

Then I turned twenty-three, and something happened (the something that happens, I think, to every daughter someday): I understood my mother. When you're a child, your parents aren't really people; they're your entire world but you can't envisage their inner lives. I knew the moment I became a woman because it was when I started thinking about what Mum must have felt all those years ago. The way I feel compelled to find something else, to follow a feeling to its conclusion – she felt it too. In effect, if not in tone, Salina's siren song is not so different from the ringing in my ears from across the Atlantic Ocean.

Those islands were small but the three of us still got lost there, mapping out entwining psychogeographies which will haunt those streets and villas and beaches forever. My memories of Favignana are vague and strange: little girls at school in their pink plaid pinafores who laughed when I couldn't speak Italian, and the weird phantasm of our landlord, placed by my five-year-old-self behind bars. But Salina was where I became a person, and I remember everything.

Those invisible maps – in my mind crisscrossing through Salina like the golden thread which Ariadne gave Theseus to find his way home – are part of the reason I haven't been back yet. I am moved, powerfully, by nostalgia, a symptom of an anchorless childhood, familiar to people with divorced or (and, in my case) expatriated parents. In the absence of a family home which belongs to us forever, my brain makes a home out of memories. Compared with my busy urban life now, that home can feel a little bizarre, like a weird dream I don't know how to parse.

Once or twice in my memory, the sea was filled with jellyfish. Barely a centimetre of water between each pulsating transparent body, stopping you in your tracks as you stepped onto the beach ready to be accepted, as you were every day, into its familiar depths. The jellyfish of my childhood, I found out today, were mauve stingers, but we called them 'medusa' in shrieked tones as we emerged gasping from underwater to alert each other. Only for the benefit of English tourists did we occasionally stoop to 'jellyfish', a term which holds so little myth and so little of the power of those strange creatures, simultaneously terrifying and utterly passive in their reliance on the tides, their lack of agency in whom their tendrils caught, especially when their tentacles came unstuck and floated, imperceptible, until they found their way into your snorkel or brushed, electric, against your ankle.

As I read up about these steady antagonists of my childhood, I try to close the distance between myself and those years which were once my life and now are just half my life. I recall their smell under the hot summer sun when we would fish one out with a net or some driftwood (we felt a keen restless urge to return to the sea and refused to wait for these faceless opponents to drift away). Underwater, they have a certain grace and otherworldliness, but on land, they felt disconnected enough from any kind of beauty that we happily smashed them with rocks and poked holes in them with sticks. There was a certain harmless violence to our childhood, the only real victims being half-dead jellyfish or (and even then only karmically-speaking) the bullies at school. Was it any surprise when we had weekly earthquake drills at school and kept a bag by the door (granola bars, Juno's fourth-favourite stuffed animal, my pink fluffy diary, factor 30 suncream and that nit comb) in case an eruption caused a tidal wave? Nature, that close up, has a way of taking you with it.

So, no, I haven't been back yet. When I think about Salina, I see the three of us as we were. Juno, charmingly chubby like a François Boucher painting, stuffing oranges in her mouth and never, ever, crying when she cut her knees open on the *scogli*. Mum looks exactly the same now as she did then – the only person I know who seems to carry the sun with them, in their body, no matter where we are – but in my mind's eye I see two small blonde children clutching at her hands and her attention. Me, very skinny and very tanned, and writing endless plans in my diary about what we were going to do when summer came (put on a play, build a rowing boat, befriend a stray kitten).

Going back would mean pretending that there is not an us which will always be there.

We are sitting on the terrace, painting erupting volcanoes on sea-smoothed volcanic stones. We are roasting sausages and marshmallows over an open fire on the beach. We are picking caper flowers and tucking them behind each other's ears. We are half-asleep on the blue bus home, Mum in between us, a head on each of her knees. We are swimming in that perfect sparkling sea, the whole world right there between our bodies.

WHERE THEY ARE NOW

Piero has grown a mango tree.

Zaccaria still does not have a mobile phone.

Giuseppina still makes cauliflower pasta and can still climb the mountain in flip-flops. Rodolfo's sudden death from a heart attack left the Zangaris feeling as if they had lost their magnetic north.

Emma and Gaetano now have six children. When Emma needs peace, she takes a cup of tea to the piazza.

Max is in a cargo ship travelling from the Straits of Bosphorus to the Bristol channel.

Ilana has the co-ordinates of Lingua tattooed on her ankle and is going to university in England.

Elettra still excavates the complexities of human emotion, and speaks and writes about them with words that resonate like poetry.

Pippo and Anna now live in Genoa.

A journalist from *L'Espresso* did visit the island and write an article about Pollara. Law cases have happened. Reputations have been challenged and defended. Nothing has been built.

I have never been back to Favignana, but I searched for Michel at his university in Siracusa, and discovered he had died of a heart attack. He was still in his thirties.

Izzy, despite her early schooling, got a double first at Cambridge and is a writer. Juno is at Bristol University writing a dissertation on Roman sex workers. When she graduates, she wants to do a master's, travel Europe and live in a van.

Juno finally persuaded Izzy to return to Salina. She texted me from Lingua yesterday. 'It's so beautiful, Mummy, and everyone is so lovely to us. I know what every plant does. Of course you wanted to bring us up here, how could you not?'

ACKNOWLEDGEMENTS

To Ruth, Juliet and Emma, my rocks and places of safety. To Mum and my late father, who showed me what unconditional love is, and to my Belford siblings, Heather and James, for fun, love, squabbles, laughter, tears and surreal memories of a 1960s childhood with a bossy big sister. Special love to Jackie.

To Rod O'Reilly for all our meandering riverside conversations; to Stephen Cherry for writerly insights, and for having the wisdom and empathy to recognise that some things are unforgiveable; and to Anne O'Reilly for a wonderful friendship (and an unswerving knack for good advice on anything I might throw at her). To Mary, Nicky, Katharine, Alicja, Tim, Chris Shoe, Chris James, Gregor and Antony, my swimming friends, who not only made Cambridge feel like home but make it hard to think of leaving.

To Patti Trimble for suggesting I turned an email into an opening chapter, and for reading numerous versions of this book with insight and generosity.

To Pina, my Salina sister, who Izzy and Juno grew up loving like an auntie, and to everyone on Salina who took us to their hearts and always made us feel welcome. To Giorgia, Katerina, Rosaria, Federica, Annamaria, Elena, Vera, Valentina and all the summertime children – Teo, Mia, Diego, Lauretta, Carlotta, Vincenzo, Lavinia, Daniele, Blue (and the future Arianna), Nico, Anna, Olmo, Nina, Paolo, Mattia and Viola.

To Giuseppina for being our adopted nonna, and to Gaetano, Max, Ilana, Chiara, Alex, Corallina and Ondina.

To Ilana (again) for being a fantastic travel companion, and to Giulia Frigieri for electrifying Juno and the Zangari girls with her passion for photography.

Grazie infinite too to my agent Tom Cull, whose belief that I should finish this book changed my life, and to Hannah and Charlotte at September for their humanity, approachability and deep good sense. Thanks as well to Liz Marvin for meticulous and stimulating copy editing and to Katie Read of Read Media for inspirational publicity.

And finally, to Izzy and Juno who have always been and always will be the best things in my life.